opportunity cost
Scarce resource

MICROECONOMICS

A Programmed Book

Keith Lumsden

Stanford University

Richard Attiyeh

University of California, San Diego

George Leland Bach

Frank E. Buck Professor of Economics and Public Policy
Stanford University

MICROECONOMICS

A Programmed Book

SECOND EDITION

PRENTICE-HALL, INC., Englewood Cliffs, New Jersey

MICROECONOMICS
A Programmed Book

Keith Lumsden
Richard Attiyeh
George Leland Bach

13-581439-1
Library of Congress Catalog Card Number: 70-119487

Current Printing (last digit):
10 9 8 7 6 5

Prentice-Hall International, Inc., *London*
Prentice-Hall of Australia, Pty. Ltd., *Sydney*
Prentice-Hall of Canada, Ltd., *Toronto*
Prentice-Hall of India Private, Ltd., *New Delhi*
Prentice-Hall of Japan, Inc., *Tokyo*

Printed in the United States of America

Preface

Our aim in writing this book and its companion piece *Macroeconomics* was
to provide students, in a brief period of time, with a working knowledge of
basic economics. It was our hope that these two books would prove a valuable
tool as the primary reading material in courses that were of short duration
(e.g., the one quarter course) or as introductory or supplementary material
in more comprehensive courses. Both the reactions of instructors who have
used the first editions and the results of a nationwide experiment* designed to
evaluate their effectiveness lead us to believe that our objectives have been
largely fulfilled. In a study involving 48 colleges and universities, students who
read these books as supplementary material scored significantly higher than
other students on the Test of Understanding College Economics. Furthermore,
and of greater importance, students who spent 12 hours studying either of
these books learned as much micro or macroeconomics as students who completed seven weeks on the same topics in a conventional course. On the basis
of these results, we reached the following conclusion:

> We feel that these results have important implications for the organiza-
> tion and teaching of the introductory course. Within the profession many
> believe that the introductory course should prepare a student to think in-
> telligently about major economic problems in modern society and that
> this goal can best be accomplished by teaching a few basic principles and
> applying them to a number of important problems. We are in agreement
> with this view. This study has shown that by using programmed learning
> materials the basic micro and macroeconomic theory can be taught in a
> relatively short period of time. Therefore, more time can be devoted to

*See our paper "The Efficiency of Programmed Learning in Teaching Economics:
The Results of a National Experiment" *American Economic Review,* LIX, No. 2, May
1969, pp. 217-223.

teaching students how to apply the theory to social problems, both by going more deeply into the more important problems and by actually covering those topics scheduled for the end of the term that often fall victim to the school calendar. The use of these materials can have other advantages: First, the student can gain a good overview of the entire course at the very beginning which helps him to put topics covered in the remainder of the course in meaningful perspective. Second, because a course taught in this manner emphasises the usefulness of economic theory in a problem solving context, it promises a positive impact on the most important single factor in the learning process: namely, student attitude towards the subject.

Much of the increase in flexibility and teaching efficiency afforded by this text stems from its characteristics as a programmed book. A program is designed to develop complex ideas in small, carefully constructed steps. Each step, or frame, requires written responses focussing on key concepts, thereby ensuring continuous participation and involvement by the student. Furthermore, since the correct responses appear at the bottom of each page, it is possible for the student to see immediately whether he is grasping the material, thereby either reinforcing his interest or delineating areas that need further work. In this edition, to accommodate typical study patterns, the material has been divided into a larger number of shorter chapters. In addition, a brief test has been appended to each chapter to meet student requests for more review.

Because of its analytical nature, economics lends itself well to the programming technique. Much of the material in both micro and macroeconomics can be usefully broken down into frames which have desired responses that are both basic and unambiguous. In this text, we analyze the way a market system will lead to an efficient allocation of resources. In studying the efficiency of such an economic system, situations in which resources will not be efficiently allocated through the market mechanisms are examined. While this edition has been expanded to include imperfect competition, most of our attention is directed towards the operation of a perfectly competitive system. Since the text is intended to give the reader a thorough grounding in basic microeconomic theory, considerable attention is paid to the basic analytical tools including a new chapter on diagramatic exposition. In this edition we have incorporated many of the suggestions made by instructors and students, as well as alterations indicated by detailed data from our study.

We are extremely grateful to Charles Briqueleur and Robert C. Walters of Prentice-Hall Inc., for their assistance in preparing the book for publication.

Keith Lumsden
Richard Attiyeh
George Leland Bach

Contents

How to use this book

This book is divided into small paragraphs, or frames, each of which requires responses. To be sure you learn as much as possible WRITE IN your responses before you check the answers at the bottom of the page. Keep the answers covered with a slider until you have made your response. Some responses simply involve choosing the correct word or phrase from the alternatives shown. This can be done simply by circling the correct alternative or crossing out the incorrect one.

Since no prior economics knowledge is presumed, the book begins at an elementary level. Furthermore, since the logical development proceeds in very small steps, you should find that you have no difficulty in making the correct responses. This indicates that you are learning the material. Studies have shown that in the ten to twelve hours required for the average student to read this book carefully, he will learn as much microeconomics as do students of the same ability studying the same topics in seven weeks of the typical conventional course.

MICROECONOMICS

A Programmed Book

1

Introduction: The Nature of Economic Problems

Why read this book? Why study economics?

Can you answer the following?

Why is anyone willing to pay Willie Mays over $100,000 per year just to play baseball?

Why is there a shortage of schools and hospitals when there is no shortage of horror comics and pop records?

Why doesn't your hardworking professor earn as much, or more, than a glamorous movie star?

Why are automobiles produced by only a few firms whereas wheat is produced on a great number of farms?

Why is the price of something essential like water so low when the price of something frivolous like diamonds is so high? If you cannot answer these questions satisfactorily, study economics: read this book.

If you have not read the preface, make sure that you fill in the blanks, or delete the wrong responses in blanks where you are given a choice, before comparing your responses with those at the bottom of the page. Reading the book in this way should ensure that you will learn as much microeconomic theory as a fellow student after seven weeks of a typical course. After completing the book, come back and work out the economic implications of this statement.

In a programmed text we proceed from the simple to the complex. Our first example, is, therefore, simple, but enlightening.

1.1

Suppose your father, wishing to encourage you to study more, made the following proposition: For every point of your grade point average (GPA), this term, he will pay you $4 per day. If your GPA is 2.0 you will receive $8 per day. If

1

an *A* is equivalent to 4 points, a *B* 3 points, a *C* 2 points, and a *D* 1 point, an *A*

average would be worth $ __16.00__ per day. Two *B*'s and two *C*'s

would be a __(2.5/2.0/1.5)__ GPA and therefore, would be worth only

$ __10.00__ per day.

1.2
You realize immediately that the higher your grades the __(higher/lower)__ will
be your income from your father. Since more time devoted to studying means
higher grades, the way to increase your income from your father is to spend

__(more/less)__ time studying.

1.3
The more time you spend studying however, the __less__ time you
have left for other income earning pursuits, such as waiting on tables, working
for the library, or cutting lawns.

1.4
Your father surmised that the reason your GPA fell last semester was that you
took outside jobs to earn income. He realized that in order to earn such income

you were devoting __time__ to outside jobs that could otherwise have
been spent studying.

1.5
Thus your father's proposition is really an attempt to encourage you to spend

__more__ time studying and __less__ time on outside jobs.

1.6
The more time spent on outside employment the __more__ will be your
income from outside sources. However, the more time spent on outside employ-

ment the __less__ time will be available for study and the __lower__

Answers
1. 16 · 2.5 · 10
2. higher · more
3. less
4. time
5. more · less
6. higher · less · lower

will be your GPA. Therefore, the more time spent on outside employment, the

lower will be your income from your father.

1.7
Suppose each day, on an average, you have six hours which are uncommitted to

sleeping, eating, going to class, and pure entertainment. You have __6__

hours per day which may be used to earn _income_ by studying or from
outside employment.

1.8
You know that income from your father depends upon your _GPA_,

which in turn depends upon the _time_ you spend studying.

1.9
Income from outside employment depends upon the hourly wage paid and the

number of _hours_ you are employed.

1.10
Since you have six hours to allocate each day, your total daily _income_
will be composed of GPA income from your father and/or wage income from outside employment. The more hours per day you devote to outside employment

the _greater_ will be your income from that source, but the

smaller will be the number of hours available for study.

1.11
The smaller the number of hours devoted to study the _lower_ will be

your GPA and the _lower_ will be your income from your father.

Answers
6. lower
7. six · income
8. GPA · time
9. hours
10. income · greater · smaller
11. lower · lower

1.12
Thus an increase in income from outside employment means a(n) ___decrease___
in income from your father.

1.13
In other words, there is a cost associated with earning income from an outside
job that is over and above the work effort involved. This cost is the income that

you could have earned by spending that time ___studying___ . Economists
call this *opportunity cost.*

1.14
When you are forced to choose from alternatives you must give up one thing to

get another. What you give up is the ___opportunity___ cost of what you get.

There is an opportunity ___cost___ in taking an outside job because it
is necessary to take time away from something else. It is impossible, given that
you have only six hours to study and/or work, to increase time spent working

without ___decreasing___ the time spent studying.

1.15
Likewise, in this example, it is impossible to increase income from outside em-

ployment without ___decreasing___ income from your father. This loss of

income from your father is the ___opportunity___ cost of the outside income
you earn.

1.16
What your father hopes to accomplish from his proposal is a(n) ___increase___

in hours devoted to studying and a(n) ___decrease___ in hours devoted to

outside jobs. He hopes to do this by raising the ___opportunity cost___
of the outside income you can earn.

1.17
Suppose your aim is to earn as high a daily income as possible, either from
studying or outside employment or a combination of both. What would you do?

Answers
12. decrease
13. studying
14. opportunity · cost · decreasing
15. decreasing · opportunity
16. increase · decrease · opportunity cost

a. *spend six hours studying*
b. *spend six hours working*
c. *I do not have enough information to answer the question*

_____(a/b/c)_____

1.18

Quite correct, you do not yet have enough information. Some of the information necessary to answer the question is how your GPA changes as you vary the
time spent studying. Suppose we agree on the relationship shown in Table 1.1:

Table 1.1
Study Time and GPA

Average Hours Spent Studying per Day	GPA
6	4.00
5	3.75
4	3.33
3	2.75
2	2.00
1	1.08
0	0.00

If you devoted all your uncommitted hours to studying you would, on average,
study six hours per day; your resultant GPA would be 4.00 and at $4 per point

your father would pay you $ ____16.00____ per day. In this case your in-

come from outside employment would be $ ____0____ . Your total

daily income therefore would be $ ____16.00____ .

1.19

Remember your goal is to earn the highest possible daily ____income____
from both sources combined. Do you now have enough information to decide

how to allocate your six hours to achieve this end? ____(yes/no)____

1.20

If you devoted five hours to studying, your GPA would be ____3.75____ .
Since your father pays you $4 per point your income from him would be

$ ____15.00____ .

Answers
17. *c*
18. 16 · 0 · 16
19. income · no
20. 3.75 · 15

1.21
Now five hours devoted to studying leaves _____1_____ hour(s) free for
outside employment. If you can only earn $0.50 per hour on outside employ-
ment, your five hours studying plus one hour on the outside will give you a total

income of $ __15.00__ + $ __.50__ which equals

$ __15.50__ .

1.22
This solution is clearly __(less/more)__ satisfactory to you, compared with

studying six hours per day, since your total income is now __less__
than before.

1.23
If, however, your outside employment paid $2 per hour, your five hours study-

ing plus one hour working outside would yield a total income of $ __17.00__

which is higher than the $ __16.00__ from studying six hours per day.

1.24
Thus, given that your aim is to maximize (make as large as possible) your daily
income, there are several things you must know in deciding how to allocate your

six hours per day. You must know how much __income__ you can earn

from your father by studying different amounts of __time__ . And, you

must know how much __income__ you can earn by spending different

amounts of time that could be used __studying__, but are used instead
working at outside jobs.

1.25
The same kind of calculation is made, consciously or subconsciously, when you
decide to spend the evening studying in the library or going out on a date. You

Answers
    21. 1 · 15 · .50 · 15.50
    22. less · lower
    23. 17 · 16
    24. income · time · income · studying

cannot easily quantify in dollars "the library" versus "a date" but somehow you make the decision. When you feel studying in the library is worth more to you (in "psychic income") than going out on a date—you go to the library. Similarly

in this example, where you are trying to maximize ___income___ , when you can earn more income by switching a study hour to outside employment, you

(should/should not) make that switch.

1.26

This simple problem, concerned with the best way to allocate your six hours, is really an economic problem. Economics is concerned with the best way to allo- cate scarce resources among various alternative uses to make some individual or group as well off as possible. In our simple example the scarce resource to be

allocated is ___(time/income)___ . The alternative uses of your time are outside

work and ___study___ . And, you are as well off as possible when your

daily ___income___ is maximized.

1.27

When economists think about the economy as a whole, the scarce resources are all those things which help produce the goods and services we want. Roads,

machine tools, schoolteachers and farmland are examples of ___scarce___ resources.

1.28

Some of the alternatives society faces are more schools or more hospitals, more butter or more guns, more pop records or more classical records. Just as in our simple example income from outside work has an opportunity cost of income

from your father, so in the real world there are ___opportunity___ costs. In order to produce more of one good, let us say, spaghetti, it is necessary to give up some amount of other goods. This latter amount, of course, is the

___opportunity cost___ of the extra spaghetti.

Answers
25. income · should
26. time · studying · income
27. scarce
28. opportunity · opportunity cost

1.29

We do not have enough _resources_ to produce all the goods and services
everyone wants. It is for this reason that we must choose what to produce. And

it is for this same reason that we say the economy's resources are _scarce_ .

1.30

Because resources are _scarce_ we cannot have everything we want.
Consequently, as a nation, we are faced with the economic problem of deciding

how to use our _scarce_ _resources_ .

1.31

Before we try to use economic analysis to understand our complex economy, let
us try to master our simple example. That is, before you try to comprehend how

society can use its _scarce_ _resources_ to its best advantage,
let us solve the economic problem of how to use your scarce resource, which is

time , to maximize your daily _income_ .

1.32

From the information you already have it is possible to construct a table of figures that will permit you to see the best allocation of working time. This is the

allocation that _(minimizes/maximizes)_ your daily income.

1.33

Table 1.2 showing the relevant information, is incomplete. Fill in the blanks.
To do so you will need to remember that your father is willing to pay you

$ _4.00_ daily per each point of your GPA.

Answers
    29. resources · scarce
    30. scarce · scarce resources
    31. scarce resources · time · income
    32. maximizes
    33. 4.00

Table 1.2

Time Allocation and Income

Hours Spent in			Daily Income		
Employment (1)	Studying (2)	GPA (3)	Employment (4)	Father (5)	Total (6)
0	6	4.00	$ 0	$16	$16
1	5	3.75	2	15	17
2	4	3.33	4	a) 13.32	b) 17.32
3	3	2.75	6	c) 11	d) 17
4	2	2.00	8	8	16
5	1	1.08	10	4.32	14.32
6	0	0.00	12	0	12

1.34

From Table 1.2 it is possible to determine the allocation of time that maximizes

your income. This allocation is ___4___ hours spent studying and

___2___ hours in employment. In this way you can earn a total of

$ ___17.32___ per day.

1.35

By looking at this allocation problem in a slightly different way, it is possible to
develop an analytical tool that is very useful in dealing with more difficult economic problems. As we saw above, an allocation problem concerns the use of

some ___scarce___ resource so as to ___maximize___ something.

1.36

For the economy as a whole we would be concerned about how to use the

nation's ___scarce___ supply of land, labor, and capital (its resources) to

___maximize___ social welfare. In our simple example, you must decide how

to use your limited ___time___ to maximize your daily ___income___ .

Answers

Table 1.2. a) 13.32 · b) 17.32 · c) 11 · d) 17
34. 4 · 2 · 17.32
35. scarce · maximize
36. scarce · maximize · time · income

1.37

We solved your allocation problem by calculating, for every possible allocation of six hours, the resulting total income and by choosing the allocation with the

maximum total income.

1.38

An alternative way to look at the problem is to start with a particular allocation, say five hours studying and one hour working, and to determine how total income changes as you change the allocation of time. If there is some way to

change the allocation to increase total income, then you _(should/should not)_ make the change. If there is no change that will increase total income, then you

must already have the _allocation_ of time that gives the _maximum_ total income.

1.39

Let us find out what happens when you reallocate one hour of your study time to outside employment. Beginning with a five hour study-one hour work combination, from Table 1.2 (which is reproduced in frame 43) you can see that an

increase in one hour of study time would raise your GPA from _3.75_

to _4.00_. Correspondingly the income you receive from your father

would rise from $ _15_ to $ _16_.

1.40

That is, starting from a level of study of five hours per day, an increase in studying of one hour per day adds $ _1.00_ in income from your father. This, of course, is the difference between an income of $16 per day associated

with a GPA of _4.00_ and an income of $ _15.00_ associated with a GPA of 3.75.

1.41

The increase in studying time must come from an equal _decrease_ in time spent working. Consequently your income from outside employment would

Answers

37. maximum
38. should · allocation · maximum
39. 3.75 · 4.00 · 15 · 16
40. 1 · 4.00 · 15
41. decrease

fall from $2 to $ � _____ . Your new total income in this case would

be �, ⎰6 _____ , which would be ▯ *less* than its initial level.

1.42

Carefully trace what is happening. Adding one study hour from five to six hours

per day would increase your GPA; it also would ▯ *increase* the daily in-

come from your father by $ ▯ *1* . The accompanying decrease of
one working hour would reduce daily income from outside employment by

$ ▯ *2* . This latter amount is the opportunity ▯ *cost*
of the extra income from your father.

1.43

Would you increase your total income by making this change? Essentially, you

would give up $ _____ *2* of income from working in return for

$ _____ *1* of income from studying, which is a net _____ *(gain/loss)*

of $1. In other words your total income would *(increase/decrease)* by the

amount of $ ▯ *1* .

For your convenience Table 1.2 is reproduced here.

Table 1.2
Time Allocation and Income

Hours Spent in			Daily Income		
Employment (1)	Studying (2)	GPA (3)	Employment (4)	Father (5)	Total (6)
0	6	4.00	$ 0	$16	$16
1	5	3.75	2	15	17
2	4	3.33	4	13.32	17.32
3	3	2.75	6	11	17
4	2	2.00	8	8	16
5	1	1.08	10	4.32	14.32
6	0	0.00	12	0	12

Answers
41. 0 · 16 · lower
42. increase · 1 · 2 · cost
43. 2 · 1 · loss · decrease · 1

1.44

Clearly, it *(would/would not)* pay to change a 5-1 study-work combination to 6-0. But what about a change in the other direction? From Table 1.2 you can

see that a decrease in study time to four hours would mean a ~~decrease~~ in your GPA from 3.75 to 3.33 and a decrease in income from your father of

$ _____

1.45

Even though this change reduces income from your father by $1.68, it would still be worth making if the hour saved from studying could be used to earn

more than $ _____ from outside employment. Since you can earn $2 per hour by working, the change from a 5-1 study-work allocation to 4-2

would ___~~increase~~___ your total income by $ ___20.00___ .

1.46

In this case, the $ ___1.68___ you lose from your father by ~~studying one~~

hour less is more than made up for by the $ ___2.00___ you can earn by using that hour working on an outside job.

1.47

Thus, it is clear that the change from 5-1 study-work allocation to 4-2 is worth making. Does this, by itself, necessarily mean that the 4-2 combination is best?

_____*(yes/no)*_____   In principle, it is possible that further changes in the direction of less study and more work would lead to further increase in total

___~~income~~___ .

1.48

Consider the possibility of changing to a 3-3 study-work combination. The de-

cline in study from four to three hours would lead to a ___*(gain/loss)*___ in

income from your father amounting to $ ___2.32___ , while the extra

hour worked would increase your outside income by $ ___2___ .

Answers

    44. would not · decrease · 1.68
    45. 1.68 · increase · 0.32
    46. 1.68 · 2
    47. no · income
    48. loss · 2.32 · 2

1.49

In this case, since the _____ (gain/loss) _____ in income from your father is not

matched by the _____ gain _____ in outside income, the change _____ (is/is not) _____
worth making.

1.50

You have seen that a change from the 4-2 study-work combination to either 5-1

or 3-3 _____ decrease _____ your total income. Therefore, the 4-2 study-work com-

bination must yield a _____ maximum _____ of total income.

1.51

What we have seen is that whether you consider this problem by looking at the
total income earned from alternative allocations or by considering changes in

income from _____ changes _____ in allocations you arrive at the same solution.
This is true because at a point of maximum income a change in any direction

will _____ decrease _____ income.

1.52

The approach that concentrates on changes in allocations economists call

marginal analysis. When using _____ marginal _____ analysis you consider things
at the margin rather than looking at the total.

1.53

In our example, we could say that a shift from 3-3 study-work combination to

4-2 would yield an increase in income from your father of $ _____ 2.32 _____
which is the *marginal benefit* of this change. And, we could say that the accom-

panying loss in outside income of $ _____ 2.00 _____ is the *marginal cost* of the
change.

1.54

In shifting from a 3-3 study-work combination to 4-2, since the _____ marginal _____

benefit exceeds the _____ marginal _____ cost, the change _____ (is/is not) _____
worth making.

Answers

49. loss · gain · is not
50. decreases · maximum
51. changes · reduce
52. marginal
53. 2.32 · 2
54. marginal · marginal · is

1.55

When you increase your study time, there are both benefits and costs because

your time is scarce. Since time is ___scarce___ you cannot increase study

time without taking ___time___ away from some other use. As a result,

you not only get the marginal ___benefit___ of increased income from your

father by studying more, you also must bear the marginal ___cost___ of
decreased income from outside employment.

1.56

Generalizing from this example, we can establish several important economic
principles: First, it is necessary to make choices, whenever resources (e.g. time)

are ___scarce___ .

1.57

Second, whenever a choice must be made there is an opportunity ___cost___
involved. When you choose an apple over an orange, the orange is the

___opportunity cost___ of the apple.

1.58

Third, however your resources are allocated to begin with, when you consider a

change in that allocation there are both a marginal ___benefit___ and a

marginal ___cost___

1.59

Finally, a change is worth making only when the ___marginal___

___benefit___ is greater than the ___marginal cost___ .

Answers

55. scarce · time · benefit · cost
56. scarce
57. cost · opportunity cost
58. benefit (cost) · cost (benefit)
59. marginal benefit · marginal cost

1.60

These facts of economic life hold true whether we consider your simple problem of allocating your time or the complex problem of allocating the economy's

many ___scarce___ resources.

1.61

The war in Vietnam provides a case in point. To carry out this war it was neces-

sary to use substantial quantities of the nation's ___scarce___

___resources___. Sadly, the greatest cost incurred was the substantial loss of human life—a loss which cannot be measured solely in economic terms.

1.62

Over and above this tragic loss of life there also was an additional enormous opportunity cost. If the war had been avoided, the resources used to carry

out the war (could/could not) have been used to produce civilian commodi-ties that American families and businesses could have put to good use. If there had been no war, the land, labor, and capital used to produce jet fighters,

napalm, and mortars (could/could not) have been used to produce new schools, better health services, and more clothing.

1.63

This is the classic choice between "guns and butter." In deciding to expand the

war the government chose to reallocate resources to produce ___more___

guns and ___less___ butter. The political and strategic gain resulting

from more "guns" is the marginal ___benefit___ from this reallocation, while the lower living standards resulting from less "butter" is the marginal

___cost___ .

1.64

Those who supported the government's Vietnam policy obviously

believed that the marginal ___benefit___ outweighed the marginal

___cost___ .

Answers

60. scarce
61. scarce resources
62. could · could
63. more · less · benefit · cost
64. benefit · cost

1.65

Those who opposed the war held the opposite view. To them, reallocating resources from fighting, let us say, poverty in the United States to fighting communism in Vietnam *(increased/decreased)* the welfare of the American people.

1.66

Another example in which the concepts of scarcity, opportunity cost, and marginal analysis are useful is the battle over the California redwood forests. As you know, redwood trees make both beautiful forests and handsome lumber. Unfortunately, if you cut a forest for lumber it is *(just as/no longer)* beautiful to look at. Furthermore, there are not enough redwoods to fully satisfy people's desires for both beautiful forests and handsome lumber. If society chooses to preserve a forest rather than use the wood for lumber, the foregone lumber is the ___opportunity cost___ of the beautiful forest.

1.67

In economic terms, then, we have said that redwoods are a natural resource that is ___scarce___ and for which there are many alternative uses. Consequently, for every grove of redwoods we *(have no/must make a)* choice.

1.68

Whichever choice is made, we must give up one of the alternatives. That is, we will have to accept the ___marginal___ cost. If we choose to cut a grove, we must face up to the loss of a beautiful forest.

1.69

It will pay to cut the grove, however, only if the marginal ___benefit___ of the extra lumber outweighs the marginal ___cost___ of one less redwood grove.

Answers

65. decreased
66. no longer · opportunity cost
67. scarce · must make a
68. marginal
69. benefit · cost

1.70

In these examples, we have shown how an economist analyzes social problems. But one other point should also have been made clear to you. Before you can compare the marginal benefit and marginal cost of any change, you must know what they are. In both of the policy problems discussed it was necessary to make subjective value judgments before you could make any decision. In all economic problems you must know people's preferences as well as their alternatives before you can make a rational decision.

REVIEW QUESTIONS

Questions 1 and 2 are based on the following statement:

"The question facing our government is whether to build a new highway system or establish public libraries throughout the country during the next three years. Resources for both projects are not available. It must be one or the other."

1.1

The fundamental economic problem being faced by the nation is one of

a. consumers' choice.
b. government decision making.
c. scarcity of resources.
d. shortage of labour.

1.2

The opportunity cost of the new highway system mentioned in the paragraph above

is ___ b ___.

a. greater than the economy can afford.
b. national libraries.
c. the money required to pay for it.
d. the resources required to build it.

Answers
   1. c
   2. b

1.3

Which word(s) in the expression "more guns or more butter" reflect(s) limited

resources for any society?   _C̶ and_

a. guns, butter.
b. more.
c. both (a) and (b).
d. or.

1.4

Those who argue that our economy should be producing more tons of butter

and fewer cases of guns are arguing that   _B̶ C̶_   .

a. the benefit from a ton of butter is greater than the benefit from a case of guns.
b. the marginal benefit of butter is greater than the marginal benefit of guns.
c. the benefit obtained from using one more unit of resources to produce butter is greater than the benefit from using it to produce guns.
d. the marginal cost of butter is less than the marginal cost of guns.

1.5

Economic goods are termed scarce goods because they _a̶_  .

a. are not available in sufficient quantities to satisfy all wants for them.
b. are not produced in sufficient quantities to satisfy the effective demand for them.
c. cannot be increased in quantity to any significant extent.
d. are of primary importance in satisfying the needs of a society.

Answers
  3. d
  4. c
  5. a

2

Marginal Analysis

2.1

In Chapter 1 you learned that whenever resources are ~~scarce~~ a choice must be made among the alternative uses of those resources. Because resources are scarce, whenever they are put to one use there will be the

~~opportunity~~ cost of the benefit that would have resulted had they been put to an alternative use.

2.2

For example, as was discussed in Chapter 1, to carry out the Vietnam War, it

was necessary to use ~~resources~~ that could have been used to satisfy domestic wants. That is, the civilian commodities that could have been pro-

duced with the resources used to fight the Vietnam War were the ~~opportunity~~ cost of the war.

2.3

This can be seen in terms of Table 2.1 and Figure 2.1 which illustrate with the example of "guns and butter" the alternative combinations of military and

civilian output that could have been produced with society's ~~resources~~ .

Answers
1. scarce · opportunity
2. resources · opportunity
3. resources

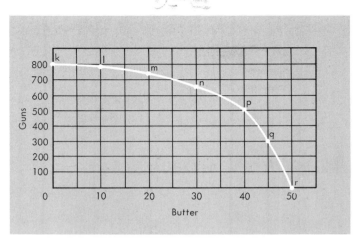

Table 2.1 Production Alternatives	
Guns	*Butter (Tons)*
800	0
780	10
730	20
660	30
500	40
300	45
0	50

FIGURE 2.1. Guns vs Butter
Production Possibility Curve

The curve shown in Figure 2.1 shows the production of guns and butter from all possible resource allocations. For this reason it is called a ~~_____~~ ~~_____~~ curve.

2.4
If all resources for some given time period (let us say one week) were devoted to the production of guns we would be able to produce ~~_____~~ guns and nothing else. We would be at point ~~_____~~ on the production possibility curve.

2.5
Now, if a small amount of resources were devoted to the production of butter, as at the point *l*, we would be giving up ~~_____~~ guns to obtain ~~_____~~ tons of butter.

Answers
  3. production possibility
  4. 800 · *k*
  5. 20 · 10

2.6

The point *q* represents ▨▨▨▨ guns and ▨▨▨▨ tons of

butter. By moving from *k* to *q*, therefore, we would be giving up ▨▨▨▨

guns to obtain ▨▨▨▨ tons of butter.

2.7

Is it worth moving from *k* to *q*? *(yes/no/don't know.)* ▨▨▨▨

2.8

The reason we do not know if it is worth moving from *k* to *q* is because we do
not know how society values guns vs butter. We do not know, for this society,

in moving from *k* to *q*, whether the benefit of ▨▨▨▨ more tons of

butter is worth the cost of ▨▨▨▨ fewer guns.

2.9

This example is similar to all resource allocation problems in economics. What
proportion of resources should be allocated to the production of different goods?

The ▨▨▨▨ curve tells what outputs of each good
will be associated with different resource allocations. The economic problem is:
Which of the different combinations of goods that can be produced with society's

limited ▨▨▨▨ should be produced?

2.10

How to allocate scarce resources to make society as well off as possible is the

▨▨▨▨ problem.

2.11

To understand the economic problem of choice from among alternative resource
allocations let us consider again our simple work-study example from Chapter 1.

You will recall that the objective was to maximize the ▨▨▨▨ you

Answers
6. 300 · 45 · 500 · 45
7. don't know
8. 45 · 500
9. production possibility · resources
10. economic
11. income

could earn by allocating your time between work and study. In this example,

your scarce resource was _____.

2.12
The alternative feasible combinations of work and study time can be seen in
Table 2.2 and Figure 2.2.

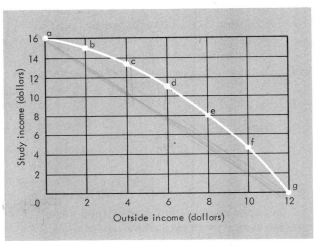

Table 2.2
Income Alternatives

Study		Outside Work	
Hrs.	In-come	Hrs.	In-come
6	$16	0	$ 0
5	15	1	2
4	13.32	2	4
3	11	3	6
2	8	4	8
1	4.32	5	10
0	0	6	12

FIGURE 2.2. Income
Possibility Curve

The points *a, b, c, d, e, f,* and *g* represent the different combinations of study

income plus outside income obtainable from _____ hours, the
amount of the scarce resource available.

2.13
Point *a* for instance, represents study income of $ _____ and out-

side income of $ _____. This combination of income is obtained

from _____ hours of studying and _____ hours of
outside work.

Answers
11. time
12. 6
13. 16 · 0 · 6 · 0

2.14

Point *d* represents study income of $ ~~____~~ and work income of $ ~~____~~ . This point corresponds to ~~____~~ hours of studying and ~~____~~ hours of outside work.

2.15

If we took all possible study-work combinations, we would obtain a smooth curve connecting points *a* through *g*, as in Figure 2.2. For instance, 5½ hours of outside work would yield an outside income of $ ~~____~~ and ½ hour of studying would yield a study income greater than zero but less than the $ ~~____~~ that could be obtained from one hour of studying. The point so derived would lie on the curve in Figure 2.2 between the points ~~____~~ and ~~____~~ .

2.16

The curve in Figure 2.2, then, is the income possibility curve that gives all of the alternative combinations of work and study ~~____~~ that are possible to attain with the six hours available to you. The economic problem, of course, is to pick the allocation of time that yields the ~~____~~ income.

2.17

In this simple case it is possible to find the best allocation of time by inspecting Figure 2.2. In more complex situations such a straightforward approach is not possible. For that reason it will be useful to consider in detail the marginal approach that was developed in Chapter 1. You will recall that given any initial situation you can imagine allocating one unit more of your resources to some particular use. This change will involve a benefit, which is called the ___(total/marginal)___ benefit, and a cost, which is the ~~____~~ cost.

2.18

In our example, we can imagine allocating one more unit of time (an hour) to studying. The extra income from your father as a reward for the ensuing higher

Answers

14. 11 · 6 · 3 · 3
15. 11 · 4.32 · *f* · *g*
16. income · maximum
17. marginal · marginal

grade point average is the  of studying.
But because you can study more only by working less there is an opportunity
cost involved. The income you give up by work ~~ne~~ hour less is the marginal

_____ of studying.

2.19

It is helpful to analyze these concepts with the help of diagrams. Look at Figure 2.3. Along the horizontal axis we me~~...~~ the hours worked in outside

employment and along the vertical axis we measure the hourly _____

_____ that can be earned from outside employment.

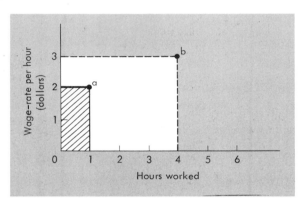

FIGURE 2.3. Income from Outside Employment Depending
on Hours Worked and the Wage Rate

2.20

Two points are plotted in Figure 2.3. Each point represents a particular combination of hours worked and wage rate. Point *a* stands for one hour worked

at a wage rate of $ _____ per hour. Point *b* represents _____

hours worked at a wage rate of $ _____ per hour.

Answers

18. marginal benefit · cost
19. wage rate
20. 2 · 4 · 3

2.21

If you worked one hour per day at a wage rate of $2 per hour, your daily in-

come would be $ ~~A~~ . In Figure 2.3. this is represented by the
area of the smaller rectangle, which is found by multiplying length by height.
The length is the same as hours worked and the height is the same as the

~~_____~~ ~~_____~~ . Therefore, the area of the rectangle and

dollars of daily income will be *(equal/unequal.)* They will both be equal to

the number of ~~_____~~ ~~_____~~ times the hourly

~~_____~~ ~~_____~~ .

2.22

If you worked four hours at a wage rate of $3 per hour you would earn

$ ~~_____~~ . In Figure 2.3. this is represented by the ~~_____~~
of the larger rectangle.

2.23

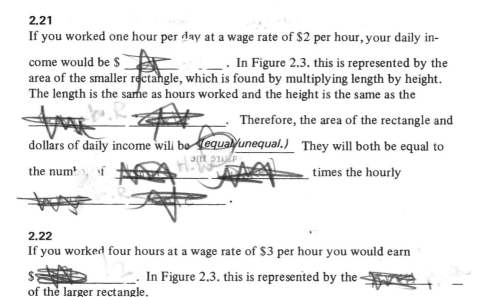

FIGURE 2.4. Income, Hours, and a Wage of $2

In Figure 2.4 the points *a, b, c, d, e, f, g* are all associated with the same wage

rate of $ ~~_____~~ per hour but with different numbers of

~~_____~~ worked. The point *b* for instance is associated with one hour

Answers
    21. 2 · wage rate · equal · hours worked · wage rate
    22. 12 · area
    23. 2 · hours

worked at $2 per hour. With what number of hours worked are *a*, *d* and *f*

associated? *a)* _____ 0 _____ *d)* _____ 3 _____ *f)* _____ 5 _____.

2.24

As in Figure 2.3, the _____ area _____ of the various rectangles in Figure 2.4

will represent daily income from different numbers of _____ hours _____
worked at a wage rate of $2 per hour.

2.25

The rectangle, for instance, whose corners are *0, 5, f* and *a* will have an area of

_____ 10 _____ units, representing an income of $ _____ 10 _____. The

area is calculated by multiplying the length, _____ 5 _____ units by the

height, _____ 2 _____ units. Daily income is calculated by multiplying

_____ hours worked _____ (on the horizontal axis) by a _____ wage _____

_____ rate _____ on the vertical axis.

2.26

Suppose that instead of income earned from working, we were interested in
income forgone by not working. This is shown by the area of the rectangles in
Figure 2.5.

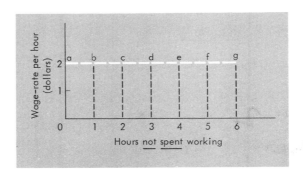

FIGURE 2.5. Income Forgone I

Answers
    23. 0 · 3 · 5
    24. areas · hours
    25. 10 · 10 · 5 · 2 · hours worked · wage rate

The vertical axis again measures the _____ W . R . _____ but
now the horizontal axis measures hours _____ N . ~w . _____
working.

2.27
Thus if the total number of hours not spent working is six (that is, all the hours
you have free to allocate daily) the income forgone, or the income you give up

by not working, will be $ _____ 12 _____ . This is calculated by multiplying

the wage rate of $ _____ 2 _____ by the number of hours not spent working,

in this case _____ 6 _____ .

2.28
In Figure 2.5 the $12 income forgone will be the area of the rectangle whose

corners are 0, _____ 6 a _____ , _____ g _____ , and _____ b _____ .
This area (06ga) is _____ 12 _____ units and is found by multiplying the

length of the rectangle, _____ 6 _____ units, by the height _____ 2 _____
units.

2.29
Figure 2.6 represents a situation in which the number of hours not spent working

is four. Thus the income forgone by not working will be $ _____ 8 _____ .
Since you have six hours available, however, and four are NOT spent working,

_____ 2 _____ hours MUST be spent working. The income from such work

will be $ _____ 4 _____ and will be represented by the *(shaded/unshaded)*

rectangle. The _____ marginal _____ loss or income forgone by not working is

represented by the _____ sh . _____ rectangle.

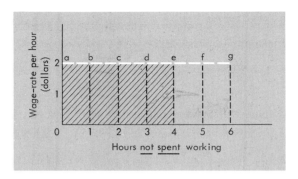

FIGURE 2.6. Income Forgone II

2.30

Now, consider the line connecting *a* through *g*. What does the height of that line indicate? It shows you for any level of hours worked the income you would give up by working one hour less. Thus it shows you the *(marginal/total)* income lost by not working. Remember, the change in income from a unit increase in time worked is the _____ income, so the change from a unit decrease in time worked is the _____ lost by not working.

2.31

For example, if you were working four hours, an increase in one hour worked would add $ _____ to your income, so that at five hours worked $2 would be your _____ income from work. Similarly, if you were *not* working four hours, and decided to work one hour less, you would then *not* be working five hours and would earn $ _____ less. That is, $2 would be your _____ , _____ lost by not working.

2.32

The line *a g* in Figure 2.6 gives the _____ lost by not working. Think about the effect of increasing your study time by one hour. Every hour of the six hours available spent studying is an hour not spent working. If you study four hours, there are _____ hours not spent working.

Answers
    30. marginal · marginal · marginal income
    31. 2 · marginal · 2 · marginal income
    32. marginal income · 4

2.33

If you want to increase study time by one hour, then you must reduce time spent working by one hour. The income lost thereby is shown in Figure 2.6 by the height of the line *a g*, which is the ~~~~~~~~~~~ income lost by not working. Therefore, Figure 2.6 shows the work income lost by studying one more hour. That is, it shows the ~~~~~~~~~~~ cost of studying.

2.34

Figure 2.7 is the same as Figure 2.6 except that the axes have been relabeled.

In Figure 2.7, the horizontal axis shows hours spent ~~~~~~~~~~~ , which you know is the same as hours not spent ~~~~~~~~~~~ . The vertical axis shows the ~~~~~~~~~~~ of studying, which you know is the work income lost by ~~~~~~~~~~~ one less hour.

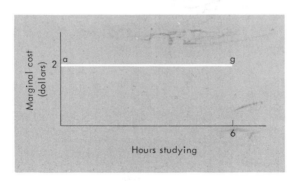

FIGURE 2.7. Marginal Cost of Studying

2.35

Let us now consider how to represent the marginal benefits from studying. Table 2.3 repeats data from Chapter 1.

Answers
  33. marginal · marginal
  34. studying · working · marginal cost · working

Table 2.3
Study Income, Total and Marginal

Hours Spent Studying	Income from Your Father	Marginal Income
6	16	1
5	15	1.68
4	13.32	2.32
3	11	3
2	8	3.68
1	4.32	4.32
0	0	

The third column gives your income; that is the income gained from one extra hour of studying (or the income lost from one hour

_____ of studying).

2.36

If instead of studying for one hour you decide to study for two hours, your

total income from your father will increase from $ _____ .32 to

$ _____ ; that is by $ _____ . 3 .68

2.37

This increase in income is due to the additional hour of study or, in other

words, the _____ income in this example is $ _____ .

2.38

Proceeding in the opposite direction: If you were originally studying for two

hours per day, your daily income from your father would be $ _____ .
If you now decided to study one hour less, the daily income would fall to

$ _____ or decrease by $ _____ .

Answers
   35. marginal · less
   36. 4.32 · 8 · 3.68
   37. marginal · 3.68
   38. 8 · 4.32 · 3.68

2.39

Whether an increase from 1 to 2 in time spent studying or a decrease from 2 to

1, the marginal ~~ＭＡＡＲ~~ *income* would be $ ~~ＡＡＡ~~ *3.68*.

2.40

In Figure 2.8 we show the relationship between hours spent studying and marginal income.

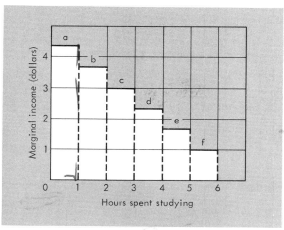

FIGURE 2.8. Study and Income I

In going from zero to one hour studying, total study income increases from zero

to $ ~~ＳＡＡ~~ *4.32*. This ~~ＡＡＡＲＮ~~ *m-* income is represented in Fig-

ure 2.8 by the rectangle *a*. The area of rectangle *a* is ~~ＡＡＡ~~ *4.32* units.

2.41

Adding another hour of studying (that is bringing the total study time up to

two hours) adds $ ~~ＢＡＡ~~ *3.68* to study income. This marginal

~~ＡＡＯＶＲ~~ *m-c.* is represented by rectangle ~~ＶＡ~~ *b* whose area

is ~~ＱＡＯ~~ *3.68* units.

2.42

Thus total study income from two hours of studying will be the increase in income from the first hour of studying plus the ~~increase~~ in income from the second hour of studying. In Figure 2.8 this will be the area of rectangle *a* plus the area of rectangle *b*, or _____ units plus _____ units, giving a total of _____ units.

2.43

Thus the total income from two hours of studying is $ _____ .

2.44

Similarly, the sum of the areas of rectangles *a*, *b*, *c*, *d*, *e* and *f* in Figure 2.8 is the total _____ from six hours of study. This total is $ _____ .

2.45

For simplicity we have considered the marginal income associated with one-hour changes in time spent studying. This has resulted in the step graph of Figure 2.8. If we consider smaller time increments, for instance quarter hours, we shall still have a step graph but the steps will be smaller; that is one quarter hour of additional study time will add ___(more/less)___ to daily income than will one hour.

2.46

Of course, adding together the increases in income from four quarter hours ___(will/will not)___ yield the same increase in income attributed to one extra hour.

2.47

This is demonstrated in Figure 2.10, where we consider in detail rectangle *a* of Figure 2.9. The area of rectangle *a* represents the amount of ___income___ attributable to the first hour of study. The height of the rectangle represents

Answers
    42. increase · 4.32 · 3.68 · 8
    43. 8
    44. income · 16
    45. less
    46. will
    47. income

the ~~marginal income~~ from increasing study time from zero hours to one hour. The width of the rectangle represents the additional ~~hour~~ spent studying, which in this case is ~~one~~ hour.

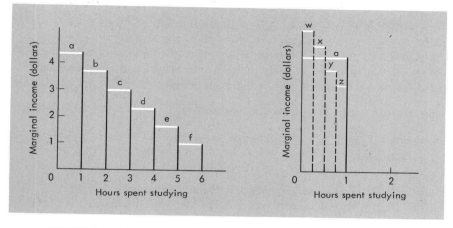

FIGURE 2.9. Study and Income I   FIGURE 2.10. Study and Income II

2.48

Just as in Figure 2.9 the first hour of study added ___(more/less)___ to study income than the second hour; so in Figure 2.10 the first quarter hour adds ~~More~~ to study income than the second quarter hour, which in turn ~~adds more~~ to study income than the third quarter hour, and so on.

2.49

In other words, as study time increases, the marginal income from studying (increases/decreases).

2.50

Originally, when we considered rectangle *a*, we assumed that the first quarter hour and the second, third or fourth quarter hour added ___(equal/unequal)___ amounts to study income.

Answers

47. marginal income · hour · one
48. more · more · adds more
49. decreases
50. equal

2.51

Now, when we consider each quarter hour separately, we see that the first quarter hour of study time adds ___(more/less)___ to study income than the second, which adds _____ than the third, and so on. That is, _____ income declines as study time _____

2.52

In Figure 2.10 the area of rectangle w represents the study income attributable to the first quarter hour of study time, the area of rectangle x represents the study income attributable to the second quarter hour of study time. As a result, both areas taken together represent study _____ attributable to the first _____ / _____ hour of study time.

2.53

What does the total area of rectangles w, x and y represent?

_____

What does the height of rectangle y represent?

_____

2.54

Now since income from the first hour of studying is known to be $4.32, it follows that income from the first four quarter hours of studying must also be $_____·, just as income from the first _____ minutes of studying must also be $4.32 and just as income from the first 60 × 60 seconds of studying must be $_____.

2.55

In other words the area of the four rectangles w, x, y, and z must equal the area of rectangle _____.

Answers

51. more · more · marginal · increases
52. income · half
53. income attributable to the first ¾ hours of study-time · marginal income attributable to the third quarter hour
54. 4.32 · 60 · 4.32
55. *a*

2.56

As we take smaller and smaller time intervals on the horizontal axis, the number of "steps" in the graph in Figure 2.10 will *(increase/decrease)*, each succeeding step becoming *(smaller/larger)* and *(smaller/larger)*.

2.57

As the steps become smaller the graph comes closer to being a straight line. If we divided the first hour, for instance, into minutes instead of quarter hours as in Figure 2.10, we would have _____ rectangles instead of 4 and if we divided it into seconds we would have 3,600. The greater the number of subdivisions, the _____ will be the "steps" in the graph.

2.58

As we imagine subdividing the horizontal axis into more and more, smaller and smaller units, e.g. milliseconds, the graph will become closer and closer to being a _____ line as in Figure 2.11.

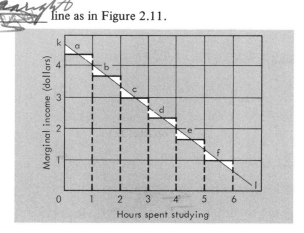

FIGURE 2.11. Study and Income III

2.59

In Figure 2.11 the line *kl* results from taking smaller and smaller intervals of the horizontal axis. The _____ under the line *kl* will represent study _____ from studying six hours.

Answers

56. increase · smaller · smaller
57. 60 · smaller
58. straight
59. area · income

2.60

This area will equal the ~~area~~ of the six rectangles *a, b, c, d, e* and *f*. The unshaded areas now included by the line *kl* will equal the unshaded portions of each of the rectangles left outside by the line *kl*.

2.61

In Figure 2.12 the point *s* on line *kl* is associated with h_1 hours of studying and a marginal income of ~~i_2~~. The point *t* is associated with ~~h_2~~ hours of studying and a marginal income of ~~i_1~~.

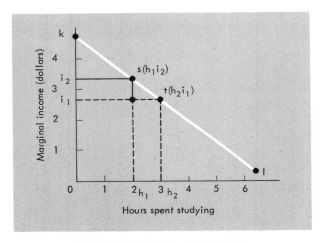

FIGURE 2.12. Study and Income IV

2.62

A movement from *s* to *t* occurs when you increase study time from ~~h_1~~ to ~~h_2~~ with a corresponding decrease in marginal income from ~~i_2~~ to ~~i_1~~.

2.63

As you increase hours studying, even though your marginal ~~income~~ decreases, your total income ~~increases~~.

Answers

60. areas
61. $i_2 \cdot h_2 \cdot i_1$
62. $h_1 \cdot h_2 \cdot i_2 \cdot i_1$
63. income $\cdot$ increases

2.64

In increasing studying time from Oh_1 to Oh_2, your total income ~~increases.~~ by the area $h_1 h_2 ts$ in Figure 2.12.

2.65

Another approach would be to say that total study income attributable to Oh_1 hours of study is represented by the area of figure $Oh_1 sk$.

Correspondingly study income related to Oh_2 hours of study is ~~$Oh_2 vtk$~~.
The difference between those two areas $h_1 h_2 ts$ in Figure 2.12 is attributable to

the ~~increase~~ in study time of ~~$h_2 - h_1$~~.

2.66

Now reconsider Figure 2.5 (repeated here as Figure 2.13) which shows the income forgone by not working.

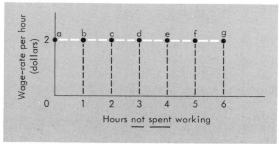

FIGURE 2.13. Income Forgone I

The area of the large rectangle 06*ga* that represents the income forgone by not

working at all, equals $ ~~12~~ . The area of any of the smaller

rectangles equals ~~income 2~~ forgone by not working that extra hour.
The income forgone by not working any hour equals the wage that would have

been paid for an hour's work; in this case $ ~~2~~ .

Answers
64. increases
65. $Oh_2 tk$ · increase · $h_1 h_2$
66. 12 · income · 2

2.67

In order for any activity to be worth undertaking, its benefit must exceed the

opportunity cost. The ~~opportunity~~ cost, as you will recall from Chapter 1,
is the benefit that could be derived from the best alternative activity. In deciding whether to study one hour, you must take into account the income
forgone by not working that hour. The income forgone by not working is the

~~opportunity~~ cost of studying.

2.68

For example, if you were to study one hour, your study income would be $4.32,

but you would also lose $ ~~2~~ by not working that hour. The

benefit from studying one hour is $ ~~4.32~~ , while the ~~opportunity~~

cost is $2. Since the benefit from studying one hour is *(greater/smaller)* than

the ~~opportunity cost~~ of studying one hour, it *(will/will not)*
pay you to study at least one hour.

2.69

With this in mind consider Figure 2.14 which is a combination of the figures with

which you are familiar. The line *lm* shows the ~~marginal~~ income from

studying, while line *ab* shows the ~~marginal~~ income forgone by not
working. The marginal income from studying is, of course, the marginal

(benefit/cost) from studying, while the marginal income forgone by not

working is the marginal ~~cost~~ of studying. At two hours spent

studying, the marginal benefit of studying is *(greater/less)* than the
marginal cost.

Answers
    67. opportunity · opportunity
    68. 2 · 4.32 · opportunity · greater · opportunity cost · will
    69. marginal · marginal · benefit · cost · greater

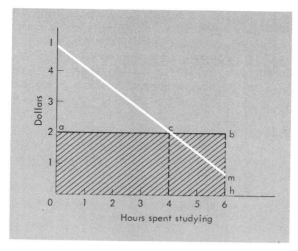

FIGURE 2.14. Study and Work Employment Income

2.70

At point *c*, lines *lm* and *ab* intersect. This point *c* corresponds to ~~four~~ hours of studying.

2.71

To the left of *c,* that is, up to four hours of studying, the line *lm* lies

(above/below) the line *ab,* showing that the ~~marginal~~ income

from studying is (greater/less) than the marginal income forgone by not working.

2.72

Thus, at any point less than four hours of studying, your income will increase

if you spend more time ~~studying~~ and less time ~~working~~.

2.73

Above four hours of studying, however, the ~~marginal~~ benefit from

studying is (greater/less) than the marginal cost of studying. At any

point above four hours of studying it would pay you to (increase/decrease)

Answers
70. four
71. above · marginal · greater
72. studying · working
73. marginal · less · decrease

time spent studying. Only at four hours spent studying, where the

~~marginal~~ benefit and cost are equal, will there be no incentive
to change the amount of time spent studying. Thus, the point where total

income from both studying and working is a maximum must be ~~four~~

hours studying and ~~two~~ hours working.

2.74
We have seen that the *optimum*, or best, position is where the ~~marginal~~

benefit and ~~marginal~~ cost are ~~equal~~. Only at such a
position will it be impossible to improve your position by making a change.

2.75
Whenever the marginal benefit of some activity exceeds the marginal cost it

will pay to *(increase/decrease)* that activity. And, whenever the marginal
benefit falls short of the marginal cost, the activity should be

(increased/decreased).

2.76
This principle applies to any situation where a choice of different combinations
is involved. Taking more of one always involves giving up more of the other.

As a result, there will always be an opportunity ~~cost~~ that must be
compared to the benefit of taking more of one. And the best combination will

be that for which the marginal ~~benefit~~ and marginal ~~cost~~
are equal.

REVIEW QUESTIONS

Questions 1 and 2 are based on the following diagram:

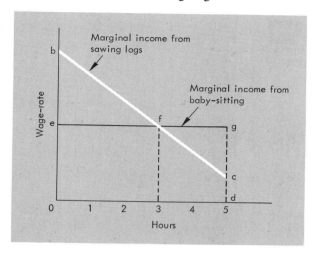

2.1

You have 5 hours to spend working. Which of the following statements are true?

a. The more time you spend sawing up logs, the less income you earn per hour of sawing.

b. The hourly wage rate you can earn baby-sitting is 0e.

c. To maximize daily income you would have to both saw logs and baby-sit.

d. All of the above.

2.2

You have 5 hours to spend working. Which of the following statements are true?

a. Daily income would be maximized by spending 3 hours sawing logs and 2 hours babysitting.

b. The maximum daily income you can earn is 0bfgd.

c. After 3 hours of log sawing the marginal income from log sawing is less than the marginal income from babysitting.

d. All of the above.

Answers
  1. d
  2. d

3

The Theory of Consumer Choice

3.1

In Chapters 1 and 2 we studied the principles of optimal resource allocation. In this chapter we shall study how an individual allocates income to make himself as well-off as possible. For most individuals, income is a scarce

_____ to be allocated among many alternatives. In economic jargon we say that the individual attempts to maximize utility (satisfaction) subject to an income constraint.

3.2

If, between the next two pages of this book, you found a dollar bill which was a gift from me to you (this is purely hypothetical, you realize) how would you spend it? The answer is fairly obvious; you would spend it in such a way

that you would receive maximum_____ (satisfaction) from the dollar.

3.3

There exist many ways to spend the dollar: you have many wants you would like to satisfy and manufacturers have produced many commodities they would like you to purchase. But you cannot buy them all; you cannot satisfy all your

_____ because you have an _____ constraint.

Answers
1. resource
2. utility
3. wants · income

3.4

You will use your limited income, in this example $1, to purchase those commodities which will satisfy you as completely as possible in such a situation. That is, you will attempt to _____ your _____ subject to your _____ constraint.

3.5

You know what you like better than anyone else. Subject to legal consideration, most people in this country are free to spend or allocate their _____ as they wish. As we shall see, it is the way that consumers like yourself allocate their _____ which tells manufacturers what commodities people want most.

3.6

Manufacturers respond to consumers *preferences* as seen through their spending habits. An economy operating in such fashion is said to allocate its scarce _____ through a *free enterprise* system.

3.7

Some people argue that consumers do not always know their best interests, and there should be limits in the way resources are allocated through a _____ _____ system to reflect _____ wants. For instance, it is argued that horror comics should be banned because they are not "good" for people. The same arguments are used in regard to alcohol, cigarettes, and some automobiles. In the U.S. economy, however, many people allocate part of their income to the purchase of horror comics, alcohol, cigarettes, and automobiles, and manufacturers of those items observe consumers' signals (dollar votes) and produce the above goods as we would expect under the functioning of a _____ _____ system.

3.8

A free _____ system does not itself make value judgments as to what people should or should not buy, but operates under the assumption that

Answers
4. maximize · utility · income
5. income · incomes
6. resources
7. free enterprise · consumers' · free enterprise
8. enterprise

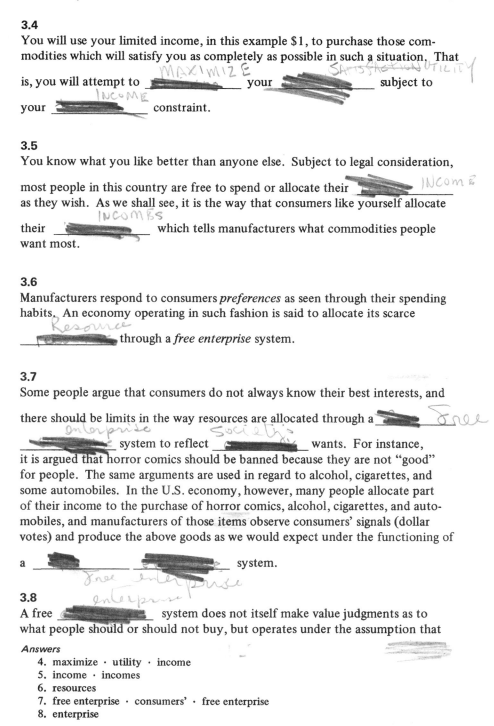

Consumers [handwritten] know their interests best. We shall study how consumers signal with dollar votes in competitive markets for goods and services to indicate to manufacturers their (income/preferences). Manufacturers in turn hire scarce

resources [handwritten] and produce the goods and services consumers want if profits are sufficient in those fields of production. Manufacturers, we assume, are motivated by a profit incentive, ____(or/not)____ by their judgments as to what people *should* buy.

3.9
It is important to remember that manufacturers are concerned with people's wants only to the extent that those wants are backed by dollar votes. You may want an expensive sports car very badly, but manufacturers will not be overly

concerned with such a want unless you have ____*dollar*____ votes to support the want and unless you are prepared to express your preferences by actively bidding in the market. We shall show that in a free enterprise system it is through a price mechanism that resources are allocated in accordance with consumer

____*preferences*____ as expressed by dollar votes.

3.10
Despite having many ____*wants*____ most consumers, for all practical purposes, have limited means of satisfying their ____*wants*____. Limited means for most people take the form of limited incomes or limited budgets available for expenditure on consumer goods and services. In any time period we normally assume, therefore, that each consumer (a consumer can be thought of as a family unit as well as one individual) has a budget constraint. That is, we

assume the consumer is limited by his ____*income*____ from purchasing all the goods and services he desires.

3.11
Within the limits of the budget or income constraint, however, the consumer attempts to make his satisfaction or utility from consuming goods and services as large as possible. Expressed more rigorously we say that the rational consumer in any time period attempts to maximize his utility subject to a ____*budget constraint*____

Answers
8. consumers · preferences · resources · not
9. dollar · preferences
10. wants · wants · budget
11. budget constraint

3.12

Thus a consumer will change his expenditure pattern if the change yields him a higher level of ~~utility~~. He will continue to change his expenditure patterns until he cannot ~~increase~~ his total utility by a reallocation of his expenditure. Only then will the consumer ~~maximize~~ his total utility. And only then will the consumer be in equilibrium, i.e. have no incentive to alter his expenditure patterns.

3.13

When will the consumer be in equilibrium? As we shall see, he will be in ~~equilibrium~~ when the utility he receives from the last dollar spent on any good or service just equals the utility received from the last dollar spent on any other good or service. Then and only then will he ~~maximize~~ his total utility.

3.14

After a certain point has been reached, the utility received from consuming additional units of a good decreases for an individual. The extra utility derived from consuming an additional unit of a good is known as the marginal utility of that good. Thus, after a certain point has been reached in the consumption of a good, the ~~marginal utility~~ of that good decreases as consumption increases.

3.15

As you sit in a soda parlor one afternoon, for instance, after you have consumed a few chocolate sundaes the ~~utility~~ you derive from, let's say, your fourth sundae will be less than that derived from your third, and the ~~utility~~ derived from the fifth will be even less than that from the fourth, and so on. In fact a sixth sundae may give you no utility or satisfaction at all and a seventh could give you pain rather than pleasure by making you sick. This would be an example of negative utility from the seventh sundae, and under normal circumstances you presumably would not consume a seventh sundae

Answers
12. utility · increase · maximize
13. equilibrium · maximize
14. marginal utility
15. utility · utility

even if it were free. Since you normally would want to ~~*maximize*~~

your total utility, in this example six sundaes would yield you ___ *(more/less)* ___
utility than seven sundaes.

3.16
In this example, when seven sundaes are consumed the ~~*marginal*~~

~~*utility*~~ becomes negative. This means that total utility is decreasing
when a seventh sundae is consumed; it does not mean that total utility is nega-

tive. ___ *(true/false.)* ___

3.17
In some given time period, how many sundaes will you consume if you have to

pay for them? As a rational ~~*consumer*~~ you will consume additional

sundaes as long as the ~~*utility*~~ from each successive dollar spent on

sundaes gives more ~~*utility*~~ than can be obtained from any alternative
purchase. At the point where the last dollar spent on a sundae gives no more

~~*utility*~~ than the last dollar spent on any other good, you will buy no
more sundaes.

3.18
If the last dollar spent on a chocolate sundae gives you less ~~*utility*~~

than the last dollar spent on a hamburger, then your total ~~*utility*~~
will be higher if you consume the hamburger rather than the sundae. In general,

you obviously ___ *(will/will not)* ___ spend another dollar on good *A* if the utility
received from that additional consumption is less than the utility you would
have received from the additional consumption of an extra dollar's worth of
some other good *B*.

3.19
It is only when the last dollar spent on each good yields the same utility that

___ *(total/marginal)* ___ utility will be a maximum.

Answers
15. maximize · more
16. marginal utility · true
17. consumer · utility · utility · utility
18. utility · utility · will not
19. total

3.20

If you are in equilibrium consuming both hamburgers at 50¢ each and hotdogs at 25¢ each, then the last hamburger consumed will have to yield you

(half the/the same/twice the) satisfaction of the last hotdog consumed. If 50¢ spent on a hamburger gives you the same utility as 25¢ on a hotdog, you should

buy more ~~hotdogs~~ and fewer ~~hamburgers~~. You will maximize

utility when the last dollar's worth of each yields the same ~~utility~~, or expressing this another way, when the marginal utility of hotdogs divided by

the price of hotdogs equals the ~~marginal utility~~ of ham-

burgers divided by the price of hamburgers. In this example $\dfrac{MU \text{ hotdog}}{25¢}$ =

$\dfrac{MU \text{ hamburgers}}{50¢}$. For the ratio to be equal, the marginal utility of your last

hamburger must be ~~twice~~ the marginal utility of your last hotdog.

3.21

Diagramatically we show this relationship in Figure 3.1.

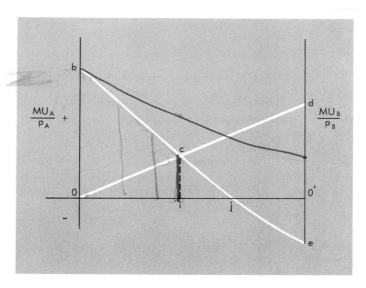

FIGURE 3.1. Utility Maximization with Two Goods and Income *00'*

Line $00'$ along the horizontal axis represents the income which you may spend

on goods A and B. Your aim is to maximize _____ subject to an

_____ (or budget) constraint.

3.22

The more income you spend on A the _____ income will be available to spend on B. If, for instance you spend $0i$ on good A, only

_____ will be available to spend on B. The line *bce* shows the
marginal utility per dollar spent on A. It slopes downward from left to right

because the greater the consumption of a good, the _(higher/lower)_   the

_____ utility of that good. As you spend more income on A the

_____ per dollar of A declines.

3.23

In fact, after a certain amount of income has been spent on A, the marginal
utility of A (MU_A) per dollar becomes negative; that amount of income is

_____

3.24

Income not spent on A is spent on good B. Considering Figure 3.1 from the

$d0'$ vertical axis we see that the MU_B per dollar falls from $0'd$ to _____
as we spend more and more income on B. Does MU_B ever become negative?

_____, the last amount spent on B yields _____ mar-
ginal utility.

3.25

Does that imply that by spending all your income on B the total utility you

would derive would be zero? _____ . Quite correct—the answer

is no; you must not confuse _____ utility with total utility.

Answers
  21. utility · income
  22. less · $i0'$ · lower · marginal · marginal utility
  23. $0j$
  24. 0 · no · zero
  25. no · marginal

The former refers to the utility derived from the *last* unit of good *B* consumed, whereas the latter refers to the utility derived from *all* units of good *B* consumed.

3.26

The total utility you would derive from spending all your income *00'* on good *B* would be _____ *area under O d* _____

(Remember how we calculated study income in Chapter 2?)

3.27

If you missed the answer to the previous frame, go back and quickly review the relevant part of Chapter 2. Now to really test your understanding! The total utility you would derive from spending all your income, *00'*, on good *A* would be

_____ *Obj − Obj* _____

3.28

How should you divide your income between goods *A* and *B*? You will recall from the hamburger-hotdog example that if you want to maximize utility, you should consume two goods in such amounts that the last dollar spent on each

good yields the same _____ *utility* _____ . In this example, if you wish to

_____ *maximize* _____ utility from the income *00'* spent on goods *A* and *B*, you should allocate this income so that the last dollar spent on *A* will yield the same

_____ *utility* _____ as the last dollar spent on *B*. This is equivalent to saying that

$\dfrac{MU_A}{P_A}$ must equal _____ $\dfrac{m U_B}{P_B}$.

3.29

This will occur in Figure 3.1 when you spend _____ *0i* _____ of your income

on *A* and _____ *i0'* _____ of your income on *B*. At this point the marginal

Answers

26. the area under the line *0CD* or the area of *0'd0*
27. the area *0bj*, minus the area *j0'e*. After you spend *0j* income on *A* the marginal utility becomes negative. Just like your sundaes.
28. utility · maximize · utility · $\dfrac{MU_B}{P_B}$
29. *0i* · *i0'*

utility per dollar is the same for both goods and is equal to  *iC* .

That is $\dfrac{MU_A}{P_A} = \dfrac{MU_B}{P_B}$

3.30
When your income is allocated in this optimal fashion, total utility will be equal
to the utility derived from spending *0i* on *A*, which is represented by the area

~~*Obci*~~ , plus the utility derived from spending *i0′* on *B*, which is

represented by area ~~~~ *0dci*

3.31
Any different allocation of income will yield a (smaller/larger) total
utility and, as you can see by trying it out on Figure 3.1, will be represented by
a smaller total area.

3.32
Figure 3.2 is a repeat of Figure 3.1; the only difference being that your

~~income~~ has increased from *00′* to *00″*. Even though your income
is higher, the utility obtained from the first unit of *A* and the first unit of *B*

will be unchanged. The $\dfrac{MU_A}{P_A}$ curve will intersect the left vertical axis at point

b and the $\dfrac{MU_B}{P_B}$ curve will intersect the new right vertical axis at point

d′ ~~~~ .

Answers
29. *iC*
30. *0bci* ·· *0′dci*
31. smaller
32. income · *d′*

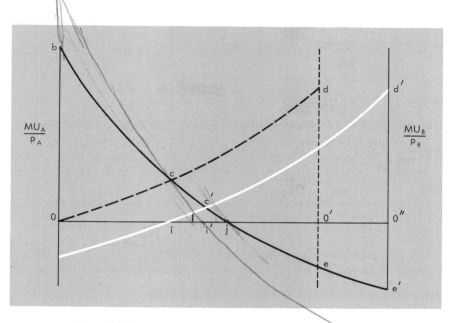

FIGURE 3.2. Utility Maximization; Same Goods-Higher Income

3.33

Now, as before, if you spend $0i$ on good A, the $\dfrac{MU_A}{P_A}$ will be _____.

But, now that your income is higher, if you spend $0i$ on A, you must spend

_____(more/less)_____ on B than before. And since, as expenditure on a good in-

creases, the marginal utility _(increases/decreases)_ the $\dfrac{MU_B}{P_B}$ must be

_____(higher/lower)_____ than previously. Consequently, the $\dfrac{MU_B}{P_B}$ curve will now

lie to the right and below its position in Figure 3.1.

3.34

When you had an income of only $00'$ and spent it all on B, the marginal utility

of the last dollar spent on B was _(positive/zero/negative)_. If you now spend

Answers
   33. ci · more · decreases · lower
   34. zero

all of income $00''$ on B the marginal utility of your last expenditure on B will

be ___negative___ .

3.35
The MU per dollar graphs now intersect at _____ ~~c'~~ . This means that

your utility will be maximized when you allocate _____ ~~0i'~~ of your

income to A and _____ ~~i'0''~~ to B.

3.36
But note a very important point. At the point of utility maximization marginal

utilities divided by respective price are both (*lower/higher*) than they were

before. The reason is because you are now consuming ___more___ of
both commodities and the more you consume of a commodity in some given

time period, the (*higher/lower*) is its marginal utility.

3.37
Thus, the marginal utilities of both commodities consumed are lower than before

because you are consuming ___more___ of both commodities. Consequent-

ly, the lower marginal utilities indicate that you are (*better off/worse off*) , or

that your total utility is (*greater/less*) than before.

3.38
Thus, given you are restricted to only two commodities, and given that marginal
utilities are positive, an increase in income will lead to an increase in

~~total~~ utility; ~~marginal~~ utilities, however, will decline.

You will maximize ~~total util~~ when the last dollar's
worth (or cent's worth) of expenditure on A yields the same satisfaction as the

last dollar's worth of expenditure on B—in other words when $\dfrac{MU_A}{P_A} = \dfrac{MU_B}{P_B}$.

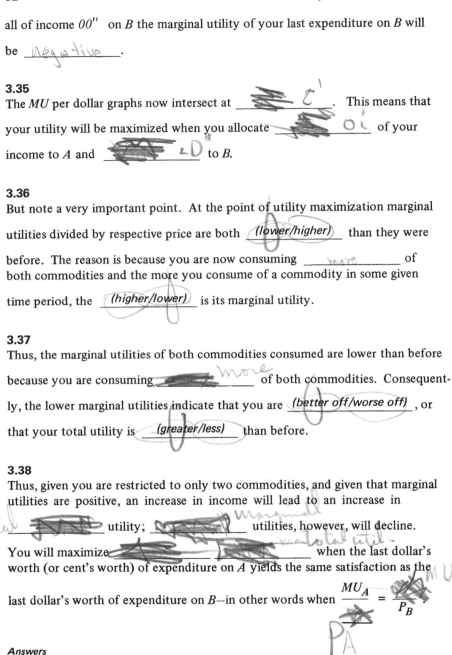

Answers
   34. negative
   35. c' · $0i'$ · $i'0''$
   36. lower · more · lower
   37. more · better off · greater
   38. total · marginal · total utility · P_A · MU_B

3.39

Figures 3.1 and 3.2 can be interpreted in a different way. The $\frac{MU_A}{P_A}$ curve can be interpreted as showing the marginal ~~(benefit/cost)~~ of expenditure on A. The $\frac{MU_B}{P_B}$ shows the marginal benefit of expenditure on B and, therefore, shows what you give up when you spend an extra dollar on A. Consequently, the $\frac{MU_B}{P_B}$ curve shows the marginal ~~(benefit/cost)~~ of expenditure on A.

3.40

As you remember from Chapters 1 and 2, the allocation which maximizes total benefit is where ~~_____~~ benefit and ~~_____~~ cost are equal. As you have already seen, the same criterion applies to the allocation of income for expenditure among different goods. Utility is maximized when $\frac{MU_A}{P_A}$, which is the ~~_____~~ of expenditure on A, is equal to $\frac{MU_B}{P_B}$, which is the ~~_____~~ of expenditure on B.

3.41

Assume you are in equilibrium in this two-commodity world, so $\frac{MU_A}{P_A} = \frac{MU_B}{P_B}$.

Now assume the price of commodity A falls; this will cause $\frac{MU_A}{P_A}$ to become ~~(less/greater)~~ than $\frac{MU_B}{P_B}$. To restore equality, i.e. to make $\frac{MU_A}{P_A} = \frac{MU_B}{P_B}$, you will reallocate your income between A and B buying more ~~_____~~ and less ~~_____~~ than before.

Answers

39. benefit · cost
40. marginal · marginal · marginal benefit · marginal benefit
41. greater · A · B

3.42

As you consume more A, however, the marginal utility of each additional unit

consulted will ~~*decrease*~~ and thus the ratio $\dfrac{MU_A}{P_A}$ will ~~*decrease*~~.

As you consume less of B, conversely, the ratio $\dfrac{MU_B}{P_B}$ will ~~*increase*~~.

3.43

You will cease reallocating income when equality is restored; i.e. when $\dfrac{MU_A}{P_A}$ =

$\dfrac{MU_B}{P_B}$. Then and only then will total ~~*utility*~~ be a maximum.

3.44

The last three frames have shown why the quantity of good A purchased was

(greater/lower) at a lower price. This condition holds for most goods.
Variables other than price, however, affect the quantity of any commodity
purchased and to fully understand we must take into account all factors affecting
consumers' purchases. Price, however, is one of the most important variables

and we would expect people to buy ~~*more*~~ steak at $1.00 per
pound than at $5.00 per pound.

3.45

Let us arbitrarily choose a time period of one week, and, given that you are a
steak consumer, let us consider the factors which might influence the amount
of steak you would purchase. The price of steak, one would expect, would
certainly influence how much you purchase. And we would further expect that

the lower the price of steak the ~~*greater*~~ the amount of steak you
would purchase.

Answers
    42. decrease · decrease · increase
    43. $\dfrac{MU_B}{P_B}$ · utility
    44. greater · more
    45. greater

3.46

One might also find, however, that if in a given week the local supermarket had lobster, chicken, and lamb at greatly reduced prices, you might buy no steak during that week. Consequently, we would expect that the ~~_____~~ of goods you might substitute for steak would affect the amount of steak you would buy.

3.47

Perhaps the only way you like your steak is barbecued outdoors over an oak-chip fire. You also do not like to barbecue outdoors unless the weather is pleasant. Consequently, we would expect that if we chose a week in which the weather was predicted to be inclement, you would, in all probability, buy no steak that week. Thus, we can see that in this specific example the amount of steak you might buy would depend upon the ~~_____~~ Pound for pound, sausage and hamburger tend to be cheaper than steak, and if indeed your income is very low, you might not be able to afford steak. Thus, we would expect that ~~_____~~ would be another factor which would influence the amount of steak you would buy.

3.48

We could expand the list of items which would affect the amount of steak you would buy in any given week, and we can see that the amount of steak demanded in any week depends not only on the price of steak but also on many other factors. To the extent that those other factors are important in the determination of the amount of steak demanded, we cannot neglect all factors except ~~_____~~ when considering demand for steak.

3.49

Suppose we wished to explore the relationship between your demand for steak and the number of your guests. If you plan to serve each person half a pound of steak, then the relationship is simple.

Answers
  46. prices
  47. weather · income
  48. price

Table 3.1
Number of Guests and Quantity of Steak Demanded

Quantity of Steak That Would Be Bought (lbs)	Number of Guests
½	0
1	1
1½	2
2	3
2½	4
3	5

Even if you have no guests we are assuming you have a steak yourself. From ~~increase~~

Table 3.1 we see that the quantity of steak that would be bought ~~increase~~ as the number of guests increases.

3.50
Since we are concerned only with the relationship between your ~~demand~~ for steak and the number of guests, we assume that anything else that could affect your demand for steak does not change during the time period under consideration. For instance, we assume the price of steak is fixed, since if steak were to increase in price to $20 per pound after you bought one pound for $2 you would probably buy chicken rather than steak for your guests.

3.51
On the assumption that everything else remains unchanged Figure 3.3 shows what quantity of ~~steak~~ you would buy today for different numbers of ~~guests~~.

Answers
49. increases
50. demand
51. steak · guests

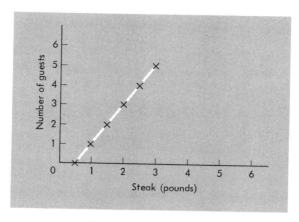

FIGURE 3.3. $D_s = f(g)$

3.52

We could repeat this process with all the items that affect your demand for steak. If we were to draw graphs similar to Figure 3.3 then we would have lines which sloped upwards to the right, as in Figure 3.3, whenever the quantity of steak demanded *(increased/decreased)* along with the variable being considered. In Figure 3.3, for instance, the quantity of steak demanded ~~increases~~ as the number of guests increases.

3.53

If we choose an item where the reverse relationship exists, for instance the price of steak, we would have a graph which would be *(downward/upward)* sloping to the _____ *(left/right)_____* , since at higher prices smaller quantities of steak would typically be demanded, other things remaining unchanged.

3.54

Let us hold everything except the price and quantity of steak constant for now. By "everything" we mean all items we have considered and all items we have not considered that might affect the quantity of steak you would purchase in any given week. We wish to see the amount of steak you would purchase at different prices during a given week. If you look at Table 3.2 you will see that if the price of steak were $ _____ per pound or $ _____ per

Answers
52. increased · increases
53. downward · right
54. $5 · $4

pound, you would not purchase any steak during the week. You will further

see that if the price of steak were ~~————~~ lower, you would purchase more
steak during that week.

Table 3.2
Individual Demand for Steak

Prices per Pound	Pounds of Steak That Would Be Purchased per Week
$5	0
4	0
3	1
2	2
1.50	3
1	5
.79	9
.50	15

3.55
In Figure 3.4 we have plotted the points from Table 3.2 and joined the points by
a smooth curve. Points lying on the curve between any given points are approxi-
mations as to what you would buy if prices lay in between any of the quoted
prices. We make this approximation in converting Table 3.2 into Figure 3.4 for
the sake of simplicity.

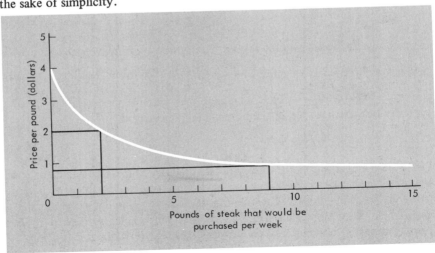

FIGURE 3.4. Individual Demand for Steak

Answers
54. lower

What we have produced in Figure 3.4 is your individual _____ curve for steak for the specified week. And we can further see that at no two different prices below $4 would the _____ of steak demanded by you be the same.

3.56

Let us look carefully at Figure 3.4 because much more lies behind your simple _____ for steak than would appear. First, there is a time period involved, which in this case happens to be one week. However, if the time period became ten weeks instead of one week, we would expect that the quantities of steak you would purchase at each of the various prices in

Table 3.2 would be _____ than the existing quantities where the

time period is _____ _____. Consequently, the de-

mand curve in Figure 3.4 __(does/does not)__ reflect the situation where the time period is ten weeks.

3.57

Let us look carefully at Figure 3.4 and see exactly what it says. Figure 3.4 says that holding everything else constant, you would in a given week buy

_____ pounds of steak if the price were $2 per pound, whereas you

would buy _____ pounds of steak if the price were $.79 per pound.

If the price were $2.50 per pound, you would buy between _____

and _____ pounds of steak.

3.58

Thus, if we hold everything else constant we can tell from your _____

_____ how much steak you _____ buy at given prices.

3.59

Your demand curve for steak, therefore, is really a hypothetical curve showing

the quantities of steak you _____ buy at different prices

_____ everything else were held constant.

3.60

One day in your local supermarket you are about to buy two pounds of steak
at $2 per pound when the attendant at the meat counter announces that he
is reducing the price of steak to $1 per pound. When this occurs, you end up
purchasing five pounds of steak. Has the meat attendant's decision to change
the price of steak from $2 per pound to $1 per pound changed your demand

curve? The answer is _____. What you have done is move from
one position on your demand curve to a new position on the same demand
curve. If everything else remains unchanged, then neither the position nor the

shape of your _____ _____ in Figure 3.4 will change.

3.61

Let us now be more rigorous about the curve in Figure 3.4. First, we have a
given time period. Second, there are certain factors such as your income,

number of guests, weather, and so on that ___*(can/cannot)*___ affect the
amount of steak you will buy in any week. Those factors, other than price,
which influence the amount of steak you buy are parameters. In Figure 3.4

we assume that those _____ are fixed and do not change.

3.62

Thus, in Figure 3.4 we see that movements along this demand curve tell us

that the quantities which would be purchased _____ as price falls.
Since prices and quantities change or vary, they are known as variables. Given
that the parameters are fixed, we know that the quantity of steak you will buy

will depend upon the _____ of steak. For this reason we say that
quantity is the dependent variable, i.e. because the quantity taken will

_____ on the price of steak.

Answers
59. would · if
60. no · demand curve
61. can · parameters
62. increase · price · depend

3.63

It is highly unlikely, however, that the price of steak in the area in which you live will depend upon the quantity of steak you buy. And for this reason

~~(price/quantity)~~ is known as the independent variable. ~~(price/quantity)~~ is known as the dependent variable.

3.64

The position and shape of the demand curve in Figure 3.4 will depend upon the

~~————~~, and if changes occur in any of the ~~————~~, then the position and shape of the demand curve will change. Since we will ulti-

mately show how resource allocation in a price system responds to ~~————~~ preferences, it is important to know that some of the parameters determining the position of your demand curve in Figure 3.4 are your tastes and preferences.

3.65

Now it is highly likely that parameters will change over time. For instance, it would be highly unusual if your tastes, income, and prices of all other goods were to remain unchanged over time. Consequently, it is highly unlikely that

the position and the shape of your ~~————~~ for steak will remain unchanged over time. But this change in the position and

shape of your ~~————~~ for steak over time must

be carefully distinguished from a movement along your ~~————~~

~~————~~ for steak in a given time period.

3.66

A demand curve is actually a hypothetical situation. It shows what would

happen, given the parameters, if the ~~————~~ of steak were to

change. That is, it tells us what ~~————~~ of steak you would buy

at various hypothetical prices, given no change in any of the ~~————~~

Answers

   63. price · quantity
   64. parameters · parameters · consumer
   65. demand curve · demand curve · demand curve
   66. price · quantity · parameters

3.67

Let us consider a change in one of the ~~_____~~ which will cause your demand curve to shift. A change in the price per pound of steak, all other things remaining unchanged, will cause your demand curve for steak to shift.

(true/false)

3.68

Imagine that the prices of lobster, lamb, and chicken fall to very low levels during some specified week, but the price of steak which is $2 per pound does not change. Had there been no changes in any of the parameters (including the

prices of lobster, lamb, and chicken) you would have purchased ~~_____~~ pounds of steak during that week. Given that you enjoy lobster, lamb, and chicken, however, we would expect you to take advantage of the low prices of those items and consume them during the week, possibly to the exclusion of steak. If indeed this did occur, the quantity of steak you would buy at a

price of $2 per pound would fall to ~~_____~~. At a price of $1.50

per pound for steak, however, given the new set of ~~_____~~ (lobster, lamb, and chicken much cheaper than they were in Figure 3.4), you would pur-chase one pound of steak, at $1 per pound two pounds of steak, and at $.50 per pound twenty pounds of steak. Thus, compared with Figure 3.4, you now

have a new ~~_____~~ ~~_____~~ for steak, because some of the

~~_____~~ that determine the position and shape of your ~~_____~~

~~_____~~ for steak have changed.

3.69

If you look at your new demand schedule for steak alongside your original one

(Figure 3.5), we can see there has been a(n) _(downward/upward)_ shift of your

demand curve, to the _(left/right.)_ This has occurred because there has

been a change in some of the ~~_____~~ that determine the position of

the ~~_____~~ ~~_____~~ ; not because the price of steak has changed.

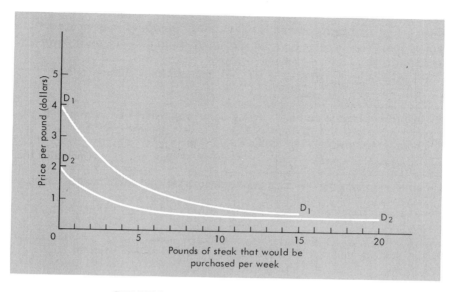

FIGURE 3.5. Shift in Demand Curve for Steak

3.70

Let us now imagine that your income increases substantially. In considering

your demand curve for steak, income is treated as a *(variable/parameter.)*
With a higher income you can now afford to buy more steak as well as more
of many other goods. But if indeed you do buy more steak at the going price
than you did with your original income, we would say there had been a

(shift of/movement along) your demand curve.

3.71

With your increase in income you would now have a new ~~~~~~~~~~~

~~~~~~~~~~ for steak because one of the ~~~~~~~~~~, which
determine the position and shape of your demand curve, had changed. In
relation to the position of your old demand curve, we would expect this new

demand curve to be _*(higher/lower)*_ and to the _*(right/left)*_ .

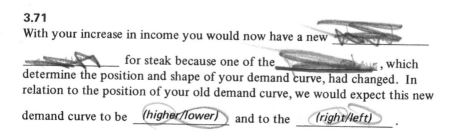

3.72

In the blanks after each question put in the most appropriate statement concerning your demand curve for steak (shifts upward to the right/shifts downwards to the left/does not change).

a. The price of lamb is drastically reduced, and you enjoy consuming lamb.

_____ *D. to left* _____

b. The price of lamb is drastically reduced, but you would buy lamb under

no circumstances because you dislike it. ____ *no change* _____

c. Farmers are bringing fewer animals to the market, and consequently there

is less steak in the stores. ____ *no change* _____

d. The government imposes a $.20 per pound tax on the price of steak.

_____ *no change* _____

e. You are given the gift of a new barbecue and barbecuing weather is perfect.

_____ *upward right* _____

f. A friend of yours, who is a hunter, gives you a side of venison, and you have

no freezer. ____ *downward to left* _____

g. The supermarket has a special discount sale on steak. ___ *no change* ___

3.73

In Figure 3.4 and 3.5 we see that demand curves slope downwards from

____ *left* ____ to ____ *right* ____. Or, in other words, the higher the

price of a good, other things remaining equal, the ___ *smaller* ___ is the
quantity normally bought. Let us see why this should be so. The first and most
obvious reason is that at a lower price, given your income, you can afford to buy

____ *more* ____ of that good since each unit costs less. If, for instance, you

Answers

72. a. shifts downwards to the left
    b. does not change
    c. does not change
    d. does not change

73. left · right · smaller · more

    e. shifts upwards to the right
    f. shifts downward to the left
    g. does not change

have only $5, and the price of steak is $5 per pound, you could buy only one pound of steak; whereas, if steak were $2.50 per pound, you could buy

_____2_____ pounds of steak.

3.74

Second, at lower prices you tend to buy ___more___ of a good because this good now becomes relatively more appealing when compared to substitutes. Let us imagine that lamb and steak both sell for one dollar per pound, and at those prices you buy one pound of each. Let us now imagine that the price of lamb does not change, but the price of steak falls to $.50 per pound. You may well decide to buy more steak for the first reason, i.e. steak is now cheaper and you can afford to buy more. But also, you may now decide to buy ___steak___

instead of lamb because the price of steak has ___fallen___ whereas the price of lamb has remained unchanged.

3.75

Another example would be the housewife who would prefer to cook with butter rather than oleomargarine, but who cannot afford to do so at existing prices.

If the price of butter falls, she can afford to buy ___more___ butter because of the price reduction. But she may also decide to cook now with butter, not because butter is even cheaper than oleomargarine at the reduced price, but because the relative difference in prices may be so small that she substitutes butter for oleomargarine in cooking.

3.76

There is still a third way we can look at our downward sloping demand curve. For the first pound of steak you purchase you are prepared to pay a relatively high price, but you will not purchase two pounds of steak for the same price.

You will only purchase two pounds of steak at a ___lower___ price,

i.e. you ___(are/are not)___ prepared to pay the same price for the second pound of steak. Presumably this is because the second pound of steak will not give you as much satisfaction as the first pound of steak. This tendency to associate diminishing satisfaction or utility with each additional unit of a good consumed in a given time period is known as the *law of diminishing marginal utility*.

Answers
73. two
74. more · steak · fallen
75. more
76. lower · are not

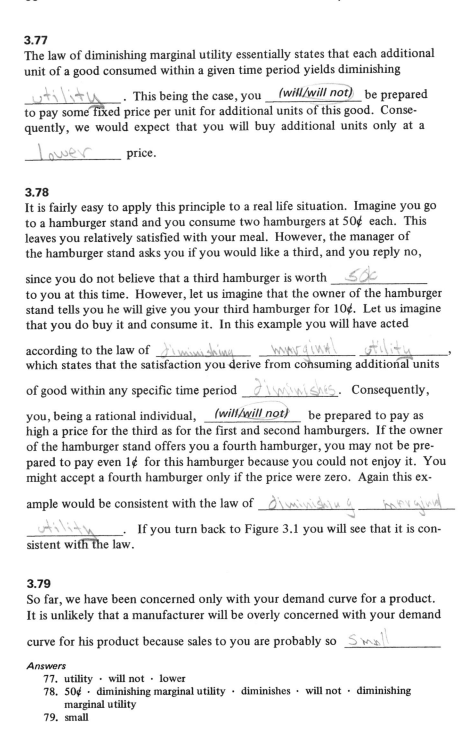

3.77

The law of diminishing marginal utility essentially states that each additional unit of a good consumed within a given time period yields diminishing

___utility___ . This being the case, you ___(will/will not)___ be prepared to pay some fixed price per unit for additional units of this good. Consequently, we would expect that you will buy additional units only at a

___lower___ price.

3.78

It is fairly easy to apply this principle to a real life situation. Imagine you go to a hamburger stand and you consume two hamburgers at 50¢ each. This leaves you relatively satisfied with your meal. However, the manager of the hamburger stand asks you if you would like a third, and you reply no,

since you do not believe that a third hamburger is worth ___50¢___ to you at this time. However, let us imagine that the owner of the hamburger stand tells you he will give you your third hamburger for 10¢. Let us imagine that you do buy it and consume it. In this example you will have acted

according to the law of ___diminishing___ ___marginal___ ___utility___ , which states that the satisfaction you derive from consuming additional units

of good within any specific time period ___diminishes___. Consequently,

you, being a rational individual, ___(will/will not)___ be prepared to pay as high a price for the third as for the first and second hamburgers. If the owner of the hamburger stand offers you a fourth hamburger, you may not be prepared to pay even 1¢ for this hamburger because you could not enjoy it. You might accept a fourth hamburger only if the price were zero. Again this ex-

ample would be consistent with the law of ___diminishing___ ___marginal___

___utility___. If you turn back to Figure 3.1 you will see that it is consistent with the law.

3.79

So far, we have been concerned only with your demand curve for a product. It is unlikely that a manufacturer will be overly concerned with your demand

curve for his product because sales to you are probably so ___small___

Answers

77. utility · will not · lower
78. 50¢ · diminishing marginal utility · diminishes · will not · diminishing marginal utility
79. small

as to appear negligible. One would *(expect/not expect)* the owners of the local supermarket to be concerned whether or not in any given day you pur-

chase a loaf of bread, because the sale of one loaf of bread *(will/will not)* substantially affect the sales or profits of the supermarket. This is an important assumption, but as you can well see a very reasonable one in a freely competitive economic system. In such a system we assume that no single individual can make any significant difference to the price of a good by purchasing or not purchasing in any given market. The influence of any single individual in a market in a

freely competitive economic system is *(negligible/substantial)*.

3.80

However, when we consider the total demand in any given market, we are summing up all the individual demands in this market, and we

(would expect/would not expect) manufacturers to be concerned with total demand. Total or market demand will be the subject of Chapter 4.

REVIEW QUESTIONS

3.1

A consumer who wants to maximize utility should increase his consumption of

a good ____D____ .

a. if the marginal utility of that good is positive.
b. if the marginal utility of that good is greater than the price of that good.
c. if the marginal utility of that good is greater than that of some other good.
d. if the marginal utility per dollar spent on that good is greater than that of some other good.

3.2

A consumer's demand curve for a good ____A____ .

a. assumes the prices of all other goods to remain constant.
b. indicates the going price of that good.
c. will shift if the price of the good changes.
d. all of the above are correct.

Answers
79. not expect · will not · negligible
80. would expect
1. d
2. a

3.3
A consumer buys only wine and cheese. In spending all his income, his marginal utility of wine is 3 and his marginal utility of cheese is 1. The price of wine is $8 and the price of cheese is $2. If the consumer wants to maximise utility he

should buy ____*B*____.

a. more wine and less cheese.
b. less wine and more cheese.
c. more wine and more cheese.
d. less wine and less cheese.

3.4
If the price of a good rises, a consumer who previously was maximizing utility

will buy less of the good because its marginal utility ____*C*____.

a. will now be negative.
b. will now be lower.
c. per dollar will now be lower.
d. per dollar will now be higher.

3.5
A consumer who wants to maximize utility and is deciding whether to consume

an additional unit of a good must consider ____*D*____.

a. the marginal utility of that good.
b. the resulting reduction in the amounts of other goods he consumes.
c. the marginal utility of other goods he consumes.
d. all of the above.

Answers
   3. b
   4. c
   5. d

4

Market Demand

4.1
Aggregate demand schedules and curves are simply found by adding together individual ___demand___ schedules and curves.

4.2
Table 4.1 and Figure 4.1 show A's demand for steak in some given time period for a given set of parameters.

Table 4.1
Family A's Demand for Steak

Price per Pound	Pounds of Steak That Would Be Purchased
$5	0
4	2
3	4
2.50	5
2	6
1	8
0	10

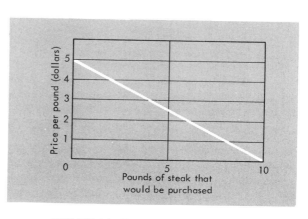

FIGURE 4.1. Family *A*'s Demand for Steak

Answers
1. demand

As might be expected the higher the price the ___lower___ the quantity that would be purchased.

4.3

Table 4.2 and Figure 4.2 show *B*'s demand for steak, again for some given

___time___ period and given set of ___parameters___ such as income and prices of other goods.

Table 4.2
Family B's Demand for Steak

Price per Pound	Pounds of Steak That Would Be Purchased
$3	0
2	5
1.50	7½
1	10
0	15

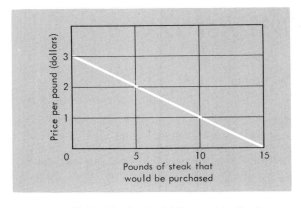

FIGURE 4.2. Family *B*'s Demand for Steak

4.4

Family *B*'s demand curve for steak ___(is/is not)___ identical to family *A*'s demand curve. Although the slope of the curve is different, it remains true

that the ___(greater/smaller)___ the price, the greater the quantity demanded.

4.5

Let us now combine the two demand schedules. At $1 per pound family *A*'s purchases would be eight pounds of steak and at $1 per pound family *B*'s purchases would be ten pounds. Therefore, taken together, both families would

purchase ___18___ pounds at $1 per pound. From Tables 4.1 and 4.2 compute the quantities of steak that would be purchased by both families at the following prices.

Answers
2. smaller
3. time · parameters
4. is not · smaller
5. eighteen

Prices	Quantities (Pounds)
$5	0
3	4
2	11
1	18
0	25

4.6

Figure 4.3 is derived in the same manner in which Figures 4.1 and 4.2 were derived; the relevant prices and quantities from your answers (the correct answers!) in frame 5 are plotted.

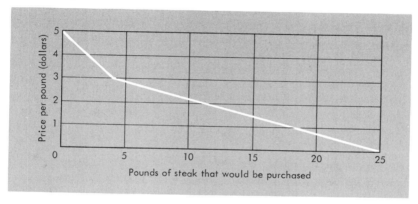

FIGURE 4.3. *A*'s and *B*'s Demand Curve for Steak

The combined curve exhibits the same properties as the individual curves; the

higher the ___price___ , the smaller the quantity that would be purchased, or, for *A* and *B* to be willing to purchase larger quantities, there must be

___lower___ prices.

Answers
5. 0 · 4 · 11 · 25
6. price · lower

4.7

We could repeat the whole procedure for all steak buyers in some town and

arrive at the aggregate ___demand___ schedule for steak for this community.
This is the schedule that meat suppliers would be interested in.

4.8

In each demand curve we have considered so far, we have seen that at different

prices, ___different___ quantities are demanded. The concept that measures
the responsiveness of the quantity demanded to price changes, is known as
price elasticity of demand. Rigorously, price elasticity of demand is defined in
the following way: price elasticity of demand = percentage change in quantity/
percentage change in price, which written symbolically is

$$E_{d\ (price)} = \frac{\Delta Q}{Q} \Big/ \frac{\Delta P}{P}, \text{ where } \Delta \text{ means "change in."}$$

Because there is an inverse relationship between price and quantity demanded, the

ratio $\frac{\Delta Q}{Q} \Big/ \frac{\Delta P}{P}$ would be _(positive/negative)_. In order to make elasticity a

positive amount, elasticity is defined as follows:

$$E_{d\ (price)} = \underline{\ -\frac{\Delta Q}{Q} \Big/ \frac{\Delta P}{P}\ }.$$

4.9

With "price" elasticity of demand we are considering percentage change in quan-

tity and percentage change in ___price___. If we wish to consider
"income" elasticity we would measure the responsiveness of quantity taken to

income change. The identity would read: ___income___ elasticity of
demand = percentage change in quantity/percentage change in income or

$$E_{d\ (income)} = \frac{\Delta Q}{Q} \Big/ \frac{\Delta Y}{Y}, \text{ where } Y \text{ represents } \underline{\ income\ }.$$

Answers
   7. demand
   8. different · negative · $-\dfrac{\Delta Q}{Q} \Big/ \dfrac{\Delta P}{P}$
   9. price · income · income

Here the sign may be positive or negative. The ratio is positive when increases in income (+) are accompanied by increases in the quantity purchased (+) and

when decreases in income (–) are accompanied by ___decreases___ (–) in the quantity purchased. When an inverse relationship exists, e.g. income increases (+) accompanied by quantity purchased decreases (–), income elasticity

of demand will be ___negative___ . Goods, with such a property, like inferior cuts of meat, are called inferior goods.

4.10
Unless we state otherwise, however, when we speak of elasticity of demand, we shall mean price elasticity of demand. Price elasticity of demand = *percentage change in quantity* / *percentage change in price*

4.11
The reason we are concerned with elasticity of demand is because we wish to

know, given a set of ___parameters___ determining the position of the demand

curve for a good, how the quantity demanded will change as ___price___ changes. Let us consider a good such as salt. Let us imagine the typical housewife purchases one pound of salt every month, and one pound of salt costs $.10. Let us further imagine that the price of salt rises to $.20 per pound, i.e.

a ___100___ percent increase in the price for salt. What do you think will happen to the amount of salt purchased by the typical housewife in any month at the new price? Salt is an essential purchase of the housewife for everyday cooking. And, since salt is so trivial as far as the budget is concerned, in all probability the amount of salt purchased per month will not change.

4.12
Let us look at this in economic terms. If every housewife feels the same way

as our typical housewife, that is, she ___(does/does not)___ alter her purchases of salt even though the price of salt doubles, then we know that if we look at an

aggregate demand curve for salt, we shall discover that the same ___quantity___ would be purchased at the price of $.10 per pound as at the price of $.20 per

Answers
9. decreases · negative
10. percentage change in quantity/percentage change in price
11. parameters · price · 100
12. does not · quantity

pound. Or, saying the same thing, the amount of salt demanded at a price of

$.10 per pound ___*(is/is not)*___ the same as the amount demanded at $.20 per pound.

4.13
Let us put the values from this example into the formula for price elasticity of demand-percentage change in quantity/percentage change in price. In this

example the percentage change in quantity obviously equals __zero__,

and the percentage change in price equals __100__. Thus, the price elasticity of demand for salt in going from a price of $.10 per pound to a price of $.20 per pound equals percentage change in quantity/percentage change in

price = __zero__.

4.14
When we have a value for price elasticity of demand that is less than one, we say we have *inelastic demand* over that range of prices. When we get a value equal to one, we say we have *unitary elasticity of demand* over that price range; and when we get a value greater than one, we say we have *elastic demand* over that range of prices. Thus, in the example in the previous frame comparing prices of salt at $.10 per pound and at $.20 per pound and the corresponding quantities purchased, we would say that demand over this range is

(inelastic/of unitary elasticity/elastic).

4.15
What elasticity of demand really tells us is the responsiveness of quantities that would be bought to changes in price. In our salt example, the responsiveness of the quantity of salt that would be bought given the change of price we con-

sidered was __zero__, and consequently in this price range demand

was __inelastic__.

Answers
    12. is
    13. zero · 100 · zero
    14. inelastic
    15. zero · inelastic

4.16

As you might guess, at the other end of the spectrum, if a relatively small change in price brings about a relatively large change in the quantity that would be demanded, we would say that demand was ___elastic___ in that range of prices.

4.17

Our third case would occur where a 1 percent increase in price would bring about a 1 percent *(increase/decrease)* in quantity that would be demanded. We would say that in this case elasticity of demand is ___unitary___.

4.18

Let us choose a couple of examples to see whether the demand is elastic or inelastic over given price ranges. Imagine, that the makers of a popular brand of cigarettes, such as Kansers, were to increase the price of Kansers cigarettes by $.10 per pack, and further assume that the price of all other cigarettes did not alter. Now since many people believe that any one brand of cigarettes has several close substitutes, we would expect smokers to switch from Kansers to some other brand of cigarettes. If this were to occur, then sales of Kansers cigarettes would ___decrease___ because of the price increase causing people to switch to close ___substitutes___.

4.19

If the observed percentage decrease in the quantity of Kansers cigarettes demanded were greater than the percentage increase in price, we would say that the demand for Kansers cigarettes was ___elastic___ over this price range.

4.20

Let us imagine the reverse situation. Imagine Kansers are reduced by a few cents per pack, and this causes many people who normally smoke other brands to switch to Kansers. In this case the percentage *(increase/decrease)* in quantity taken would be large, whereas the percentage *(increase/decrease)*

Answers
16. elastic
17. decrease · unitary (one)
18. decrease · substitutes
19. elastic
20. increase · decrease

in price would be small. Over this price range we would again say that the demand for Kansers cigarettes was __e̶l̶ᴀ̶s̶t̶i̶c̶__ .

4.21

If a 1 percent decrease in the price of Kansers cigarettes led to only a 1 percent __i̶n̶c̶r̶e̶a̶s̶e̶__ in the quantity of Kansers taken, the demand for Kansers cigarettes over this price range would be of unitary elasticity.

4.22

Consider the following, however. If a small increase in the price of all cigarettes had a negligible effect on the quantity of cigarettes demanded, *ceteris paribus* (*cet. par.* = with other things remaining equal) the demand for cigarettes would be __i̶n̶e̶l̶ᴀ̶s̶t̶i̶c̶__ over this price range, even though the demand for any particular brand were elastic over the same price range.

4.23

We may have a demand curve that over a certain range of prices will be elastic, over another range of prices will be of unitary elasticity, and over still another range of prices will be inelastic. For instance, look at the following table. The symbol ΔP means change in price and ΔQ means __c̶h̶ᴀ̶n̶g̶e̶__ in quantity. If we were to plot columns 1 and 4 on graph paper, we would have a __d̶e̶m̶ᴀ̶n̶d̶__ __c̶u̶r̶v̶e̶__ for cameras. The position of this __d̶e̶m̶ᴀ̶n̶d̶__ __c̶u̶r̶v̶e̶__ is determined by __p̶ᴀ̶r̶ᴀ̶m̶e̶t̶e̶r̶s̶__ , the independent variable is __p̶r̶i̶c̶e̶__ , and the dependent variable is __q̶u̶ᴀ̶n̶t̶i̶t̶y̶__ .

Answers

20. elastic
21. increase
22. inelastic
23. change · demand curve · demand curve · parameters · price · quantity

Table 4.3
Demand Schedule for Cameras

(1)	(2)	(3)	(4)	(5)	(6)	(7)
						Elasticity =
P	ΔP	$\dfrac{\Delta P}{P}$	Q	ΔQ	$\dfrac{\Delta Q}{Q}$	$-\dfrac{\Delta Q}{Q} \Big/ \dfrac{\Delta P}{P}$
$30			16			$\dfrac{1}{.2} > 1$ (elastic)
	− 6	− .2		16	1.00	
$24			32			$\dfrac{.25}{.17} > 1$ (elastic)
	− 4	− .17		8	.25	
$20			40			$\dfrac{.15}{.15} = 1$ (unitary elasticity)
	− 3	− .15		6	.15	
$17			46			$\dfrac{.11}{.12} < 1$ (inelastic)
	− 2	− .12		5	.11	
$15			51			$\dfrac{.04}{.07} < 1$ (inelastic)
	− 1	− .07		2	.04	
$14			53			

4.24

When plotted, columns 1 and 4 would give us a normally shaped <u>demand</u> <u>curve</u>, sloping <u>downward</u> from <u>left</u> to <u>right</u>.

4.25

Column 2, headed ΔP, is a change in <u>price</u>. The first entry in the column is the change in <u>price</u> from $ <u>30</u> to $ <u>40</u>.

4.26

The last entry in column 2 is the change in <u>price</u>, going from a price of $ <u>15</u> to $ <u>14</u> and equals $ <u>−1</u>.

Answers

24. demand curve · downward · left · right
25. price · price · 30 · 24
26. price · 15 · 14 · −1

4.27

What we have computed in column 3 is change in price divided by the original price. The numbers in this column are *(positive/negative)* because we are recording *(increases/decreases)* in price. In computing $\dfrac{\Delta P}{P}$ in column 3 the denominator "P" is $30 and not $24. If we were going from a price of $24 to $30, our change in price would not have a ___minus___ sign in front of it, and the denominator in this case would be $ ___24___.

4.28

When we are considering decreases in price, we have a ___minus___ sign, whereas when we are considering increases in price, we would not have a

___minus___ sign. Of more immediate concern at this point, however, is that the value $\dfrac{\Delta P}{P}$ in column 3 would be different depending upon which denominator we used. Using a denominator of $30 and a ΔP of –$6, we get $\dfrac{\Delta P}{P}$ equal to ___–2___ ; whereas, had we used the denominator of $24 and a ΔP of $6, we would have had a $\dfrac{\Delta P}{P}$ of ___.25___. This is one of the problems in using this rather crude way in calculating price elasticity of demand. However, a rigorous formulation would consider only infinitesimal changes in prices and quantities. When we do this, the problem disappears.

4.29

In column 4 in our table, we have the quantities of cameras that would be demanded at various prices, and we can see that as prices fall, the quantity of cameras that would be demanded ___increases___. In column 5, as we did in column 2, we calculate the increase in quantity that would be purchased at different prices. Column 6 is similar to column 3, although each ΔQ in column 5 is positive because as you go down column 4 the quantity that would be demanded *(increases/decreases)*.

Answers
  27. negative · decreases · minus · 24
  28. minus · minus · –.2 · .25
  29. increases · increases

4.30

Column 7 gives us calculations for price __elasticity__ of demand. We

derive this by dividing the figures in column __6__ by the cor-

responding figures in column __3__ .

4.31

Let us consider our first calculation. Here we see that as the price of cameras
changes from $30 to $24 each, the quantity of cameras that would be pur-

chased increases from __16__ to __32__ . We further

see, however, that the percentage change in price is __less__ in
absolute value than the percentage change in quantity.

4.32

Consequently, in going from a price of $30 to $24 per camera, the demand

for cameras in this price range is __elastic__ .

4.33

In going from a price of $24 to $20 per camera, the percentage change in

__price__ is again __smaller__ in absolute value than the

percentage change in __quantity__ ; and consequently, within this price

range, demand is also __elastic__ .

4.34

Thus, considering both those price changes, we can state our results in layman's

terms and say that a change in price brings about a relatively *(smaller/greater)*
change in the quantity of cameras that would be demanded.

4.35
In going from a price of $20 per camera to $17 per camera, we see that the value

for $\frac{\Delta P}{P}$ equals – _____.15_____ . The corresponding $\frac{\Delta Q}{Q}$ is also

_____.15_____ . And consequently, the ratio of – $\frac{\Delta Q}{Q}$ / $\frac{\Delta P}{P}$, i.e. the price

elasticity of demand equals _____one_____ .

4.36
Again in layman's terms we would say that the percentage decrease in price in

this price range just _____equals_____ in absolute value the percentage increase

in quantity that would be purchased, giving us _____unitary_____ _____elasticity_____
in this price range.

4.37
We can continue in the same fashion with the remainder of the table, and we
see that in both cases where we go from a price of $17 to $15, and then from

$15 to $14, the percentage change in _____quantity_____ is smaller in absolute

value than the percentage change in _____price_____ in both instances. Consequently, over those price ranges we would say the demand curve was

_____inelastic_____ .

4.38
Putting the results of the previous frame in layman's language, we would say

that a change in price would bring about a relatively _____smaller_____
change in the quantity demanded.

4.39
While economists cannot tell why some people prefer good *A* over good *B*
and why other people prefer good *B* over good *A*, general statements can be

Answers
    35. .15 · .15 · one
    36. equals · unitary elasticity
    37. quantity · price · inelastic
    38. smaller

made about when demand for a product is likely to be elastic over some price range and when demand is likely to be inelastic over a price range. When we discussed salt, we argued that the demand for salt over moderate price changes

was likely to be ___inelastic___, one reason being that salt normally consumes a negligible portion of a family's income. This means that a small change

in price *(would/would not)* significantly alter the amount of salt the typical housewife would purchase.

4.40

For most people salt is also a necessity, and there are very few items one can substitute for salt in the kitchen. We can take our salt example and generalize

it by saying the demand for a good is likely to be ___inelastic___ when expenditure on that good consumes a very small portion of the weekly in-

come or weekly budget, and demand is also likely to be ___inelastic___ when the good in question has no close substitute.

4.41

Examples of necessities would be your urgently requiring the services of a dentist or surgeon. If you required an appendectomy, and if a hospital attendant were to tell you that the surgeon's fee for performing an appendectomy was $200, you would in all probability agree to have the operation performed. If, however, the hospital attendant then told you that he had made an error and the surgeon's fee was $225, it is highly unlikely that you would change your mind about the operation. In this example, therefore, the demand for

surgeons' services is ___inelastic___, implying that for a given moderate price

change the amount of a surgeon's services demanded ___(will/will not)___ vary significantly with the prices charged.

4.42

Goods which are consumed together are known as complementary goods. Left

shoes and right shoes are examples of ___complementary___ goods, whereas

yellow pencils and blue pencils are ___substitute___ goods. As we might expect, the demand for many complementary goods is inelastic. One requires gasoline before one can drive an automobile; since one is consuming gasoline as one consumes an automobile's services, automobiles and gasoline are

complementary goods.

4.43
If the price of gasoline were to increase a few cents per gallon, one

(would/would not) expect sales of gasoline to fall significantly. If this

were to be the case, the demand for gasoline would be ___inelastic___.

However, one brand of gasoline is a very close ___substitute___ for another
brand of gasoline. And if indeed the price of one brand of gasoline were to
increase but all others were to remain unaltered, we would expect sales of the

higher priced brand to ___decrease___ significantly. Thus, a good which has

very close substitutes tends to be characterized by an ___elastic___
demand.

4.44
From the previous frames we can draw important inferences. If we are dealing
with one good for which there is no close substitute, demand is likely to be

___inelastic___, but if we are dealing with a brand of a good for which there

are very close substitutes, demand for that brand is likely to be ___elastic___.

4.45
Demand is likely to be ___inelastic___ where
a. the amount of money involved is very small,
b. no close substitutes are available,
c. the buying of this good cannot be postponed.
d. there is a large variety of possible uses for this good.
It should be remembered in discussing elasticity of demand that we are con-

sidering relatively ___small___ price changes.

Answers
42. complementary
43. would not · inelastic · substitute · decrease · elastic
44. inelastic · elastic
45. inelastic · small

4.46

How would you classify the following goods—as complements or substitutes?

a. Automobile tires and automobiles minus tires. _Complements_

b. Black and white films and color films. _Substitutes_

c. A film and a camera. _C._

d. Two $5 bills and a $10 bill. _S._

e. Coca Cola and Pepsi Cola. _S._

f. Shirts and trousers. _C._

4.47

As you might expect, many goods are neither perfect substitutes nor perfect complements, but lie somewhere between those two extremes. However, generally we would expect demand for substitutes to be __elastic__, whereas demand for complements is likely to be __inelastic__.

4.48

Let us now explore the importance of elasticity and inelasticity. Let us consider the case of one good: light bulbs. Since light bulbs have very few close substitutes, we would expect the demand for them to be __inelastic__. Let us now imagine that all manufacturers of light bulbs got together (colluded) and decided to increase the price of all light bulbs by 10 percent. Since the demand for light bulbs is relatively __inelastic__, we would not expect there to be a significant __reduction__ in the quantity of light bulbs purchased; and consequently, we would expect that the total income manufacturers of light bulbs would receive after they started charging the higher price would be __greater__ than it was before. This would occur because the price had risen, whereas the quantity purchased had changed *(more than/less than)* proportionately. Consequently, the total revenue (price X quantity) received from the sale of light bulbs would __increase__.

Answers

46. complements · substitutes · complements · substitutes · substitutes · complements
47. elastic · inelastic
48. inelastic · inelastic · reduction · greater · less than · increase

4.49

Total revenue is a technical term used by economists to describe, in this example, the total income received from the sale of light bulbs, and, as you might expect, we calculate total revenue by multiplying the number of light bulbs sold by the

_____price_____ of light bulbs.

4.50

Thus, we see that in situations where demand is inelastic, total revenue will move in the same direction as price. If price is increased, total revenue will

___increase___ , whereas if price is decreased, total revenue will _decrease_ .

4.51

Business firms are concerned with many items besides total revenue, but total revenue is an important consideration. Thus, elasticity is an important concept to businessmen. Let us take the example of the demand curve which is completely inelastic over a given price range. This means that in this given

price range the quantity purchased __(will/will not)__ be independent of the price charged.

4.52

Thus, if the businessman who supplies this market wishes to obtain the highest total revenue from sales in this market within the given price range, he will

charge the _highest_ price in this range. If he were to charge a lower

price, the quantity of the good purchased _(would/would not)_ change, but

the ___total___ _revenue_ from sales of this good would be

lower .

4.53

At the other end of the spectrum, let us imagine a very elastic demand curve.

In this case a small decrease in price will lead to a large _increase_

Answers

    49. price
    50. increase · decrease
    51. will
    52. highest · would not · total revenue · lower
    53. increase

in the quantity demanded (this is a *(shift of/movement along)* the demand
curve), and the total revenue will be ___higher___ at the lower price.

4.54

We can now see that where demand is elastic total revenue *(will/will not)*
move in the same direction as price, because a small price decrease will lead

to a large ___increase___ in quantity bought, whereas a small price increase would lead to a large ___decrease___ in quantity bought.

4.55

Between the two, elastic demand and ___inelastic___ demand, we have
unitary elasticity of demand. In this third case total revenue is unaffected by

price change. A 1 percent increase in price will lead to a 1 percent ___decrease___
in quantity taken. Consequently, ___total___ ___revenue___, which

equals quantity multiplied by ___price___, will be the same before and
after the price change.

Table 4.4
Demand Schedule for Cameras

(1)	(2)	(3)	(4)	(5)	(6)	(7)	(8)
						Elasticity $= $	
P	ΔP	$\dfrac{\Delta P}{P}$	Q	ΔQ	$\dfrac{\Delta Q}{Q}$	$-\dfrac{\Delta Q}{Q} \Big/ \dfrac{\Delta P}{P}$	$P \times Q$
$30			16			$\dfrac{1.00}{.2}$ > 1 (elastic)	480
	– 6	– .2		16	1.00		
$24			32			$\dfrac{.25}{.17}$ > 1 (elastic)	768
	– 4	– .17		8	.25		
$20			40			$\dfrac{.15}{.15}$ = 1 (unitary elasticity)	800
	– 3	– .15		6	.15		
$17			46			$\dfrac{.11}{.12}$ < 1 (inelastic)	782
	– 2	– .12		5	.11		
$15			51			$\dfrac{.04}{.07}$ < 1 (inelastic)	765
	– 1	– .07		.2	.04		
$14			53				742

Answers
53. movement along · higher
54. will not · increase · decrease
55. inelastic · decrease · total revenue · price

4.56

If we turn to Table 4.4, which shows our demand curve for cameras and look at column 8, we have a column $P \times Q$ (price times quantity) which shows

_____total_____ _____revenue_____ for cameras.

4.57

Column 8 is derived by multiplying the figures in column 1 by the relevant figures in column 4. For instance, we can see that if the price of cameras

were $30 each, the quantity demanded would be _____16_____ , and

the total revenue which the camera store would collect would be $____480____ .

4.58

If the price of cameras were $24 instead of $30, we see that the quantity de-

manded would be _____32_____ instead of 16. I.e., a 20 percent decrease

in price would lead to a _____100_____ percent increase in the quantity taken.

4.59

We can see from column 8, however, that since this percentage change in

quantity is _____(greater/less)_____ in absolute value than this percentage change

in price, over this range of prices demand is ____elastic____ .

4.60

We said before that total revenue and price move in the ____(same/opposite)____ direction when the demand is inelastic. This is verified in our example in column 8 because we see that as the price of cameras falls from $30 to $24,

total revenue rises from $480 to $ ____768____ . Thus, prices and total

revenue move in the ____opposite____ direction.

Answers
56. total revenue
57. 16 · 480
58. 32 · 100
59. greater · elastic
60. opposite · 768 · opposite

4.61

If we proceed to the last two rows in Table 4.4 we discover that a decrease in

price from $15 to $14 results in an ___increase___ in the quantity of

cameras demanded from ___51___ to ___53___. In this

example the percentage change in price is ___7___, and the per-

centage change in quantity is ___4___, showing that the demand

for cameras in this price range is ___inelastic___.

4.62

We saw, however, that in the case of ___inelastic___ demand total revenue
moves in the same direction as price (this is substantiated in column 8),

since with a price decrease from $15 to $14 total revenue ___decreases___
from $765 to $742.

4.63

If we plot the demand curve from the data in Table 4.4, we have a demand curve

which slopes downwards from ___left___ to ___right___, which

in the upper left hand corner would be *(inelastic/elastic)*, and which in the

lower right hand corner would be *(inelastic/elastic)*. If indeed the curve were
continuous, it would have to pass through a point of unitary elasticity where a

small decrease in price would just be matched by a small ___increase___
in quantity that would be demanded. And we can see from Table 4.4 that this

point lies in the price range $ ___20___ to $ ___17___.

4.64

The demand curves we have considered so far we would describe as normal de-

mand curves. Those curves slope downwards from ___left___ to

___right___, indicating that at higher prices a ___smaller___ quantity
would be purchased.

Answers
61. increase · 51 · 53 · 7 · 4 · inelastic
62. inelastic · decreases
63. left · right · elastic · inelastic · increase · 20 · 17
64. left · right · smaller

4.65

Just as there are exceptions to most rules, so there are exceptions to our normal demand curves. Some people believe (often for good reasons)that "you only get what you pay for," and if they see a good priced lower than what they expect it to be, they may have some doubts as to the quality of this good, whereas if this good were priced higher, they might be prepared to buy it. Thus, this could lead to a situation which would be the reverse of our normal demand curve situa-

tion. At a higher price people would actually buy ___more___ of the good than they would at a lower price, and consequently, the demand curve for this

good for the group of people who think in this fashion *(would/would not)* slope downwards from left to right.

4.66

Similar to this type of situation is the situation involving prestige goods. Prestige goods, such as mink coats, may be bought by some people simply because

the price of mink coats tends to be relatively ___high___. If the price of mink coats were very low and many people had them, mink coats would no

longer be a ___prestige___ good, and consequently, those people who buy

them for ___prestige___ reasons would not purchase mink coats at lower prices. Again we would have an example of a demand curve for mink coats by

this group of people which would not slope ___downwards___ from

___left___ to ___right___.

4.67

There is another famous case of a nonnormal sloping demand curve, involving an inferior good, which refers to the demand for potatoes by Irish peasants. [You should recall that an inferior good is a good whose income elasticity of

demand is *(negative/positive)* i.e. where increases in income (+) are associated with decreases in quantities purchased (-).] Irish peasants were very poor people who could only afford to buy very cheap food, and potatoes comprised a substantial portion of their normal diet. In good times, however, when Irish farmers had bumper crops of potatoes, the price of potatoes tended to fall. Since potatoes consumed a large portion of the Irish income or budget for the typical peasant family, a fall in the price of potatoes would mean that each

Answers
65. more · would not
66. high · prestige · prestige · downwards · left · right
67. negative

family could buy the same quantity of potatoes as they normally did at the

higher price for ___less___ money. Consequently, they would have

___(some/no)___ income left to spend on other goods after their purchase
of potatoes.

4.68

With this income the Irish peasant could now afford to buy other goods such as
meat, milk, and cheese. But since families could now enjoy meat, milk, and
cheese, they did not require as many potatoes, and consequently, the peasants
would buy fewer potatoes. Here we have an example which shows that through

a ___fall___ in the price of potatoes, Irish peasants could afford to buy

some expensive foods, and consequently, would eat ___fewer___ potatoes.
In terms of the demand curve for potatoes, we can see that at a lower price

___fewer___ potatoes were purchased than previously at the higher price.
Again we have an exception to the rule where the demand curve for potatoes in

this instance ___(does/does not)___ slope downwards from left to right.

From demand let us now turn our attention to supply.

REVIEW QUESTIONS

4.1
For most people ___D___ .

a. red taxi-cabs are perfect substitutes for yellow taxi-cabs.
b. right gloves and left gloves are complements.
c. socks and shoes are complements.
d. all of the above are true.

4.2
Goods A and B are substitutes; goods A and C are complements. Other things

unchanged, a rise in the price of A will cause ___C___ .

a. an increase in the demand for B.
b. a decrease in the demand for C.
c. both (a) and (b).
d. an increase in the demand for C.

Answers
67. less · some
68. fall · fewer · fewer · does not
1. d
2. c

4.3

Mr. Burger's linear demand curve for ham touches both the price and quantity axes.

The price elasticity of demand is __________.

a. greater than 1 near the price axis and less than 1 near the quantity axis.
b. less than 1 near the price axis and greater than 1 near the quantity axis.
c. equal to 1 near both axes.
d. equal to 0 near both axes.

4.4

Mr. Packer says that no matter the price, he will buy tickets to all his team's home games. The price elasticity of Mr. Packer's demand for tickets is

__________.

a. greater than 1.
b. equal to 1.
c. less than 1.
d. indeterminate.

4.5

Mr. Greenbay says that the number of home games he will go to is proportional to his income. The income elasticity of Mr. Greenbay's demand for tickets is

____ß____.

a. greater than 1.
b. equal to 1.
c. less than 1.
d. indeterminate.

Answers

    3. a
    4. c
    5. b

Market Supply

5.1

In many ways a supply curve is similar to a demand curve. Each describes a relationship between the quantity and the price of a commodity. However, whereas a demand curve tells the quantities of a good that would be

demanded in any time period in any given market at different prices, a supply curve tells the quantity of a good that would be supplied in any given

time period in any given market at various _prices_ .

5.2

A supply curve is similar to a demand curve in that it represents a set of hypothetical situations. It shows how much of a good suppliers would offer

for sale in a given market in a given _time_ _period_

in response to various _prices_ .

5.3

As in the case of the demand curve, the position of the supply curve is fixed by

a set of _parameters_, which are factors that influence supply, but which

are assumed to be _(variable/constant)_. The two variables are again price and

Answers
1. demanded · prices
2. time period · prices
3. parameters · constant

quantity, price being the independent variable and quantity that would be supplied being the _dependent_ variable.

5.4

We saw in discussing demand curves that normally the higher the price, the _lower_ is the quantity that will be demanded, and consequently, most demand curves slope _downwards_ from _left_ to _right_.

5.5

In the case of a supply curve, the reverse is true. Normally, in a given time period, suppliers will only be willing to supply more of a good at a _higher_ price, *ceteris paribus.*

5.6

Since normally suppliers will only supply more of a good at a higher price, supply curves normally slope _upwards_ from _left_ to _right_.

5.7

Let us imagine you are a tomato grower, and when tomatoes are in season your plants produce approximately 100 pounds of tomatoes per day. The village store offers you 30¢ per pound for tomatoes, and at that price, each day, you supply the store with 70 pounds of tomatoes, you can 25 pounds of tomatoes, and your family consumes the remaining 5 pounds. Thus, if we were to consider your daily supply curve of tomatoes to the village store, we would know one point on that supply curve. At a price of 30¢ per pound, the quantity you would supply would be _70_ pounds.

5.8

Let us now imagine, however, that the store does not have enough tomatoes for all its customers and asks you to supply more. You answer, however, that at

Answers
3. dependent
4. smaller · downwards · left · right
5. higher
6. upwards · left · right
7. 70

30¢ per pound, you are willing to supply only 70 pounds of tomatoes per day.
The store then asks how many pounds of tomatoes you would supply at 35¢
per pound. You decide that at this price, it doesn't really pay you to can
tomatoes, so you offer 95 pounds at 35¢ per pound. Thus, we have a new point

on your daily ___supply___ curve of tomatoes. The new point is

___95___ pounds at a price of ___35___ ¢ per pound.

5.9

Even with this increased daily supply of tomatoes, the store is still not satisfied,
and now offers you 40¢ per pound for tomatoes. At this price, you decide that
your family can do without 5 pounds of tomatoes per day, and you contract
with the store to supply them with 100 pounds of tomatoes per day at a price

of 40¢ per pound. Thus, we have a third point on your ___supply___
schedule. This point tells us that at a price of 40¢ per pound, you would be

willing to supply ___100___ pounds per day.

5.10

The store, however, phones you the following day and says they still need more
tomatoes. You could actually gather more tomatoes from your plants, but it
would involve hiring additional tomato pickers and picking the plants much
more carefully than you did in the past. However, you tell the store you can
supply an additional 10 pounds of tomatoes, but because of the additional ex-
pense, you would supply 110 pounds of tomatoes per day only at 60¢ per pound.
Let us look at Table 5.1 which gives us your daily supply schedule of tomatoes.
Here we have the quantities of tomatoes you would supply at various prices.

We see that this quantity is _(greater/smaller)_ the higher the price offered.

Table 5.1
Daily Supply Schedule of Tomatoes

Price per Pound	Quantity of Tomatoes You Would Supply (Pounds)
$.30	70
.35	95
.40	100
.60	110

Answers
8. supply · 95 · 35
9. supply · 100
10. greater

5.11

Now look at Table 5.2. Here we have the daily supply schedules of farmers *A* and *B* as well as yourself. *A* and *B* are both tomato farmers who live some distance from the store and who are not prepared to supply any tomatoes at a

price of _____30_____ ¢ per pound because of transportation costs. Thus, if you, *A,* and *B* are the only potential tomato suppliers for this market, the

quantity of tomatoes that would be supplied daily at a price of _____30_____ ¢ per pound would be 70 pounds.

Table 5.2
Daily Supply Schedule of Tomatoes

Price per Pound	Quantity of Tomatoes That Would Be Supplied by (Pounds)			
(1)	*(2)* *You*	*(3)* *A*	*(4)* *B*	*(5)* *Total*
$ .30	70	—	—	70
.35	95	—	25	120
.40	100	50	50	200
.60	110	80	50	240
1.00	110	90	50	250

5.12

If the store offers 35¢ per pound for tomatoes, however, you would be willing

to supply _____95_____ pounds of tomatoes per day, *A* would be willing

to supply _____0_____ pounds per day, and *B* would be willing to supply

_____25_____ pounds per day. Consequently, the total quantity of tomatoes

that would be supplied at a price of 35¢ per pound would be ___120___ pounds per day.

5.13

At a price of 40¢ per pound, *A* finds it profitable to transport tomatoes to the store, and we see that the total (aggregate) quantity of tomatoes that

___would___ be supplied at this price would be ___200___ pounds

Answers
   11. 30 · 30
   12. 95 · 0 · 25 · 120
   13. would · 200

per day. Unfortunately for *B*, he just cannot, at any price, supply more than 50 pounds of tomatoes per day. This being the case, if we consider a price range from 40¢ per pound upwards, *B* cannot supply any more even if the price rises. Price elasticity of demand, if you recall, was a measure of the responsiveness of changes in quantity demanded to changes in price. Since we use the same procedure in calculating price elasticity of supply, *B*'s supply curve of tomatoes for

prices above 40¢ per pound will be completely   *inelastic* .

5.14

If we plot columns 1 and 5 from Table 5.2 on a graph, putting price on the vertical axis and quantity that would be supplied on the horizontal axis, we have the aggregate daily supply curve of tomatoes for our market, and as we expected,

and as can be seen in Figure 5.1, this curve slopes   *upwards*   from

____*left*____ to ____*right*____ .

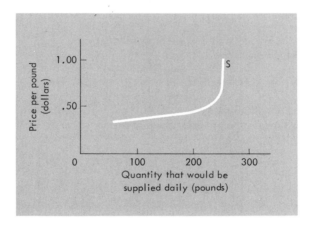

FIGURE 5.1. Aggregate Daily Supply Curve of Tomatoes

5.15

In Figure 5.1 we have price per pound on the vertical axis; price is the

__*independent*__ variable. The quantity that would be supplied daily is

plotted on the horizontal axis, quantity being the   *dependent*   variable.

Answers
13. inelastic
14. upwards · left · right
15. independent · dependent

5.16

The position of the aggregate daily ___supply___ curve of tomatoes in

Figure 5.1 is determined by a set of ___parameters___

5.17

Just as a demand curve will shift when one of the parameters determining its
positon changes, so also will a supply curve. However, when we look at Figure
5.1 and consider the quantity that would be supplied at any given price and
compare it with the quantity that would be supplied at a different price, we are

considering a *(movement along/shift of)* the supply curve.

5.18

Just as the time period under consideration is important when discussing demand curves, so is it also when discussing supply curves. In Figure 5.1 the

time period under consideration is one ___day___ . If we were to compare the supply curve in Figure 5.1 with a weekly supply curve of tomatoes, we

would see that the weekly supply curve would be to the ___*(left/right)*___ of
our daily supply curve.

5.19

Let us now imagine that a disease kills off the tomato plants of one of the suppliers. What would happen to the aggregate supply curve in Figure 5.1? It would

shift to the ___*(left/right)*___ .

5.20

If people suddenly decided that they were not going to buy any tomatoes on a
specific day, what would happen to our daily supply curve of tomatoes?

 no change

Answers
16. supply · parameters
17. movement along
18. day · right
19. left
20. it would not change

5.21

Imagine a group of tourists comes to visit our small town and wishes to purchase some of the excellent tomatoes sold by the store, which unfortunately only has sufficient tomatoes for regular customers. What will happen to the daily supply

curve of tomatoes in this situation? *no change*

5.22

As the answer to frames 20 and 21 indicate, factors that affect the position of

the demand curve ___*(do/do not)*___ necessarily affect the position of the sup-ply curve. Such factors are very likely, however, to lead to price changes and to

___*movement*___ ___*along*___ the supply curve.

5.23

As we saw in an earlier frame a supply curve can be elastic or inelastic just like a demand curve. If, in the market depicted in Figure 5.1, 250 pounds of tomatoes is the maximum amount tomato growers can supply no matter what the price offered, then our supply curve in Figure 5.1 would become a

(horizontal/vertical) line for all prices above one dollar. That is, in this range

of the curve, supply would be completely *inelastic*.

5.24

If it were true, however, that a small increase in price would bring about a relatively large increase in the quantity that would be supplied, the supply

curve in that price range would be *elastic*.

5.25

As you might expect, if a 1 percent increase in price were to bring about a 1 percent increase in the quantity that would be supplied, the supply curve

in this range would be of *unitary* *elasticity*

Answers

21. it will not change
22. do not · movements along
23. vertical · inelastic
24. elastic
25. unitary elasticity

5.26

The two concepts of price elasticity of supply and price elasticity of demand, are identical except for the fact that in the case of demand price increases are normally associated with a *(positive/negative)* change in quantity, whereas for supply, price increases are normally associated with a ___positive___ change in quantity.

5.27

Consider a famous painting such as the Mona Lisa. Since there is only one original Mona Lisa painting, the quantity of original Mona Lisas available in the world today ___*(will/will not)*___ change, no matter how high collectors are prepared to bid for this painting. Thus, no matter what price is offered, the quantity of Mona Lisas ___*(will/will not)*___ change, and consequently the supply of original Mona Lisa's is completely ___inelastic___.

5.28

If you were to draw a supply schedule for Mona Lisas with price on the vertical axis and quantity on the horizontal axis, you would have a *(horizontal/vertical)* line, which would touch the horizontal axis at the number ___One___.

5.29

At the other extreme, if a supplier of phonograph records were prepared to supply 100 records at a price of $2 each and also 1,000 or even a million records at a price of $2 each, within some specified time period *t,* then the supply curve for this record would be represented by a *(horizontal/vertical)* line as in Figure 5.2, and supply in this range would be completely ___elastic___.

5.30

Most goods and services we consume lie somewhere between the extremes of complete inelasticity and complete elasticity of supply. In a given time period, manufacturers may only be willing to supply additional units of output at a

Answers
    26. negative · positive
    27. will not · will not · inelastic
    28. vertical · one
    29. horizontal · elastic

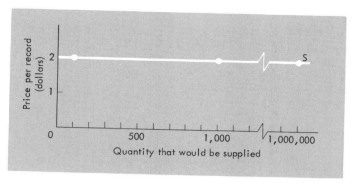

FIGURE 5.2. Supply Curve of Phonograph Records

higher price. To the extent that this is true, a supply curve will slope

upwards from _L_____ to _R_____ .

5.31

Just as in demand theory, so is it in supply theory that the time period under consideration is very important. Let us take a very short time period. Consider one day. In the morning you picked 100 pounds of tomatoes. Let us further imagine that if you do not sell your tomatoes during this day, they will spoil and become a complete loss. Now considering only the 100 pounds

of tomatoes during this specific day, you would obviously prefer a _higher____ price for those tomatoes to a lower price. Furthermore, since the tomatoes will not keep an extra day, you will be prepared to sell them to the highest bidder even though the price he may give you for them will not cover the costs of producing them. The reason you will be prepared to do this is because if you do

not sell them at all, total revenue will be ___0_____ , whereas if you sell them at any positive price, you will at least have some revenue to set against your costs.

5.32

This type of situation can be represented in Figure 5.3. Here we have your supply curve of tomatoes on the given day, and we see that the quantity you would supply would be __100_____ pounds, independent of the price you are offered.

Answers

30. upwards · left · right
31. higher · zero
32. 100

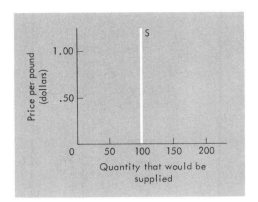

FIGURE 5.3. Supply Curve of Tomatoes on
One Given Day

5.33
Just as there are exceptions to the normally shaped demand curve so we find exceptions to the normally shaped upward sloping supply curve. For now, however,
let us assume that the supply curve slopes in the opposite direction from the

typical demand curve; that is, it slopes _____ from _____

to _____ . We shall now analyze why supply curves generally have
this characteristic.

REVIEW QUESTIONS

5.1
Which of the following could not cause a shift in the position of the supply

curve for beer? _____

a. An increase in the price of beer.
b. An increase in the population.
c. Discovery of a cheaper process for producing beer.
d. The weather.

Answers
  33. upwards · left · right
  1. a

5.2

If a 1% increase in the price of logs would bring about a 2% increase in the quantity supplied, the supply curve in this region would be  _____ .

a. inelastic.
b. of unitary elasticity.
c. elastic.
d. horizontal.

5.3

The position of a demand curve is determined by a set of parameters; price is the independent variable and quantity that would be demanded is the dependent variable. Similarly a supply curve's position is determined by a set of parameters; price again being the independent variable and quantity that would be supplied

the dependent variable. The above statements ____A_____ .

a. are true.
b. which refer only to demand curves are true.
c. which refer only to supply curves are true.
d. are false.

5.4

The shape of a normal supply curve implies that, other things remaining equal,

_____ .

a. the higher the price, the greater will be the quantity demanded.
b. the lower the price, the greater will be the quantity demanded.
c. the higher the price, the greater will be the quantity supplied.
d. the lower the price, the greater will be the quantity supplied.

Answers
2. c
3. a
4. c

5.5

Which of the following is not likely to cause a shift in the supply curve for

potatoes?   _____A_____

a. A fall in the price of meat.
b. A rise in the wage rate.
c. A fall in the price of machinery.
d. A rise in the value of land.

Answer
   5. a

Productivity and Costs

6.1

The suppliers of goods and services (output) in our economy face two basic problems:

a. how much output should they produce per time period, and

b. what is the most efficient way to produce that output.

To fully understand the behavior of suppliers (and why supply curves typically

slope ___upwards___ from left to right) we must study productivity and costs. More simply expressed, we must study how much output will result from different amounts and combinations of inputs—this is the study of productivity—and also how much will it cost to produce such outputs.

We shall begin with a simple example of a wheat farmer. We wish to find out how the wheat output from one field will change, as the farmer varies *only* the amount of labor input on this field.

6.2

Consider Table 6.1 which shows data on what would happen if, *ceteris paribus,* a farmer were to vary the amounts of labor input, which we are measuring in

___man-days___ , in one of his wheat fields. Labor is not the only factor of production involved in the production of wheat, but here we are holding all

other inputs, or factors of ___production___ , constant and we are asking

Answers
 1. upwards
 2. man-days · production

103

what happens when we vary only one input, in this case labor. That is, we are

holding ___constant___ such things as the amount of fertilizer and the amount
of mechanical aids a farmer might use.

Table 6.1
Wheat Output—One Field with Varying Labor Input

Units of Labor Input (Man-Days)	Total Product (Bushels)	Average Product per Unit of Labor Input (Bushels)	Marginal Product of Labor Input (Bushels)
0	0	—	
			40
1	40	40	
			100
2	140	70	
			160
3	300	100	
			180
4	480	120	
			170
5	650	130	
			160
6	810	135	
			150
7	960	137	
			120
8	1,080	135	
			90
9	1,170	130	
			30
10	1,200	120	
			−10
11	1,190	108	
			−50
12	1,140	95	
			−230
13	910	70	

6.3
Consider only the first two columns. We can see that as we add successive inputs

of labor, total output (product) rises until we add the ___11th___ unit of

labor. Then total output ___decreases___ and continues to do so, the more
labor input we use.

6.4
If the farmer were to employ more than ten units of labor input, total output

would be ___less___ than total output with ten units of labor input.

Consequently, it *(would/would not)* be profitable for the farmer to hire this
eleventh unit of labor input as long as he has to pay a positive price for each unit
of labor input.

Answers
   2. constant
   3. eleventh · decreases
   4. less · would not

6.5

In our example, therefore, maximum total output can be obtained when the

farmer uses _____10_____ units of labor input. This maximum is

_____1,200_____ bushels of wheat.

6.6

Column 3 is derived by dividing the figures in column _____2_____ by

the corresponding figures in column _____1_____ . Column 3, which is

also in bushels, is a measure of the _____Avg. prod. per unit of labor_____

6.7

In column 3, we can see that the average product per unit of labor input in-

creases up to the _____7_____ unit of labor input, whereafter it

_____dec._____ .

6.8

Up to the seventh unit of labor input, average product increases because the

_____total_____ product increases proportionately faster than the number of
units of labor input. The maximum average product per unit of labor input is

_____137_____ bushels, which occurs when the farmer employs _____7_____
units of labor input.

6.9

Note that while 137 bushels is the maximum average product obtained in this
example, the corresponding total output for this number of labor inputs is not a

_____maximum._____ Also observe that at _____10_____ units of labor input,
a maximum total output of 1,200 bushels is obtained, but the corresponding

average product or output per unit of labor input, which is _____120_____ ,

is not the _____max._____ average product in the table.

Answers
    5. ten · 1,200
    6. 2 · 1 · average product per unit of labor input
    7. seventh · decreases
    8. total · 137 · seven
    9. maximum • ten • 120 • maximum

6.10

Column 4 measures the marginal product of labor input, also in bushels. This column tells us what the incremental, or additional, or marginal output will be if we add one more unit of labor input. For instance, if we consider the first

two lines, total output from zero units of labor input is ___0___

bushels. Total output from one unit of labor input is ___40___ bushels. Thus, we can see that the increase in output in going from zero units of labor input to one unit of labor input (i.e. that additional or marginal prod-

uct) is ___40___ bushels.

6.11

We see also that the total output from employing three units of labor input is

___300___ bushels, and total output from employing four units of

labor input is ___460___ bushels. Thus, the difference between those

totals, in this case ___180___ bushels of wheat, is due to the addition

of the ___4th___ unit of labor input. Consequently, we would say that

the ___marginal___ ___product___ of the fourth unit of labor input is

___180___ bushels.

6.12

Now consider the output from nine units of labor input; it is ___1,170___ bushels. Adding one more unit, i.e. the tenth unit, gives us only a very small

increase in total output, i.e. an increase in total output of ___30___

units of wheat. Thus, we see that the ___marginal___ ___product___

of the tenth unit of labor input is, in this case, ___30___ bushels.

6.13

When we add an eleventh unit of labor input, we see that total output actually

___decreases___ from ___1,200___ bushels to ___1,190___ bushels.

Answers
10. 0 · 40 · 40
11. 300 · 480 · 180 · fourth · marginal product · 180
12. 1,170 · 30 · marginal product · 30
13. decreases · 1,200 · 1,190

6.14

Thus, the output attributable to the eleventh unit of labor input, i.e. the

_____marginal_____ _____product_____ of the eleventh unit, is negative in the

amount of _____10_____ bushels.

6.15

After the eleventh unit of labor input, as more labor is added, total product con-

tinues to _____decrease_____ . The marginal product of each successive unit added

remains _____negative_____ and becomes smaller and smaller.

6.16

Now look at Figure 6.1 which is derived from columns 1 and 2 in Table 6.1.
Again, we see the same story as we saw in the table. That is, total output rises

as we hire additional units of labor input and reaches a peak of _____1200_____

bushels when we hire _____10_____ units of labor input, after which total

output _____decreases_____ as we add more units of labor input.

6.17

In Figure 6.2 we have plotted average and marginal products associated with
various labor inputs. Again we see that a maximum average product of

_____137_____ bushels per unit of labor input is obtained when the farmer

hires _____seven_____ units of labor input after which average product

_____decreases_____. That is, each additional unit of labor input hired adds more
to total product than the average of all previous units of labor input up to that
point. Consequently, the average output or product curve must be

(rising/falling) up to that point. However, as soon as the marginal output of
the last unit of labor input hired is less than the average up to that point, the
marginal output curve must intersect the average output curve and cause the

average output curve to turn down and start to _____decrease_____ .

Answers
  14. marginal product · 10
  15. decrease · negative
  16. 1,200 · ten · decreases
  17. 137 · seven · decreases · rising · decrease

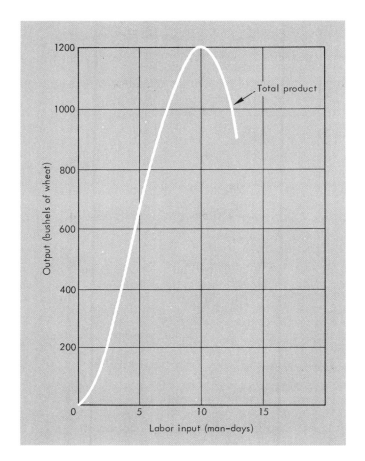

FIGURE 6.1.

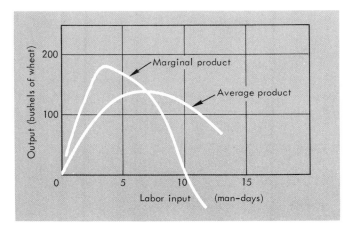

FIGURE 6.2.

6.18

Thus, it is not by chance that the marginal ___product___ curve intersects the ___average___ product curve at the ___highest___ point of the average product curve. Think about that. For instance it is not by chance that the average height of a basketball squad *(increases/decreases)* if you add a player whose height is less than the average.

6.19

Another significant point in Figure 6.2 is where the marginal product curve becomes negative. This occurs when the farmer hires the ___10th___ unit of labor input. The significance of this point is that this unit of labor input has a negative ___marginal___ ___productivity___ which means, of course, that the hiring of this unit would not cause total output to increase, but would actually cause it to decrease.

6.20

If we look back to Figure 6.1 we do discover this: total output starts to decrease when the ___11th___ unit of labor input is hired and continues to decrease as more units of labor input are added.

6.21

These relationships provide an example of the widely observed law of diminishing returns. This states that after some point has been reached, the amount of additional output obtained through adding more units of one factor input to a fixed supply of other factors will decrease. This we saw to be true in Table 6.1. We held constant all factors of production except ___labor___ , and we observed as we added successive units of labor that, after a point was reached, the additional output or ___marginal___ ___product___ of each successive unit of ___labor___ input ___decreased___.

Answers

18. product · average · highest · decreases
19. eleventh · marginal product
20. eleventh
21. labor · marginal product · labor · decreased

6.22
Thus, we would say that the example we discussed is consistent with the

_____ law _____ of _ diminishing returns _ .

6.23
To summarize, as the proportion of one factor input to other fixed factor inputs

is increased, average _ product _ of this factor input will, after a certain

point has been reached, _ decrease _ and continue to _ decrease _ .

The _ marginal _ product of the increasing factor input will also, after a

certain point has been reached, _ decrease _ and continue to _ decrease _ .
The marginal product curve will intersect the average product curve at its

_____ highest _____ point.

6.24
It should be obvious that under normal circumstances we would never expect
an entrepreneur, paying positive prices for his factor inputs, to hire an additional unit of some specific input whose marginal product was zero or

_____ neg. _____ . Is the following statement true or false? We would, therefore, never expect an entrepreneur to hire an additional unit of any input if the
marginal product of this unit were less than the marginal product of all other

hired units. _____ false _____

6.25
Do we know how many units of labor input the farmer should hire if he wishes

to maximize his wheat output? _____ (yes/no.) _____ Do we know how many units
of labor input the farmer should hire to make as high a profit as possible?

_____ No _____ .

6.26
Consider the following piece of information, however. Imagine you are told
that the farmer has to pay each man 30 bushels of wheat for a day's work.

Answers
   22. law of diminishing returns
   23. product · decrease · decrease · marginal · decrease · decrease · highest
   24. negative · false
   25. yes · no

That is, imagine the farmer lives in an economy with a barter system where people are paid in kind. Now you should be able to see how Table 6.1 relates to the farmer's decision about how much labor to hire and what to produce. If indeed the rate of pay is 30 bushels of wheat per man-day, then if the farmer were to employ one man for one day, total output would be _____46_____ bushels. If all other factors of production were free, his total costs of production would be _____30_____ bushels and his profit (output minus input cost) would be _____10_____ bushels.

Table 6.1
Wheat Output—One Field with Varying Labor Input

Units of Labor Input (Man-Days)	Total Product (Bushels)	Average Product per Unit of Labor Input (Bushels)	Marginal Product of Labor Input (Bushels)
0	0	—	
1	40	40	40
2	140	70	100
3	300	100	160
4	480	120	180
5	650	130	170
6	810	135	160
7	960	137	150
8	1,080	135	120
9	1,170	130	90
10	1,200	120	30
11	1,190	108	-10
12	1,140	95	-50
13	910	70	-230

6.27

Let us imagine that the farmer decided to hire four man-days. In this case, his total output would be _____480_____ bushels, his total costs of production (again given the assumptions in the previous frame) would be _____120_____ bushels, and his profit would be _____360_____ bushels.

6.28

Instead of making these tedious calculations, let us consider column 4, which shows the _____marginal product_____ of the last unit of labor hired. Remember that the _____marginal prod._____ is what one addi-

Answers

26. 40 · 30 · 10
27. 480 · 120 · 360
28. marginal product · marginal product

tional unit of labor input, in this case one man-day, will add to total production.

That is, it is the additional ___output___ the farmer would obtain by hiring the last unit of labor.

6.29
Suppose the farmer has been hiring three units of labor and now decides to hire a fourth. We see from column 4 that the output due to the fourth unit hired is

____150____ bushels. Thus, if indeed the farmer has only to pay the fourth unit of labor input 30 bushels, he will make a profit on that fourth unit of labor

input of ____150____ bushels.

6.30
Consider the seventh unit. Does it pay the farmer to hire this unit? _(yes/no,)_

because the output due to that unit will be ____150____ bushels, and the

costs to the farmer of hiring that unit will only be ____30____ bushels;

consequently, he will have a profit of ____120____ bushels in the hiring of that unit.

6.31
When we come to the tenth unit, however, the case is different. Here we see

that the tenth unit only adds ____30____ bushels of wheat to total out-

put, and the farmer must pay this tenth unit ____30____ bushels of wheat. Consequently, the farmer will be indifferent as to whether or not he

hires this individual unit, because he ___(will/will not)___ make any additional profit from hiring the tenth unit.

6.32
Will the farmer hire an eleventh unit of labor input? ____(yes/no,)____ because

the cost of hiring the eleventh unit is ___(greater/less)___ than the marginal product of that unit. In fact, by hiring the eleventh unit of labor it would cost the farmer 30 bushels in wages minus the marginal product of that unit, which

is –10 bushels, i.e. a total of ____40____ bushels.

Answers
28. output
29. 180 · 150
30. yes · 150 · 30 · 120
31. 30 · 30 · will not
32. no · greater · 40

6.33

Now, even though the farmer would not be prepared to hire the eleventh unit, because the eleventh unit would actually mean a loss to the farmer on that unit, this does not imply that the farmer would not be making a profit on his field if he hired eleven units of labor. Total output from the hiring of eleven

units is ____1190____ bushels and total cost is ____330____ bushels.

Consequently, the farmer would make a profit of ____860____ bushels if he were to hire eleven units of labor input.

6.34

You should be able to see that it will always pay a farmer to hire an additional

unit of labor input as long as the __marginal__ __product__ of the

last unit hired is __greater__ than the marginal cost of that unit.

6.35

The only place where it will not pay the farmer to change the amount of labor hired, and output produced, is where the marginal product of the last unit

hired is _(less than/equal to/greater than)_ the marginal cost of that unit. This

is because his profit is at a ____maximum____ at that point.

6.36

Perhaps the easiest way to see this result is to adapt one of the diagrams of Chapter 2 to this problem. Consider Figure 6.3. The marginal product of labor curve has been taken from Figure 6.2. It shows the marginal

__(benefit/cost)__ of hiring labor. The wage rate of 30 bushels per man

is shown as a __horizontal__ line. It shows the marginal __cost__ of hiring labor for each level of labor input. The line is horizontal at

____30____ bushels because the cost of hiring an additional unit of

labor is always ____30____ bushels, no matter how many units have already been hired.

6.37

As in Chapter 2 we have taken smaller and smaller increments on the horizontal

Answers
33. 1,190 · 330 · 860
34. marginal product · greater
35. equal to · maximum
36. benefit · horizontal · cost · 30 · 30

axis and have emerged with a smooth curve, i.e. the ___marginal product___
curve instead of a set of touching rectangles.

6.38
From Figure 6.3 we can see that the first unit of labor input adds ___40___

bushels to total output and the second unit ___100___ bushels. How

much does the fifth unit add? ___170___ bushels.

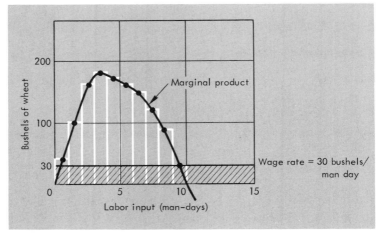

FIGURE 6.3.

6.39
Now one way we could find out how much output five man-days would produce
would be to add the output from the first man-day with the output from the
second man-day, plus the third, fourth, and fifth. In terms of the rectangles in

Figure 6.3 we would add the ___areas___ of the first five rectangles from
the origin *0*.

6.40
The sum of the areas of the first five rectangles, of course, is an approximation

of the area under the ___marginal product___ curve from zero to

five on the horizontal axis.

Answers
37. marginal product
38. 40 · 100 · 170
39. areas
40. marginal product

6.41

Similarly the area under the _____m A r q i h a l_____ _____p r o d u c t_____ curve between zero and nine units of labor input is total output from using nine units of labor input.

6.42

Now consider the labor costs of producing this output. Each man-day costs

_____30_____ bushels as is shown by the horizontal wage line. Fifteen

man-days, for instance would cost _____4 5 0_____ bushels.

6.43

Thus the area under the _____M A r g i n a l_____ _____c o s t_____ _____c u v ι e_____

from zero to fifteen on the horizontal axis represents the total _____c o s t_____
of labor to the wheat farmer of employing fifteen man-days, i.e. this area repre-

sents _____4 5 0_____ bushels of wheat.

6.44

We can collect, therefore, lots of useful information from Figure 6.3, since the

area under the _____M A r g ,_____ _____p r o d u c t_____ of labor curve represents
total output (or total benefit) from hiring some given number of labor inputs

and since the area under the wage line represents the total _____c o s t_____
of hiring some given number of labor inputs.

6.45

As long as the marginal product curve lies __(above/below)__ the wage line the
last unit of labor hired will be yielding a return greater than its cost.

6.46

In terms of the rectangles in Figure 6.3, the analysis would be as follows: the
product of the ninth unit of labor input (given by the area of the ninth large

rectangle) is _____9 0_____ bushels of wheat. The cost of the ninth unit
of labor is the wage rate (given by the ninth smaller rectangle), which is

_____3 0_____ bushels. Thus the gain in hiring the ninth unit of factor
input will be the difference between the marginal product and the wage rate

Answers
   41. marginal product
   42. 30 · 450
   43. marginal cost curve · cost · 450
   44. marginal product · cost
   45. above
   46. 90 · 30 ·

(the difference between the areas of the ninth large and small rectangles), i.e.

____60____ bushels. In deciding about hiring a tenth unit of labor the

farmer would be indifferent because the __marginal__ __product__ of

this unit just equals the __wage__ rate, i.e. the rectangles are equal.

6.47
In terms of the marginal product and wage rate curves, which allow for fractional amounts of labor input, the analysis would be slightly different. In this case,

at 8½ units of labor input, the marginal product of labor is __90__

bushels of wheat, while the wage is __30__ bushels. Since at 8½

man-days the marginal __(benefit/cost)__ of hiring labor exceeds the marginal

__(benefit/cost)__ it will pay the firm to (increase/decrease) the amount of
labor input. In fact, it will pay to increase employment until the level of labor

inputs reaches __9½__ man-days.

6.48
Would it pay the farmer to hire more than 9½ units of labor? __(yes/no,)__

because at higher levels of labor input the __marginal__ __product__

of labor is less than the __wage__ rate.

6.49
This is easily seen in Figure 6.3 in which the __marg.__ __prod.__

curve intersects and falls below the wage rate curve at a level of __9½__
man-days. The optimum number of units of labor to hire is indicated by the

point where the two curves (intersect/are zero). Thus, if the farmer can hire

fractions of man-days he (would/would not) hire as many as ten man-days.

6.50
Now try this question, which is not easy. When you have found and understood the correct answer, you will have mastered quite a bit of basic economics. In Figure 6.4 two output levels exist where profits are zero; i.e.:

Answers

46. 60 · marginal product · wage
47. 90 · 30 · benefit · cost · increase · 9½
48. no · marginal product · wage
49. marginal product · 9½ · intersect · would not

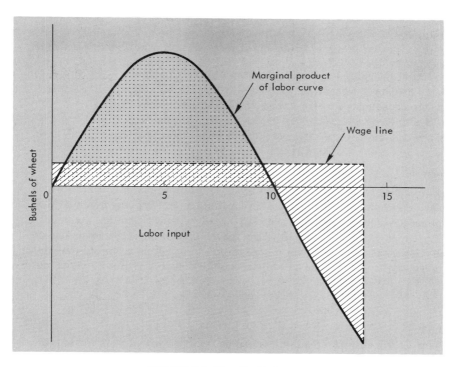

FIGURE 6.4. Zero Profit Output

those occur when the farmer hires zero units of labor and also when the farmer hires fourteen units of labor (assume all factor inputs except labor are free). Profits are obviously zero, given our assumptions, when zero units of labor are hired, since output is zero and costs are zero. In terms of Figure 6.4, what must be true if profits are zero when fourteen units of labor are hired? [Hint. How do you know, from the areas in the diagram, that the farmer is making a profit when he hires eight units of labor? When he hires 11 units?—Careful—the question is not whether a profit is made on the eleventh unit but whether profits are positive when eleven units are hired.]

_____

_____

_____

_____

_____

Answers
50. Profit will be zero, neither positive nor negative, when the area under the marginal product curve above the horizontal axis minus the area of rectangle below the wage line plus the area above the marginal product curve below the horizontal axis equals zero, i.e. when the dotted area equals the hatched area.

6.51

If, as we assume in this example, the farmer tries to maximize profit and must

pay labor the going wage rate, then the farmer should hire ___(a/b/c/d)___ :
a. 10 man-days, where *total* product of labor is maximized
b. 7 *units* man-days, where *average* product of labor is maximized
c. 4 man-days, where *marginal* product is maximized
d. 9½ man-days, where marginal product equals the wage rate.

6.52

Let us consider further the costs of the business firm. It will become obvious how important is the material we have just discussed. Suppose now that the farmer pays labor in dollars, instead of bushels of wheat, and that the price of one man-day of labor is $30. Also, for the sake of simplicity let us assume all other costs are zero. If we also assume that our farmer is a profit-maximizing individual, he will not hire an additional unit of labor input for which he must pay

$30, if that labor produces output that will sell for less than $ ___30___ .

6.53

Since, in this example, the farmer must pay workers with dollars and sells his

wheat for dollars, we must make calculations in ___dollar___ terms. Thus, in a profit-maximizing firm, labor will be hired until the dollar value of labor's marginal product is equal to the dollar cost, or wage, of a unit of labor.

The value of the ___marginal___ ___product___ of a unit of labor input is equal to the price of the product times the marginal product of that unit. If, for instance, at 8½ units of labor input the marginal product of labor is 90

bushels and wheat sells for $1 per bushel, the ___value___ of the marginal

product of labor will be $ ___90___ .

6.54

Let us now assume, more realistically, that there are costs in addition to labor costs. If the farmer rents a ten-acre field for one year at $10 per acre, then, independent of how much wheat the farmer produces, he will have to pay

$ ___100___ in rent. This is a fixed cost of production since it

___(will/will not)___ vary with the annual wheat output from this field.

6.55

If the farmer has to pay $30, however, for each man-day of labor employed, then the amount of wages he must pay ___(will/will not)___ vary with the number of units of labor input hired. These costs are known as variable costs. In this example they vary with the number of units of ___labor inputs___ hired, and hence with the output of wheat.

Table 6.1
Wheat Output—One Field with Varying Labor Input

Units of Labor Input (Man-Days)	Total Product (Bushels)	Average Product per Unit of Labor Input (Bushels)	Marginal Product of Labor Input (Bushels)
0	0	—	
1	40	40	40
2	140	70	100
3	300	100	160
4	480	120	180
5	650	130	170
6	810	135	160
7	960	137	150
8	1,080	135	120
9	1,170	130	90
10	1,200	120	30
11	1,190	108	−10
12	1,140	95	−50
13	910	70	−230

6.56

We see from Table 6.1 that, up to a point, in order to obtain more wheat, we had to hire ___more___ units of labor input, and since this hiring necessarily involves paying more wages, variable costs will indeed vary with total ___output___ of wheat. Variable costs ___(decrease/increase)___ as

Answers
54. 100 · will not
55. will · labor input
56. more · output · increase

total _____*output*_____ increases up to the maximum of 1,200 bushels when

_____*ten*_____ units of labor input are hired.

6.57

Turn now to Table 6.2. If we compare the first two columns, we can see that

_____*total*_____ _____*fixed*_____ _____*costs*_____ are independent of the
annual output of wheat. This is what we would expect, since if the farmer
commits himself to rent a ten-acre field at $10 per acre, this cost will be the
same regardless of his output of wheat; consequently, we regard it as a

_____*fixed*_____ cost.

6.58

The figures for columns 1 and 3 have been taken from Table 6.1. Given our
assumptions about other factor inputs, we see how many units of labor input
are required to produce the various quantities of wheat. We also see that in

order to produce more wheat, we have to hire _____*(more/fewer)*_____ units of
labor input.

Table 6.2
Fixed, Variable, and Total Costs in the Production of Wheat

(1) Annual Output of Wheat	(2) Total Fixed Costs	(3) Units of Labor Input (Man-days)	(4) Total Variable Costs	(5) Total Costs
0	$100	0	$ 0	$100
40	100	1	30	130
140	100	2	60	160
300	100	3	90	190
480	100	4	120	220
650	100	5	150	250
810	100	6	180	280
960	100	7	210	310
1,080	100	8	240	340
1,170	100	9	270	370
1,200	100	10	300	400

Answers
  56. output · ten
  57. **total fixed costs** · fixed
  58. more

6.59

Since labor is our only variable input, under our simplifying assumptions, the only factor input which will vary in quantity with total output will be

_____labor_____ input. Since we know the price or wage the farmer must pay for one man-day, we can calculate the labor costs corresponding to any given level of output. For instance, we see that in order to produce 650 bushels of wheat,

we require _____five_____ units of labor input. Thus, the cost to the farmer

of this labor input will be $_____150_____ .

6.60

Similarly, the labor costs to the farmer of producing 1,080 bushels of wheat

would be $_____240_____ , since this requires _____8_____ units of labor input.

6.61

Thus, we can see how we derive the figures in column 4, which is headed "Total Variable Costs." We derive those figures by multiplying the figures in column

_____3_____ by $30—the cost of one unit of _____labor_____ input.

Since the cost per unit of labor is constant and since a _____larger_____ quantity of labor input is required to produce a larger quantity of output, we would

expect total variable costs to vary in the _(same/opposite)_ direction as total output.

6.62

We derive total cost by adding together total fixed cost and _____total_____

_____variable_____ _____cost_____ , and we find, as you would expect, total

cost varies in the _____same_____ direction as output.

6.63

In Figure 6.5 we have plotted the data in Table 6.2 and, as you would expect, the total fixed costs are represented by a horizontal line, because they do not

Answers
  59. labor · five · 150
  60. 240 · eight
  61. 3 · labor · larger · same
  62. total variable cost · same

_____vary_____ with the level of output. The total cost curve is derived by

adding the ____total____ ____fixed____ ____cost____ curve to

the ____total____ ____variable____ ____cost____ curve.

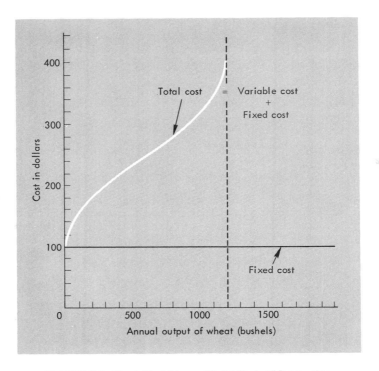

FIGURE 6.5 Fixed, Variable, and Total Costs of Production

6.64

We have reproduced Figure 6.1 here to help you see how Figure 6.5 can be derived directly from Figure 6.1 if you know the costs of the fixed and

___variable___ factor inputs.

From Figure 6.1 you can see how much wheat will be yielded from different

amounts of ___labor___ input in the field, *ceteris paribus.* Knowing the cost of the labor (and the rental cost of the field) you can calculate, therefore, how much the different outputs of wheat will cost.

Answers
    63. vary · total fixed cost · total variable cost
    64. variable · labor ·

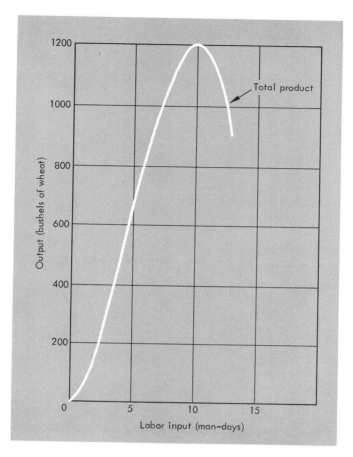

FIGURE 6.1.

6.65

If you recall, we used the data from Figure 6.1 to derive the curves in Figure 6.2 (repeated on the following page); that is, we could derive the _marginal_ product and average product of labor curves from the _total_ _product_ curve of labor.

Answers
65. marginal · total product

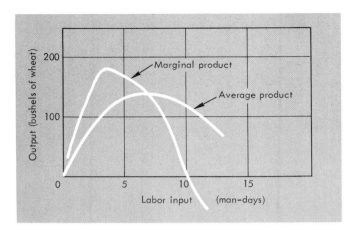

FIGURE 6.2.

6.66

In a similar fashion we are going to derive the marginal and average cost curves

of wheat from the _____ total _____ _____ cost _____ curve of wheat in Figure 6.5.

6.67

Just as it was important to see the relationship between the total product of the

variable factor input and _____ total _____ _____ cost _____ of output, so it is important to understand the relationship between marginal and average product curves and marginal and average cost curves.

6.68

With a little thought you should realize that the higher is the average product of a given amount of (in this case) labor, the lower will be the average cost of the output produced. For instance if ten bakers produce 100 loaves of bread rather

than 50 loaves, the average product will be _____*(higher/lower)*_____ and the cost per

loaf will be _____*(higher/lower).*_____ The higher the average product, the lower the

_____ Avg. _____ _____ cost _____ .

Answers
   66. total cost
   67. total cost
   68. higher · lower · **average cost**

6.69

Similarly if an additional baker produces six loaves rather than three loaves,

the marginal ___product___ of labor will be higher and the marginal

___cost___ of bread will be lower.

6.70

Let us return to our wheat example. In Table 6.3 data from Table 6.2 are repeated with some additional calculations. To simplify calculations we have assumed the only two factors of production for which the wheat farmer has

to pay are land and ___labor___. The amount of land is fixed at ten

acres and costs $10 per acre. Thus the total ___fixed___ cost is $100. The variable factor input is labor at $30 per man-day. The total cost of

production will be found by adding together ___total___ ___fixed___

___costs___ and ___total___ ___variable___ ___costs___.

Table 6.3
Total, Average, and Marginal Costs of Wheat Production

(1)	(2) Total Fixed	(3) Average Fixed	(4) Total Variable	(5) Average Variable	(6)	(7) Average Total	(8)
Output	Costs	Costs	Costs	Costs	Total Costs	Costs	Marginal Cost
0	100	—	0	—	100	—	
40	100	$2.50	30	$0.75	130	$3.25	$0.75
140	100	.71	60	.43	160	1.14	.30
300	100	.33	90	.30	190	.63	.19
480	100	.21	120	.25	220	.46	.17
650	100	.15	150	.23	250	.38	.18
810	100	.12	180	.22	280	.35	.19
960	100	.10	210	.219	310	.32	.20
1,080	100	.09	240	.22	340	.31	.25
1,170	100	.085	270	.23	370	.32	.33
1,200	100	.083	300	.25	400	.33	1.00

6.71

Average fixed costs are found by dividing ___total___ ___fixed___

___costs___ by output; average variable costs are calculated by dividing

Answers
69. product · cost
70. labor · fixed · total fixed costs · total variable costs
71. **total fixed costs**

_____t._____   ___и в'_____   ___C._____   by __output__

and average total costs by dividing _____total_____ ____costs____ by
output.

6.72
Since total costs equal total fixed costs plus total __и Ariable__

___Crsts____ average total costs will equal average __fixed__

__costs__ plus __Average__ variable costs.

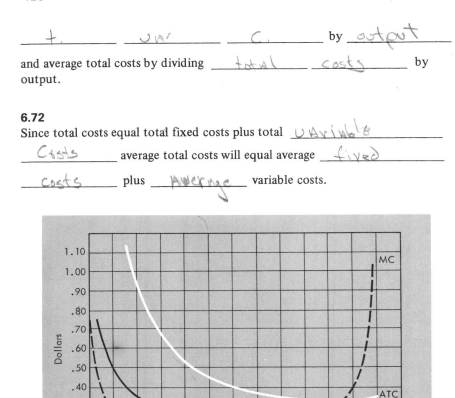

FIGURE 6.6.

6.73
We have plotted the average and marginal curves from Table 6.3 in Figure 6.6.
To avoid having too messy a figure we have omitted the average fixed cost curve

that, if included, would be a line of (constant/increasing/~~decreasing~~) height and
that would measure the distance between the average total cost curve and the

__Avg.__ __Var.__ __Cost__ curve.

6.74

The average total cost and average variable cost curves first decrease to minimum

points, after which they __increase__.

6.75

Although we derive the marginal cost curve in Table 6.3 from total cost figures,

we could also derive the marginal cost from total __variable__ cost figures,
since the marginal cost of producing additional wheat will be independent of the

__fixed__ __costs__.

6.76

Note two significant points in Figure 6.6. These are where the marginal cost
curve intersects the average variable cost curve and the average total cost curve.
In both instances the marginal cost curve intersects each curve at its

(minimum/~~maximum~~) point. This is no accident, but is necessarily true. We
can see from Figure 6.6 that as the marginal cost of producing additional wheat
equals the average total cost, the marginal cost curve must intersect the average

total cost curve at its __minimum__ point, since once it has intersected
the average cost curve (and once marginal costs exceed average costs), it will

cause average total cost to __rise__.

6.77

Think again about a basketball squad. If the height of a sixth player is greater than
the average height of the other five, then the addition of this sixth man will cause

the average height to __rise__.

Answers
73. decreasing · average variable cost
74. increase
75. variable · fixed costs
76. minimum · minimum · rise
77. rise

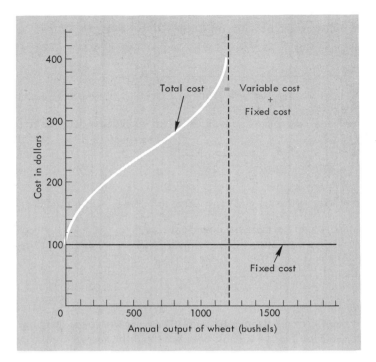

FIGURE 6.5.

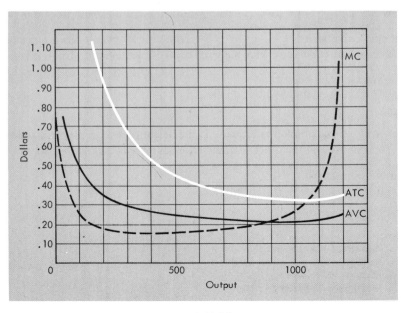

FIGURE 6.6.

6.78

Let us now consider Figures 6.5 and 6.6 together, both of which were drawn from data in Table 6.3.

Had we been given only Figure 6.6, we could have derived Figure 6.5 from it. As you observe in Figure 6.5 the difference between total cost and fixed cost is

___variable___   ___costs___ . We also see that total cost

(increases/decreases) as output increases,   *(but not at/at)*   the same rate.

6.79

Fixed cost is *(dependent on/independent of)* the level of output and is constant and equal to $ ___100___ .

6.80

Thus, if we wish to derive the average fixed cost per unit of output from Figure 6.5, we divide ___fixed___   ___costs___ by output. The curve representing average fixed cost will slope ___downwards___ from ___left___

to ___right___ , since we are dividing a constant number by increasing numbers for higher levels of output.

6.81

In a similar fashion, we would derive the average total cost curve by dividing

___total___   ___cost___ by ___output___ . This curve will

Answers
78. variable cost · increases · but not at
79. independent of · 100
80. fixed cost · downwards · left · right
81. total cost · output

first fall, reach a minimum point, and then start to rise. We see from Figure 6.6 when we plot the average cost curve that it reaches a minimum at an output

level of approximately _____ 100 _____ bushels.

6.82

We derive average variable cost in a similar fashion, by dividing total

_____ av. _____ cost _____ by _____ output _____ . Since the

difference between total cost and variable cost is _____ fixed _____ cost _____ ,
the difference between average total cost and average variable cost will be

_____ average _____ fixed _____ cost _____ . Since _____ avy _____

_____ f _____ cost _____ is smaller for higher levels of output, as
the level of output increases the difference between average total cost and

average variable cost will _____ decrease _____ .

6.83

The calculation of marginal cost is slightly more complex. Ideally we want to
know the cost of producing one additional unit of output. We know for instance
that the total cost of producing 40 bushels of wheat is $130 and the total cost of

producing 140 bushels is $160. Thus the difference in cost of $ _____ 30 _____
is the marginal cost of producing an additional 100 bushels (i.e. 140-40 bushels).

Answers

81. 1,100
82. variable cost · output · fixed cost · average fixed cost · average fixed cost · decrease
83. 30

If we treat each of those extra 100 bushels equally, we would calculate the

marginal cost of one bushel as $30/100 = $ ___ .30 ___ .

6.84

The problem we are encountering here is the same one we discussed earlier in the book. We are not making *continuous* changes but rather *discrete* changes; not plotting the marginal and average curves for every atom of output but rather considering output in "lumps." The smooth curves are drawn through those lumps

as though we had considered continuous changes. O.K.? ___ O.K. ___

6.85

Given lumpiness problems and assuming that land and labor are the only two factor inputs and also assuming that their prices are fixed in the market, it is clear that total variable cost for a given level of output will be determined by

the amount of ___ labor ___ hired. But, with a given amount of land, the

amount of labor required to produce this level of ___ output ___ is given by the product curves. Thus, given the prices of resources and the level of output,

the product curves will determine the total, average, and marginal ___ cost ___ curves. That is, the shape of the cost curves will be determined by the shape of

the ___ product ___ curves.

Answers
    83. .30
    84. O.K.
    85. labor · output · cost · product

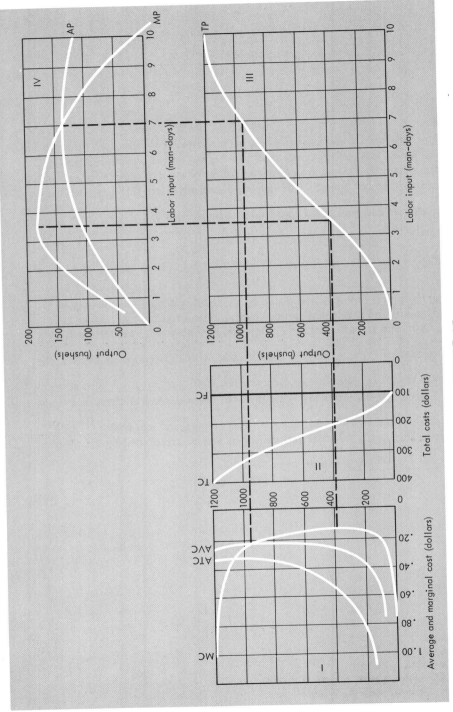

FIGURE 6.7.

6.86

Figure 6.7 shows the relationship between product and cost curves. The average variable cost curve will be inversely related to the average product of labor curve, remembering that the wage per man-day is set in the market and is constant. Thus, when the average product per man-day is rising, average variable

cost will be ___*falling*___ , and when average product per man-day is falling,

average variable cost per unit of output will be ___*rising*___ .

6.87

Another way to express the same idea would be to say that the greater the average

product of each man-day of labor the ___*(higher/lower)*___ will be the average variable cost of each bushel of wheat produced. And conversely, the less wheat a

man-day of labor can produce, the ___*(higher/lower)*___ will be the average variable cost of each unit of wheat.

6.88

By studying Figure 6.7, which combines the diagrams we have been using, the inverse relationship between average variable cost and average product of labor can be clearly seen. Part IV of Figure 6.7 shows the average and marginal product of labor curves. The average product of labor is a maximum of 137 bushels when seven units of labor are hired. At this point, where the average product is at its

maximum, the average product curve must be intersected by the ___*marginal*___

___*product*___ curve.

6.89

From Part III we see that seven units of labor input are associated with a total

output of ___*960*___ bushels. As you should recall we derived the *AP* and *MP* curves of Part IV from the *TP* curve of Part III.

6.90

Part II merely transforms the *TP* curve into a ___*total*___ ___*cost*___ curve. This is done by plotting output against total cost rather than against

Answers
    86. falling · rising
    87. lower · higher
    88. marginal product
    89. 960
    90. total cost

labor input. Total costs, in this example, include a _~~fixed~~_____

__~~cost~~_____ of $100 for land in addition to the __~~variable~~___ costs
for labor.

6.91
Seven units of labor input yield an output of 960 bushels, which are associated

with a total cost of $310, $100 for ____~~fixed~~_____~~costs~~_____

and $210 for ____~~variable~~_____~~costs~~_____. The $210 figure represents

the seven units of labor at $ ____~~30~~_____ each.

6.92
As seen earlier in this chapter, average and marginal cost curves can be derived
from total cost curves. The curves in Part I are derived from the *TC* curve of
Part II. At our output level of 960 bushels, we see in Part I that *AVC* is at a

minimum ($0.219) and is intersected at this output level by the _~~marginal~~_.

____~~cost~~_____ curve.

6.93
In Figure 6.7 a broken line traces the points we have discussed. We have shown

how the maximum ____~~avg.~~_____ ____~~product~~_____ point is reflected at

the ___~~minimum~~____ average variable cost point.

6.94
Just as the maximum value of the average product of labor yields the minimum

_____~~avg.~~___~~var.~~_____ ____~~cost~~_____, so the maximum value

of the marginal product of labor yields the ___~~min.~~___ ___~~marg.~~____

____~~cost~~_____ as you can see from the other connecting lines in Figure 6.7.

Answers
   90. fixed cost · variable
   91. fixed costs · variable costs · 30
   92. marginal cost
   93. average product · minimum
   94. average variable cost · minimum marginal cost

REVIEW QUESTIONS

6.1

A farmer wishing to maximize profit will always hire a factor of production as long as the value of its marginal product _____c_____ .

a. is positive.
b. exceeds its average product.
c. is greater than its cost.
d. is negative.

6.2

Which of the following cannot increase, other things equal, as output increases? _____c_____ .

a. Average total cost.
b. Average variable cost.
c. Average fixed cost.
d. Marginal cost.

6.3

Other things remaining the same, the higher the marginal product of a factor input, _____b_____ .

a. the higher the marginal cost of output.
b. the lower the marginal cost of output.
c. the lower the marginal product of the other factor inputs.
d. the lower the average product of that factor.

Answers
  1. c
  2. c
  3. b

6.4

If a firm is producing output at a point where diminishing returns have set in,

this means that ________ .

a. each additional unit of output will be more expensive to produce.
b. each additional unit of output will require increasing amounts of the factor of production being increased.
c. the marginal product of the variable factor of production decreases as the quantity used increases.
d. all of the above are correct.

6.5

   i. The higher the marginal product of a factor input, the lower the marginal cost of output.
   ii. The higher the average product of a factor input, the lower the average cost of output.
   iii. The higher the costs of fixed factor inputs, the lower the marginal cost of output.

Which of the preceding statements are true?

_____A_____ .

a. Only i and ii.
b. Only ii and iii.
c. Only i and iii.
d. i, ii, and iii.

7

The Competitive Firm
in the Short Run

7.1

In the previous chapter we analyzed how the productiveness of factor inputs

determined the ___costs___ of production at different output levels.
We assumed all factor inputs but one to be fixed. In this chapter and in the
next we shall continue our analysis by introducing revenue from sales as well
as cost of production and show how the profit-maximizing competitive firm
behaves—first when some factor inputs are fixed and then when all are variable.

Figure 7.1 shows four average total cost curves. These can be thought of as the
average cost curves of four firms involved in making the same product or of one
firm with four different possible scales of operation. These average total cost
curves represent different sizes or scales of operation. If each firm in Figure 7.1
sells an identical product and if each firm can sell as many units as it can possibly
produce, then the firm which could produce an output cheaper than any other

firm would be one with average total cost curve _(ATC₁/ATC₂/ATC₃/ATC₄.)_
The lowest average total cost per unit of output for this firm would be reached

at the ___lowest___ point on the average total cost curve, i.e., C_3. We also

see that this point is ___lower___ than are the corresponding points C_1,
C_2 and C_4.

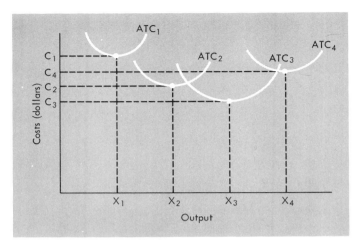

FIGURE 7.1. Various Scales of Operation

7.2

If you think of the real world around you, it is obvious that not all firms have the same size or scale of operation. You see the corner grocery store and the super-market, the small movie theater and the large movie theater. Average total cost curve 1 may represent a small grocery store, and average total cost curve 3, the supermarket. We must investigate why such situations exist and why we do not have all firms with identical average total cost curves, imitating firm 3 in our example which has the minimum point on all average total cost curves, even though each enterprise deals in the same product and even though in this exam-

ple, average total cost is lower for the *(supermarket/grocery store)* than it is for

the *(supermarket/grocery store)* at the minimum point of the respective aver-age total cost curves.

7.3

Average total cost curve 2 may represent the average total cost per unit of output in a medium-sized supermarket. Perhaps the corner grocer and then this medium-sized supermarket moved into an area which was growing in size, and the medium-sized supermarket did not wish to build too large a store, fearing that the demand in this market was insufficient for a really large-size supermarket. Thus, we would find that the minimum point on the average total cost curve of the medium-

size supermarket was ___lower___ than the minimum point on the average

Answers
2. supermarket · grocery store
3. lower

total cost curve of the ___grocery___ ___store___ , but higher than the corresponding point in our large supermarket, in this case firm 3.

7.4

Firm 4 is an enormous firm and the minimum point C_4 on its average total cost

curve ATC_4 is reached at an output of ___X_4___ which is ___higher___ than C_3, the minimum point on the average total cost curve in firm 3.

7.5

Perhaps the corner grocer plans to become larger; perhaps the medium-sized supermarket plans to expand and try to match firm 3, but the time period we are considering when we look at Figure 7.1 is known as the short run. It is very difficult to be precise, in terms of days or months, about how short or how long the short run is, and it will vary from case to case. We define the short run to be that

period of time within which fixed costs do not vary. The ___long___ run is that time period in which all costs can vary.

7.6

Let us consider a manufacturer of bedroom furniture. He has a relatively small factory on a piece of ground which he rents, and a large wood-cutting machine. This machine requires some maintenance whether or not it is used, and there is a certain amount of wear and tear on his factory building, which is also independent of the number of sets of furniture produced per time period. Thus, the manufacturer will have certain costs, whether or not he produces any furniture. These costs would include depreciation on his building, maintenance on his machines, and rent to the landowner. These costs, therefore, are

___fixed___ costs because they are ___independent___ of the level of output.

7.7

Next week will certainly be the short run for our furniture manufacturer. It

will be the short run because certain costs are ___fixed___ costs. If the manufacturer wished to double output next week, then he would have to hire

Answers
3. grocery store
4. X_4 · higher
5. long
6. fixed · independent
7. fixed

additional labor and buy more raw materials. The costs incurred in hiring more

labor and buying more material are ___variable___ costs because they vary

with the level of ___output___ .

7.8
That time period within which increased output will be forthcoming only by

increasing ___*(fixed/variable)*___ factor inputs, but during which certain costs will

be fixed and hence ___independent___ of the level of output, is the short run.

7.9
If the manufacturer decides to build a new factory, however, because of increasing demand for his bedroom furniture and also to install new machinery,
then he is altering the amount of fixed factors of production. This period would

be the ___long___ ___run___ . Thus, that period in which all

costs become variable, is the ___long___ ___run___ .

7.10
In the short run an increase in output will be associated with increased

___variable___ costs with no change in ___fixed___ costs, whereas

in the long run ___all___ costs become variable.

7.11
One may well ask why firms do not decide what scale of operation will yield
them a minimum total average cost in the long run and operate that size of
enterprise. The chief reason is because the future is fraught with uncertainty.
Firms do not know what technological changes are going to take place in their
specific line of business, nor do they know how consumers' demand may switch
from one good to another good. For instance, how big should a supermarket be?
As you might guess, the answer is not a simple one, and will depend upon such
things as projected population growth within a given area and the type of competition that may be forthcoming from other stores. Once the store has been

constructed, however, certain ___fixed___ costs have been undertaken,

Answers
    7. variable · output
    8. variable · independent
    9. long run · long run
    10. variable · fixed · all
    11. fixed

and it could be a very expensive proposition to change the size of a supermarket every week, or every month, or every year. The time period within which those

fixed costs are assumed not to vary is known as the ___short___ ___run___ ,

and the time period within which all costs are variable is known as the ___long___

___run___ .

7.12

Dry-cleaning establishments tend to be relatively small-scale business enterprises. But we find that dry-cleaning establishments tend to be much smaller in small towns than they are in large towns. One would expect that the larger-scale op-

eration would have ___(higher/lower)___ average total costs at the minimum point on the average total cost curve, but this does not say that it would be profitable to build the larger scale dry-cleaning establishment in a very small town. There might be lots of unused capacity in this larger-scale establishment in a small

town, and as we might expect, fixed costs would tend to be much ___higher___ for the larger-scale enterprise. Thus the larger firm might not be able to operate at a profit in a very small town.

7.13

General Motors is a very large organization producing thousands of automobiles per year in a very efficient fashion for that scale of enterprise. It would be absurd to have such a large enterprise producing only one automobile per year;

the ___fixed___ ___costs___ would be much too high to make an output of one automobile per year profitable.

7.14

Given the large demand for the output of General Motors, however, the company can employ men to do very specialized jobs, at which they become expert, and can use assembly line production and very expensive and elaborate machinery, because all this produces a relatively low point on the firm's average

___total___ ___cost___ curve at very high levels of output. If General Motors were to produce only a few automobiles per year, the average

Answers
11. short run · long run
12. lower · higher
13. fixed costs
14. total cost

total cost of each automobile produced would become very ___high___ compared to the situation in which they have a large output.

7.15

Larger firms may also be able to use by-products in a profitable fashion, where this may not be profitable for the smaller firm. A large furniture manufacturer, for instance, may be able to profitably sell scrap wood for firewood, whereas the amount of scrap wood which the small firm could collect might not make it profitable for the small firm to go into the firewood business. If this were true, then the average total cost of producing a bundle of firewood for the large firm would be ___lower___ than the average total cost of producing a bundle of firewood for the small firm. There are many considerations to be taken into account. Therefore, when we are trying to decide on the optimal scale of operation for a firm, we *(would/would not)* expect in the real world to find that all firms are the same size with identical cost curves.

7.16

We saw earlier how sets of parameters determined the position of demand and supply curves and how on the demand curve, normally a ___smaller___ quantity would be ___demanded___ the higher the price, and on a ___supply___ curve, a larger quantity would be ___supplied___ the higher the price. With our knowledge of costs, let us now see how, for the profit-maximizing businessman, the amount he will be willing to supply in any given time period will be determined by his costs of production.

7.17

We shall first consider the competitive firm in the short run, and we shall assume that the aim of the firm is profit maximization. We wish to know what output a firm should produce in the short run, in which certain costs are ___fixed___, given that the firm's goal is to maximize ___profit___.

Answers

   14. high
   15. lower · would not
   16. smaller · demanded · supply · supplied
   17. fixed · profit

7.18

The gross income a firm receives from the sale of its product is known as its revenue. Thus, if we use the jargon of economists, we would say that the total income received by a manufacturer from sales in some given time period (say one month) is total ___revenue___ .

7.19

When total revenue from some specific output exceeds the total cost of producing that output, then the firm will make a ___profit___ at that level of output. If, however, total costs are greater than total revenue for some specific output, the firm will make a loss at that level of output (i.e. will have a negative ___profit___).

7.20

Let us consider Table 7.1 where we have total cost, total revenue, and profit for a furniture manufacturer.

Table 7.1
Total Cost, Revenue and Profit

(1) Output	(2) Total Cost	(3) Total Revenue	(4) Profit
0	$ 1,300	$ 0	$-1,300
1	2,300	800	-1,500
2	2,800	1,600	-1,200
3	3,050	2,400	- 650
4	3,200	3,200	0
5	3,300	4,000	700
6	3,700	4,800	1,100
7	4,500	5,600	1,100
8	5,500	6,400	900
9	7,200	7,200	0
10	10,000	8,000	-2,000

This furniture manufacturer produces identical sets of bedroom furniture, each of which sells for $800. Thus, we derive the figures in column 3 in Table 7.1 by multiplying $800 by the level of ___output___ . If the manufacturer

Answers
18. revenue
19. profit · profit
20. output

sells ten sets of furniture per month, the total revenue for that month would be

$ ___8,000___ . If he sells four sets, his total revenue will be $ ___3200___ ,

and if he sells zero sets, the total revenue will be $ ___0___ .

7.21

Let us now consider the manufacturer's cost of production. When the manufacturer produces zero sets of furniture, the only cost incurred will be fixed cost. In this example fixed cost, which is the same at all levels of output, equals

___$1300___ . From columns 1 and 2 we see that total cost (variable plus

___fixed___ cost) increases as output ___increases___ .

7.22

We obtain the profit figures in column 4 by subtracting total ___cost___

from total ___revenue___ . If, in some given month, the furniture manufacturer produces zero sets of furniture (perhaps everyone is having a month's

vacation) the only cost that will be incurred will be ___fixed___ cost,

but since total revenue will be $ ___0___ , profit will be $ ___−1300___ .

7.23

We also see that if the furniture manufacturer produces one set of furniture per

month, his loss (negative profit) will be even ___greater___ than if he pro-

duces zero sets of furniture. The actual loss suffered would be $ ___1500___ .
At an output level of four sets of furniture per month, however, the manufacturer

breaks even. He suffers no loss, but neither does he make any ___profit___ .

This is because total costs are $ ___3200___ and total revenue is also

$ ___3200___ . Total revenue, at this output level, is calculated by mul-

tiplying $ ___800___ by ___four___ .

Answers
20. 8,000 · 3,200 · 0
21. $1,300 · fixed · increases
22. cost · revenue · fixed · 0 · –1,300
23. greater · 1,500 · profit · 3,200 · 3,200 · 800 · four

7.24

It is only in the range of output of ___5___ to ___8___
sets of bedroom furniture per month that the manufacturer will make positive
profit. We see that at a level of output of nine sets of furniture per month, profit

is again ___zero___ , and at higher levels of output, profit is ___neg.___ .

7.25

Given that the aim of the manufacturer is to maximize profit, it is quite obvious

from Table 7.1 that he will produce either ___six___ or ___seven___
sets of furniture per month, since either of those outputs gives us a maximum

profit per time period of $ ___1,100___ .

7.26

In Figure 7.2 we have plotted the data from Table 7.1.

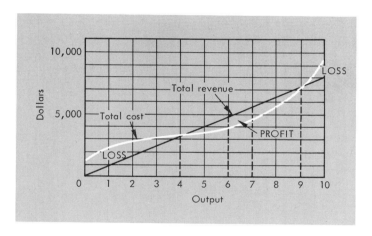

FIGURE 7.2. Total Revenue and Total Cost

Since each set of furniture sells for $ ___800___ total revenue increases

by $ ___800___ for each additional unit of output. As a result total

revenue is represented in Figure 7.2 by a ___straight___ line.

Answers

24. five · eight · zero · negative
25. six · seven · 1,100
26. 800 · 800 · straight

7.27

The total cost curve is shaped similarly to the total cost curves we have already

analyze. We see that at zero output, total cost is $ _____1,300_____ . At this

level of output total cost equals _____fixed_____ cost. As output increases,
total cost increases fairly fast at first, then more slowly for levels of output between two and seven, and then fairly sharply again for higher levels of output.
We also see that our total cost curve intersects our total revenue curve at levels

of output of _____four_____ and _____five_____ .

7.28

We see from Figure 7.2 that at an output of four sets of furniture per month,

total cost _____equals_____ total revenue and, consequently, _____profit_____
is zero.

7.29

For all levels of output less than four, total cost _____exceeds_____ total revenue
and, consequently, profit is negative. This situation is similar for levels of out-

put greater than _____nine_____ sets per month where once more total cost
exceeds total revenue.

7.30

For levels of output between four and nine sets of furniture _____total_____
~~revenue~~
~~output~~ exceeds _____total_____ _____cost_____ , and, conse-

quently, _____profit_____ is positive.

7.31

The level of profit at the monthly output of five sets of furniture could be found

by taking the vertical distance between the _____total_____ _____revenue_____

curve and the _____total_____ _____cost_____ curve at a level of output of

five sets. This distance would be $700, which would be the _____profit_____
for that level of output.

Answers
    27. 1,300 · fixed · four · nine
    28. equals · profit
    29. exceeds · nine
    30. total revenue · total cost · profit
    31. total revenue · total cost · profit

7.32
Since our furniture manufacturer wishes to maximize profit, he will choose that level of output where the distance between the ___total___ ___revenue___ curve and the ___total___ ___cost___ curve is a maximum.

7.33
Thus, our manufacturer will be maximizing ___profit___ if he produces either ___six___ or ___7___ sets of furniture per month. In both cases profit will be $___1,100___.

7.34
Just as the distance between total revenue and total cost shows (positive) ___profit___ for outputs of four to nine sets of furniture, so will this distance show ___loss___ (negative profit) for levels of output less than four and greater than nine. Thus, given the range of outputs in Figure 7.2, maximum loss would be incurred at an output level of ___ten___ sets of furniture per week, and would amount to $___2000___. The level of output that would produce the second highest loss would be ___one___ set(s) of furniture per month, where the extent of the loss would be $___1800___.

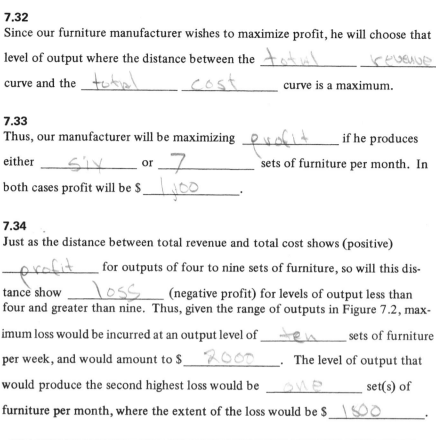

FIGURE 7.3. Profit at Different Levels of Output

Answers
32. total revenue · total cost
33. profit · six · seven · 1,100
34. profit · loss · ten · 2,000 · one · 1,500

7.35

In Figure 7.3 we have plotted profit at various levels of output. For those levels of output where the curve lies below the horizontal axis, profit is

(positive/negative) and where it lies above the axis, profit is ~~positive~~ .

If the firm is to maximize profit, it should produce ~~six~~ or

~~seven~~ sets of furniture per month. (The profit curve in Figure 7.3 reaches a peak between levels of output of six and seven. Had our units been ten sets instead of one set, then the profit maximizing output would lie somewhere between sixty and seventy sets, e.g. sixty-five. This is, you will recall, the problem of *discrete units.*)

7.36

Given our knowledge of costs, there is a more useful way we can calculate the profit-maximizing output for our furniture manufacturer. Look at Table 7.2.

Table 7.2
Marginal Cost and Marginal Revenue

(1) Output	(2) Total Cost	(3) Marginal Cost	(4) Total Revenue	(5) Marginal Revenue
0	$ 1,300		$ 0	
		$1,000		$800
1	2,300		800	
		500		800
2	2,800		1,600	
		250		800
3	3,050		2,400	
		150		800
4	3,200		3,200	
		100		800
5	3,300		4,000	
		400		800
6	3,700		4,800	
		800		800
7	4,500		5,600	
		1,000		800
8	5,500		6,400	
		1,700		800
9	7,200		7,200	
		2,800		800
10	10,000		8,000	

Answers
35. negative · positive · six · seven

In column 3, we have calculated marginal cost, which you will remember is the cost of producing (an additional/the initial) set of furniture. We see, for instance, that the total cost of producing two sets of furniture is $ _2800_ , and the total cost of producing one set of furniture is $ _2300_ .

Thus, the cost of increasing production from one to two sets of furniture is the difference between those two figures, which is $500. Thus when output is one set per month, _marginal_ cost is $500.

7.37

Similarly, the marginal cost of producing the fifth set of bedroom furniture is $ _100_ . This figure is derived by subtracting the cost of producing _four_ sets of furniture which is $ _3200_ from the cost of producing _5_ sets of furniture which is $ _3300_ .

7.38

In a similar fashion we can calculate the marginal revenue. As you might expect, marginal revenue in this case is the additional revenue collected by selling one _Additional_ set of furniture. Since the selling price of each set of furniture is the same, the extra revenue from selling an additional set of furniture is (less than/equal to) the price. Thus, in this example marginal revenue is a constant, equal to $ _800_ because price is equal to $ _800_ .

7.39

Let us now see how our marginal cost and marginal revenue columns can help us determine the profit-maximizing output. Suppose, for example, our furniture firm is producing two units of output and wants to decide whether to produce a third unit. You know from Table 7.2 that at two units of output the marginal revenue is $ _800_ and the marginal cost is $ _250_ .

Answers
36. an additional · 2,800 · 2,300 · marginal
37. 100 · four · 3,200 · five · 3,300
38. additional · equal to · 800 · 800
39. 800 · 250

7.40

If by producing an extra unit revenue is increased by $800 and cost is increased by $250, would the change be worthwhile? The answer to this question is

_____ *(yes/no)* _____ because such a change would *(increase/decrease)* profit by

$ _____ 550 _____ .

7.41

Thus, you can see that it will always pay to produce an extra unit of output as

long as the marginal revenue of an extra unit is ____ *(greater/less)* ____ than the marginal cost.

7.42

Would it pay the firm to produce a fourth unit of output? ____ *(yes/no.)* ____

What would be the extra profit if it did so? $ _____ 650 _____ .

7.43

At what level of output will there be no gain from producing an extra unit?

____ six ____ units. It is here that ____ marginal ____ revenue and

____ marginal ____ cost are equal and ____ profit ____ is a maximum.

7.44

The extra cost incurred in producing the sixth set of bedroom furniture is

____ less ____ than the extra revenue received from its sale. Thus, it is profitable to produce the sixth set. The marginal cost of producing a seventh

set is $ ____ 800 ____ , and the marginal revenue from its sale is

$ ____ 800 ____ . Thus, we would say that the manufacturer would be indifferent (he would not care from the viewpoint of maximizing profit) as to whether or not he produced and sold this seventh set. He would not, however, produce more than seven sets because that would take him beyond the point at

which ____ marginal ____ revenue ____ equals marginal cost.

Answers
   40. yes · increase · 550
   41. greater
   42. yes · 650
   43. six · marginal · marginal · profit
   44. less · 800 · 800 · marginal revenue

7.45

We can see that the manufacturer *(would/would not)* want to produce an eighth set of furniture per month, because the marginal cost of producing an eighth

set of bedroom furniture is $ ___1000___ and the marginal revenue is

only $___800___. For the eighth set, marginal ___cost___ ex-

ceeds marginal ___revenue___ and a monthly output of eight sets is there-

fore not the ___profit___ -maximizing output level.

7.46

Note, however, that even though the manufacturer would not produce this eighth set of bedroom furniture, he could still make a profit producing eight

sets of bedroom furniture, because total cost is $ ___5,500___ and total

revenue is $ ___6400___. Thus, the profit made from selling eight

sets of bedroom furniture is $ ___960___. The firm would not produce eight units even though it earns a profit at this level of output, because here

profit would not be at a ___max.___ . Since marginal revenue does not equal marginal cost at this level of output, profit would obviously be

(greater/less) at some other level of output.

7.47

Again it would not be wise for the manufacturer to produce a ninth set of

bedroom furniture, because ___marginal___ ___cost___ exceeds

___marginal___ ___revenue___ by the amount of $ ___900___ .
That is, the extra cost incurred in producing this additional set exceeds by $900

the extra ___revenue___ obtained from its sale. The manufacturer would

just break even in producing nine sets; total revenue would equal ___total___

___cost___ .

7.48

Figure 7.4 repeats the above discussion and takes advantage of one of our Chapter 2 diagrams.

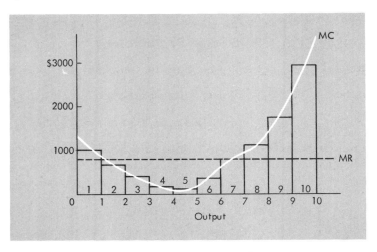

FIGURE 7.4. Profit-Maximizing Output

Adding together the ten rectangles would yield the ___total___

___variable___ ___cost___ of ten sets of furniture.

7.49

Using the continuous curve instead we know that the ___Area___

under the curve also measures the ___variable___ ___cost___

_____ of ten sets.

7.50

Using only the *MC* curve, how would you calculate the total variable cost of producing the fifth plus the sixth plus the seventh plus the eighth sets. *(CAREFUL!)*

_____

_____

Answers

 48. total variable cost
 49. area · variable cost
 50. find the area under the *MC* curve between the numbers 4 and 8 on the output axis—
   note *not* 5 and 8, since that would exclude the fifth set

7.51

The area under the *MR* curve between 0 and 10 equals the _total_

revenue from selling ten sets of furniture. This area represents

$ _8,000_ .

7.52

Thus ignoring fixed cost, as long as the area under the *MR* curve is _greater_ than the area under the *MC* curve, profit will be positive. However, as soon as the *MC* curve lies above the *MR* curve the benefits (revenue) from producing addi-

tional sets are _less_ than the costs of those additional sets. Conse-quently, the profit-maximizing entrepreneur will not produce beyond the point

where *MR* = _MC_ .

7.53

You should note that it is a necessary condition for _MR_ to

equal _MC_ for profit maximization, but not a sufficient con-dition. *MC must also be rising.* For example, the *MC* curve intersects the *MR* curve between output levels of one and two, but this is not a profit-maximizing

output level because the _MC_ curve is falling.

7.54

Thus, we can summarize what we have learned in Figure 7.4 by saying that a profit-seeking entrepreneur (businessman) will increase output up to that point at which marginal revenue equals marginal cost. It will not pay him to stop be-fore that point is reached because the marginal revenue collected from each addi-

tional set of bedroom furniture exceeds the _marginal cost_

of producing that set. _Profit_ will not be maximized by producing beyond the point at which marginal revenue equals marginal cost, because the marginal revenue collected from sales of additional sets of bedroom furniture

will be _less_ than the marginal cost of producing them.

Answers
 51. total revenue · 8,000
 52. greater · less · *MC*
 53. *MR* · *MC* · *MC*
 54. marginal cost, · profit · less

7.55

Thus, as long as producing and selling more sets of bedroom furniture adds more to total revenue than it does to total cost, it will pay the manufacturer to do so. This statement is the same as saying that a profit-seeking manufacturer should increase his output up to that point at which marginal revenue equals

marginal cost .

7.56

We derived total revenue by multiplying the selling price of each set of furniture

(which was $800) by the number of units of ___output___ per month. If we wish to calculate average revenue figures from total revenue figures, then we divide total revenue by output. In our furniture example, we would, of course,

obtain a figure of $___800___ as our average revenue for each level of output. This is a very simple point, but you should be aware of what an average revenue curve is when we draw one in our next diagram. If you were to sell three identical pencils for a total of $0.30, then total revenue from your sales

would be $___.30___. The average revenue you would obtain from

each pencil would be $___.10___, which is of course the selling price of each pencil. Thus, we see in our furniture example that average revenue is

$___800___ which is also ___marginal___ revenue.

7.57

Thus, if in this example we were to plot selling price, average revenue, and marginal revenue against output on a graph, with the prices on the vertical axis and output on the horizontal axis, we would have one horizontal line

crossing the vertical axis at a price of $___800___, representing all three. This line would also be the demand curve facing the manufacturer. This demand curve shows that the furniture manufacturer can sell as many sets as he wants at a price of $800 each. The number of sets that would be bought at

prices greater than $800 is ___zero___. Since the manufacturer can sell as many sets of furniture as he wishes at $800, but none at a price greater than

$800, it *(will/will never)* be in his interests to charge a lower price.

Answers
   55. marginal cost
   56. output · 800 · 0.30 · 0.10 · 800 · marginal
   57. 800 · zero · will never

7.58

Now look at Table 7.3. Here, we have calculated average fixed costs, variable costs, average variable costs, and average total costs from the data in Table 7.2.

Again we see that the fixed cost is constant at the level of $ ___1,300___ and is independent of the level of output. Average variable costs and average

total costs steadily decrease up to an output of ___six___ sets of furniture, after which they increase. You should remember from the discussion

earlier that the shape of the average total and average ___variable___ cost curves is determined by the corresponding average productivity curves.

Table 7.3
Total, Average and Marginal Cost

(1) Output	(2) Fixed Cost	(3) Average Fixed Cost	(4) Variable Cost	(5) Average Variable Cost	(6) Total Cost	(7) Average Total Cost	(8) Marginal Cost
0	$1,300	–	$ 0	–	$ 1,300	–	
1	1,300	$1,300	1,000	$1,000	2,300	$2,300	$1,000
2	1,300	650	1,500	750	2,800	1,400	500
3	1,300	433	1,750	583	3,050	1,017	250
4	1,300	325	1,900	475	3,200	800	150
5	1,300	260	2,000	400	3,300	660	100
6	1,300	217	2,400	400	3,700	617	400
7	1,300	186	3,200	457	4,500	643	800
8	1,300	163	4,200	525	5,500	688	1,000
9	1,300	144	5,900	656	7,200	800	1,700
10	1,300	130	8,700	870	10,000	1,000	2,800

7.59

Figure 7.5 shows all the average and marginal data for our furniture manufacturer. First look at our average total cost curve and our average revenue

Answers
   58. 1,300 · six · variable

(AR = _MR_ = p = $800) curve. We see that our average total cost

curve intersects our average revenue curve at a price of $ _800_

and at levels of output of _4_ and _9_ .

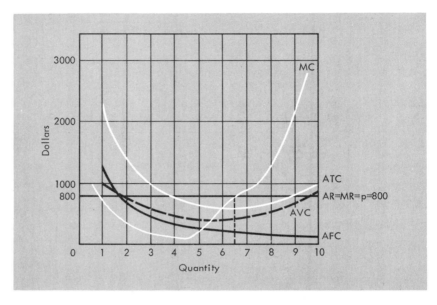

FIGURE 7.5. Cost and Revenue

7.60

Assume that four sets of bedroom furniture are being produced. At this output level, what is the significance of the intersection of the average total cost (*ATC*)

and the *AR* = *MR* = _p_ = $800 curve? The average cost of pro-

ducing four sets of bedroom furniture is $ _800_ and the average

revenue from selling four sets of bedroom furniture is $ _800_ .
Thus, the average profit from selling four sets of bedroom furniture will be

$ _0_ .

Answers
   59. MR · 800 · four · nine
   60. *p* · 800 · 800 · 0

7.61

Similarly, at an output of ___9___ sets of bedroom furniture, average total cost equals average revenue, and, consequently, ___profit___ will again be zero. Outputs of ___four___ and ___nine___ are break-even outputs.

7.62

For any level of output between four and nine sets of bedroom furniture, however, the average total cost of producing each set is ___less___ than the average revenue from the sale of each set. Consequently, a ___profit___ can be made at any level of output between four and nine per month.

7.63

What we are saying is that if the price received for each set of bedroom furniture is ___(less/greater)___ than the average cost of producing each set at some given level of output, this will be a ___profitable___ level of output, but not necessarily the most profitable level.

7.64

Thus, looking at Figure 7.5 we can see that any output is a profitable output as long as the ___average total cost___ curve lies below the ___avg. rev.___ curve.

7.65

We can also see from Figure 7.5 what will be the profit-maximizing output. You will remember that the profit-maximizing businessman will carry production up to that point at which ___marginal___ cost equals ___marginal___ revenue. And we can see from Figure 7.5 that in this example this is an output between six and seven sets of furniture per month.

Answers
61. nine · profit · four · nine
62. less · profit
63. greater · profitable
64. average total cost · average revenue
65. marginal · marginal

7.66

We can now see clearly from Figure 7.5 what we verbalized before. When output is

seven sets per month the marginal cost is $ ___1,000___ and the marginal

revenue is $ ___800___. This means the cost of producing an extra or
eighth set of bedroom furniture exceeds the additional revenue from its sale.

Eight sets of furniture, therefore, will not be the profit-___profit___
level of output. By looking at the average total cost and average revenue curves,

we can see that the entrepreneur would make a ___below___ from selling
eight sets of bedroom furniture. We know this because the average total cost

curve lies ___below___ the average revenue curve. By considering the
marginal cost and marginal revenue curves, however, we know that eight sets

per month would not yield ___maximum___ profit.

7.67

If we subtract the average total cost from the average revenue for any level of

output, the difference will equal ___profit___ per unit of output. And this
figure multiplied by the number of units of output will give us total

___profit___ for that level of output. The ___profit___ -maximizing

level of output, however, will occur where ___marginal___ ___revenue___

equals ___marginal___ ___costs___.

7.68

Let us now imagine that sets of bedroom furniture fall in price to $500 per set.

This being the case, we would have a new price line, a new ___Avg.___

___rev.___ line, and a new ___marginal___ ___revenue___ line, all
of which would coincide and all of which would touch the vertical axis at a

price of $ ___500___.

7.69

You can see from Figure 7.6 however, that if $500 per set were the ruling market
price of bedroom furniture sets there would be no level of output at which our

Answers
66. 1,000 · 800 · maximizing · profit · below · maximum
67. profit · profit · profit · marginal revenue · marginal costs
68. average revenue · marginal revenue · 500

manufacturer could make a profit because there would be no level of output at

which the ___*Avg.*___ ___*t.*___ ___*Cost*___ curve would

lie below the ___*Avg rev.*___ curve.

7.70

We may ask ourselves what should the furniture manufacturer do, since there is

no level of output at which he can operate and make a ___*profit*___ . One
possibility would be to close the plant. Then, he would not have to pay any
variable cost, because, given the prices of factor inputs, variable costs are deter-

mined by the level of output; and when output is zero, ___*var.*___

___*cost*___ will be zero. However, he would still have to pay

___*fixed*___ cost which is independent of the level of output.

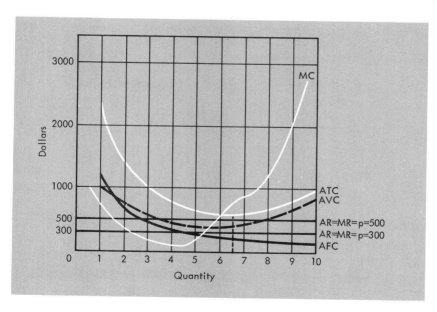

FIGURE 7.6. Cost and Revenue

Answers
69. average total cost · average revenue
70. profit · variable cost · fixed

7.71

Thus, if our furniture manufacturer were to close his plant, it would cost him

$ ___1,300___ per month, since that is the ___fixed___ cost he
incurs whether or not he produces any furniture.

7.72

Thus, the profit-maximizing (loss-minimizing) entrepreneur should close down, if

the loss incurred through closing down is ___less___ than the loss incurred
by remaining in business. Let us now consider Figure 7.6 and see if there are any
levels of output at which our manufacturer would be better off to operate, be-

cause his ___loss___ would be less than the $1,300 loss incurred if he
shuts down.

7.73

Consider an output of six sets of bedroom furniture per month. We can see that

the average variable cost then equals $ ___400___ , and we can also see
that the average revenue from selling six sets of bedroom furniture per month

equals $ ___500___ . Thus, if our furniture manufacturer were to produce
six sets of bedroom furniture per month, he would cover all his variable costs
involved in producing these sets, and, since the distance between average variable
costs and average revenue at this level of output is 100, he will have 100 times

six or $600 to set against his fixed costs, which are $ ___1,300___ .

7.74

Since at an output of six sets of furniture per month, he will have $ ___600___
to set against his fixed costs, the loss he will incur from operating at this out-

put level will be $ ___1,300___ - $ ___600___ , which equals $700.

7.75

Thus, if our manufacturer is a profit-maximizing (loss-minimizing) entrepreneur,
it will pay him in the short run to produce some output, because the loss in-

curred, for instance, in producing six sets is ___less___ than the loss that
would be incurred were he to shut down.

Answers
   71. 1,300 · fixed
   72. less · loss
   73. 400 · 500 · 1,300
   74. 600 · 1,300 · 600
   75. less

7.76

If you study Figure 7.6, you will see that there is a range of output for which the average revenue ($500) line lies above the average variable cost curve. Consequently, this will give us a range of output within which it will always be possible to earn some revenue over and above __variable__ cost, to set against __fixed__ cost.

7.77

If the price of bedroom furniture were $300 per set, would there be a level of output for which average revenue lies above the average variable cost?

__no__. Thus, there __(is a/is no)__ level of output at this selling price where our manufacturer could cover his variable costs. If the manufacturer cannot cover his variable costs it __(will/will not)__ pay him to keep on producing sets of bedroom furniture. He would be better off to shut down, since the amount used to pay his fixed __costs__ will be less than the loss incurred were he to produce any sets of bedroom furniture. This is because at a selling price of $300 the manufacturer cannot even cover his

__variable costs__, i.e. the cost of such things as raw materials and labor.

7.78

Let us summarize our findings. To have a profitable level of output __total revenue__ must exceed total cost. Therefore, average total revenue must be greater than __average total cost__.

7.79

When total cost equals __total revenue__, we have a break-even level of output, i.e. our manufacturer makes neither a __profit__ nor a __loss__ at that output level.

7.80

In the short run, the loss incurred by a manufacturer from closing down will

equal his ___*fixed*___ ___*cost*___. From a ___*loss*___
minimizing viewpoint, this closing down would be rational behavior if there is
no level of output which will yield sufficient revenue to at least cover

___*variable*___ ___*cost*___.

7.81

The selling price that will just cover variable cost occurs when price just equals

the minimum point of the average ___*variable*___ ___*cost*___ curve.

At this level of output, all ___*mean v. cost*___ will be covered,

but there will be no revenue left to set against ___*fixed*___ ___*cost*___.

If the horizontal price line lies below the ___*Avg.*___ ___*var.*___

___*cost*___ curve at all levels of output, then no output exists where
variable costs can be covered. Consequently, the loss incurred at any positive

level of production would ___*exceed*___ the loss incurred were the firm

to shut down, since the loss incurred in shutting down equals ___*fixed*___

___*cost*___.

7.82

From Figure 7.7 we can see that for any price less than p_1, output from our

profit-maximizing (loss-minimizing) manufacturer will be ___*zero*___,

since ___*variable*___ ___*cost*___ will not be covered. The loss

incurred, therefore, for prices less than p_1 will be ___*fixed cost*___

_____.

Answers
> 80. fixed cost · loss · variable cost
> 81. variable cost · variable cost · fixed cost · average variable cost · exceed ·
>   fixed cost
> 82. zero · variable cost · fixed cost

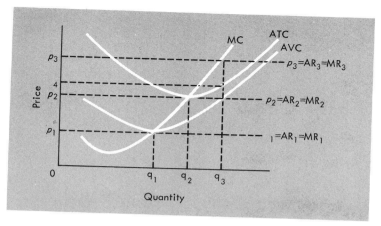

FIGURE 7.7. Short-Run Equilibrium of the Firm

7.83

For prices between p_1 and p_2 the manufacturer will still be operating at a

_____loss_____ but variable costs will be covered, and in addition some

revenue will be available to set against ____fixed____ ____cost____
for output levels less than q_2.

7.84

At a price of p_2 the manufacturer can produce an output of ____q_2____,

and all costs (____variable____ ____costs____ + ____fixed____

____costs____) will be covered; profits will be ____zero____.

7.85

For prices above p_2 it will be possible for the firm to produce at levels of out-

put where profits are (positive/negative). We have said, in terms of Figure 7.7,

that when the price is less than p_1, the firm ____(will/will not)____ produce a

positive output. When the price is greater than p_1, the firm ____(will/will not)____
produce a positive output, even though the price may be less than average
total cost.

Answers

83. loss · fixed cost
84. q_2 · variable costs · fixed costs · zero
85. positive · will not · will

7.86
Whenever the price is greater than p_1, we can determine how much the profit-maximizing firm will produce by finding where price, or marginal revenue, is

equal to __marg.__ _____cost_____. For example, if price is equal
to p_3, the firm will produce at that level of output where marginal cost is equal

to p_3. In Figure 7.7 that level of output is _____q_3_____.

7.87
We can find the equilibrium or profit-maximizing, output, therefore, for different prices by looking at the marginal cost curve. We know then that the

marginal cost curve for prices above p_1 is the firm's ___*(supply/demand)*___
curve, because the marginal cost curve tells us what outputs the firm would be willing to produce at different prices in order to maximize profit or minimize loss.

7.88
To repeat, the firm's supply curve is the same as its ___marginal___

_____cost_____ curve, because the marginal cost curve shows for different prices (greater than p_1) the profit-maximizing levels of output.

7.89
It is possible to read from Figure 7.7 the amount of profit that the firm will earn in its equilibrium position. For example, if the price is p_3, the equilibrium

level of output is q_3. The average total cost of producing q_3 is ___p_4___.
Since the price, or average revenue, is p_3, the average ___profit___ in

producing q_3 is $p_3 - p_4$, that is, average revenue minus ___avg.___

___total___ ___cost___. If average profit (profit on one unit) is
$p_3 - p_4$, then total profit must equal average profit × the number of units, or

$(p_3 - p_4) \times$ ___q_3___.

Answers
   86. marginal cost · q_3
   87. supply
   88. marginal cost
   89. p_4 · profit · average total cost · q_3

7.90

If the price were to fall from p_3, the area representing profit in Figure 7.7 would _(decrease/increase)_ until profit became zero at a price of ___ p_2 ___.

7.91

For prices between p_1 and p_2 the firm would incur a ___ loss ___. In this price range the firm would still be willing to produce a positive output, because the loss would be ___ _(greater/less)_ ___ than the loss that would be incurred were the firm to shut down. The exact output which our—in this case—loss-minimizing manufacturer would produce would be determined by the ___ Marg. Cost ___ curve.

7.92

For all prices less than p_1, the firm will shut down, since at this low price there will not be enough revenue to cover even ___ Var. Cost ___. Thus output will be ___ zero ___ for prices from zero up to p_1.

7.93

We can, therefore, derive the short-run supply curve of the firm from the cost data in Figure 7.7. The supply curve, of course, shows how many units of output would be produced per time period at various ___ prices ___, other things remaining equal. For prices above p_1, the supply curve will be the ___ Marginal Cost ___ curve.

Price	Quantity That Would Be Supplied
0	0
less than p_1	0
p_1	q_1
p_2	q_2
p_3	q_3

Answers
90. decrease · p_2
91. loss · less · marginal cost
92. variable cost · zero
93. prices · marginal cost

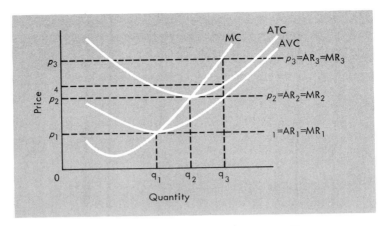

FIGURE 7.7. Short-Run Equilibrium of the Firm

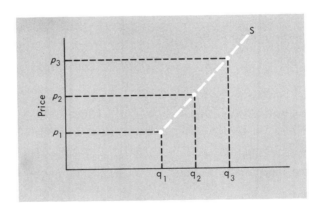

FIGURE 7.8. Short-Run Supply Curve

7.94

Let us summarize our findings. Thus far, in the short run, that time period when some costs are fixed, the equilibrium output of the firm will be that output at

which ___marginal___ ___revenue___ equals ___marginal___

___cost___ . This will be an equilibrium position in the sense that the

firm will be maximizing ___profit___ . In this short run, other levels of

Answers

94. marginal revenue · marginal cost · profit

output may yield a profit, but not a maximum profit. In the short run, therefore, once the firm has reached that ___equilibrium___ position, profit cannot
be increased by altering the output level.

REVIEW QUESTIONS

Questions 1-4 are based on the following information:

At its present level of output of 400 units, a perfectly competitive firm discovers
that its marginal cost is $4.00. At an output level of 300 units, marginal cost is
$3.00 and is equal to average total cost. The price of the commodity being pro-
duced is $5.00.

7.1
To maximize profit, the firm ___A___.

a. should increase output.
b. should keep output at the present level.
c. should decrease output.
d. will require more information to know how output should be changed.

7.2
The 400th unit adds ___D___.

a. $5.00 to total profit.
b. $4.00 to total profit.
c. $2.00 to total profit.
d. $1.00 to total profit.

Answers
  94. equilibrium
   1. a
   2. d

7.3

If the firm were to operate at that level of output where average total cost is

minimum, profits would be _____.

a. $300.
b. $400.
c. $600.
d. positive, but insufficient information exists to determine the exact level.

7.4

The firm will be in equilibrium in the short run when _____.

a. it is maximizing profit.
b. MC = MR.
c. MC = $5.00.
d. all of the above are true.

7.5

In the short run an increase in output is associated with an increase in

_____.

a. fixed costs.
b. marginal costs.
c. variable costs.
d. none of the above, necessarily.

Answers
  3. ⌣
  4. d
  5. c

8

Long-Run Equilibrium of the Firm

8.1

In Chapter 7 we considered the equilibrium position of the firm in the short run. We saw that certain costs were fixed, the size or scale of operation was set, and the profit-maximizing firm's ___marginal___ ___cost___ curve was its short-run supply curve. In this chapter we shall consider the firm in the long run, when all costs are ___(fixed/variable)___ , and when the firm may, for instance, vary the scale of operation. That is, in the long run, a firm can alter those costs that are fixed in the short run. What then will be its long-run profit-maximizing output level? To this question we now turn.

8.2

The long run is that time period when all factor inputs are variable. In the short run certain factors are fixed and, consequently, in the short run certain ___costs___ are fixed. In the long run, by contrast, there are no fixed costs.

8.3

The real world is a dynamic place. Consumers' tastes and preferences are constantly changing, new goods and services come into being, research and development discover new uses for natural resources, and technological change is

Answers
1. marginal cost · variable
2. costs

constantly occurring. Because of all this, we would be very surprised if firms ever settled for long, or even reached a long-run equilibrium position, i.e. a position from which there would be no incentive to change. However, while

firms may never reach a long-run ___equilibrium___ position from which there is no incentive to change, we define long-run equilibrium as a position toward which firms move and which would ultimately be reached, in the absence of any other changes. Thus, long-run equilibrium is an abstract concept. It is a position toward which firms would move, were other things to

(remain the same/change.)

8.4

Suppose that a tomato farmer discovered that by using his land and labor to produce lettuce he would earn a larger profit than he is currently earning by

using them to produce tomatoes. In the ___short___ run some factors are fixed and cannot, therefore, be shifted away from the production of

tomatoes. In the ___long___ run, however, it would be possible for the farmer to shift production from tomatoes to lettuce. Since it is more profitable

to produce lettuce, we can expect that in the long run the farmer *(will/will not)* shift to the production of lettuce.

8.5

In the long run, then, for a farmer to remain in the tomato-growing business, if he wishes to maximize his earnings it is not sufficient simply to earn a profit. For a farmer to continue to produce tomatoes, it is necessary that he earn a

profit that is *(larger/smaller)* than that which he can earn by using his resources to produce lettuce or any other commodity.

8.6

In Chapter 1 we discussed that there is a cost to produce a commodity that is over and above the costs that have to be paid out as wages, rent, etc. This cost is the profit that could be earned by using resources in an alternative use. It is the entrepreneur's *opportunity cost.* In our example, the profit that the tomato farmer could earn if he produced lettuce instead of tomatoes is his

___opportunity___ cost.

Answers
3. equilibrium · remain the same
4. short · long · will
5. larger
6. opportunity

8.7

In the long run, in our example, if our farmer does not receive enough revenue to

cover his ___opportunity___ cost, he will shift his resources to the production of lettuce. Earlier we said the same thing a different way: If a farmer cannot earn as much profit in the production of tomatoes as he can in the production of

lettuce, then in the ___long___ ___run___ he will shift to the production of lettuce.

8.8

If the farmer cannot cover his opportunity cost in the production of tomatoes,

it means that he can earn a ___(higher/lower)___ profit in the production of some other commodity, and in the long run will shift his resources from the production of tomatoes to the production of that commodity where the return is highest.

8.9

In our diagrams, we have included the entrepreneur's opportunity cost as one of the costs of production. Thus, in these diagrams, when a firm is earning a

profit it means that it is earning a profit that is ___(greater/less)___ than the profit that could be earned by taking advantage of any alternative opportunity.

8.10

In other words, in our diagrams when a firm is earning a profit, it means that it is earning enough profit to discourage it from shifting resources to the

production of a different commodity. Is this statement ___(true/false)___ ?

8.11

Thus, if a firm is so producing that average total cost equals average revenue, we say that the firm is not earning a profit. By this we mean that its revenue

is just enough to cover its ___opportunity___ cost but is not earning any profit in excess of what is required to keep the firm's resources in that line of production.

Answers
   7. opportunity · long run
   8. higher
   9. greater
   10. true
   11. opportunity

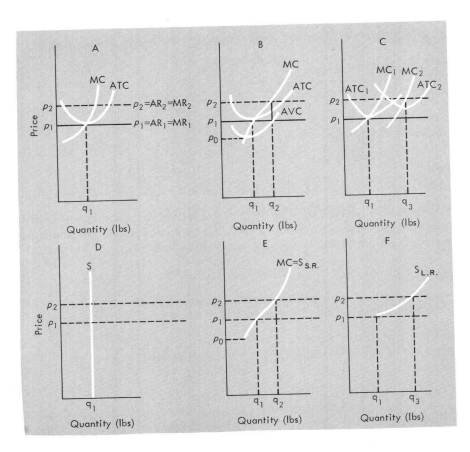

FIGURE 8.1. Cost and Supply

8.12

Let us assume for the present that we have an economy in which all firms are competitive and in which the trend is toward long-run equilibrium. In Figure 8.1 we consider a tomato grower in three different time periods. Figure A represents a normal day in the life of the tomato grower. He expects the price of tomatoes to be p_1 per lb., and thus, being a profit maximizer, will produce

tomatoes up to the point where __marginal__ __revenue__ equals

__marg__ __cost__. Thus, our tomato grower arrives in the

market with the quantity ____q_1____ for sale. Remember the grower

expects the market price to be ____p_1____ per lb.

Answers

12. marginal revenue · marginal cost · q_1 · p_1

8.13

Given that our grower has arrived in the market with a perishable cargo of

_____ q_1 _____ pounds of tomatoes, he will sell those tomatoes for whatever happens to be the market price that day. If he does not sell them, they
will spoil; thus, no matter what the market price is, the amount he will supply

during this particular day is _____ q_1 _____ pounds. Thus, if we consider
Figure 8.1D, today's supply curve of our tomato grower will be represented by

a _____ vertical _____ line touching the horizontal axis at ____ q_1 ____
pounds.

8.14

At a price of p_1 in Figure 8.1A, our grower ___*(will/will not)*___ be making

profits, since at a price of p_1 per pound average ___revenue___ just equals

_____Avg_____ _____total_____ _____cost_____, though remember the

_____Avg._____ _____total_____ _____cost_____ curve includes a normal return on investment, which covers the opportunity cost.

8.15

Now consider Figure 8.1B. The grower expects the price of tomatoes the next

day to be p_2 per pound, and thus, he will supply _____q_2_____ pounds at
the expected price; that is, he will again produce tomatoes up to the point at

which ___marginal revenue___ equals ___marginal___

___cost___. The time period we are considering here is the short run.

(This is in contrast to the long run when all ___costs___ are variable, and
it is also in contrast to the "instantaneous" time period in the previous three
frames where the grower arrived in the market with a given quantity of tomatoes,

q_1, which he would sell at whatever was the market ___price___.)

8.16

Thus there is a limited flexibility for the tomato grower in the short run as
far as the quantity he will supply is concerned. He may hire additional labor

(the factor of production that is variable in the short run) to pick his plants more intensively if the price is sufficient to warrant such action. Thus within certain limits the quantity of tomatoes our grower will supply in the short run in any given market will vary at different prices. From Figures 8.1B and E,

we see that for prices above p_0, the higher the price, the ___(greater/smaller)___ is the quantity that would be supplied.

8.17

If his expectations prove correct and the price of tomatoes the following day is p_2, how would you calculate a) the average profit per pound at an output level of q_2 and b) total profits during the day from Figure 8.1B?

a. _____

b. _____

8.18

Again from Figure 8.1B, how could we find out the output of our tomato grower in one specific day if he expected the price to be higher than p_2 per pound?

_____

_____

8.19

Below what price will output be zero and why? _____

_____

8.20

Consider now the behavior of our tomato grower in the long run. Since no factors

of production are fixed in the long run, it ___(is/is not)___ possible for the farmer to increase or decrease the scale of his operations by acquiring new land or selling land now used to produce tomatoes, as well as hiring more labor. In the

short run the firm ___(can/cannot)___ change its output, but only by increasing

or decreasing the factors of production that are ___variable___ in the short run.

Answers
16. greater
17. a) measure the distance between the AR (p_2 line) and the ATC curve at an output level of q_2 · b) multiply a) by q_2
18. look at his MC curve, which tells how much output he would supply, i.e. where marginal revenue equals marginal cost
19. p_0 · for prices below p_0 the grower cannot cover his variable costs
20. is · can · variable

8.21

Suppose that the price is p_1. We have seen in Figure 8.1B that in the short run

the firm would produce at a level of output equal to ___q_1___. At that

output, profit would be ___zero___ because average revenue would be
equal to average total cost. Of course, by zero profit we mean that the farmer is
earning just enough profit to keep him from shifting resources away from the
production of tomatoes.

8.22

Since the farmer is just covering his costs at a price of p_1, there is no incentive
for him to expand or contract operations. As a result, as can be seen in Figures

8.1C and F, at price p_1 the long-run equilibrium output will be ___q_1___.

8.23

Suppose that the price is p_2. We have seen in Figure 8.1B that in the short run
output would be expanded to the point where the short-run marginal cost equals

the ___price___. This level of output is ___greater___.

8.24

At price p_2 and output q_2 the firm ___(is/is not)___ making a profit. This
is clear from Figure 8.1B because at this point the price, or average revenue,

is ___(greater/less)___ than average total cost.

8.25

Because a profit is being earned at price p_2 at the short-run equilibrium position,

it appears that the farmer would like to ___(expand/contract)___ his scale of operations.

By adding new acreage to the production of tomatoes it ___(seems/does not seem)___
possible to add to total profit.

8.26

In order to see more clearly the long-run equilibrium position, Figure 8.1C is
reproduced in greater detail in Figure 8.2. In Figure 8.2 the long-run marginal

Answers
21. q_1 · zero
22. q_1
23. price · q_2
24. is · greater
25. expand · seems

cost (*LMC*) and long-run average cost (*LAC*) are drawn. The short-run cost

curves show how costs increase as ____(variable/all)____ factors of production are
increased in the short run. The long-run cost curves show how costs increase as

____(variable/all)____ factors are increased in the long run.

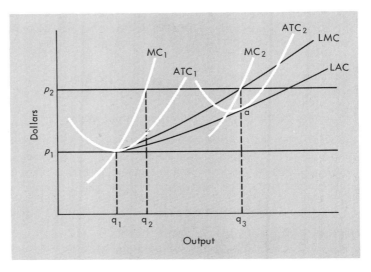

FIGURE 8.2. Long-Run Average and Marginal Cost

8.27
We can see in Figure 8.2 why at price p_2 our farmer will want to expand his
scale of operations. At output q_2 average total cost at the original scale of

operations is ____(greater/less)____ than the average total cost that would be incurred at a somewhat larger scale of operations.

8.28
We know this to be the case because at output q_2 the initial short-run average

total cost curve lies ____(above/below)____ the long-run average cost curve.

8.29

For a given output level, as long as it is possible to reduce average cost by varying

the factor inputs we assume fixed in the short run, it ___(will/will not)___ be
profitable to do so. In other words, if at the short-run equilibrium level of output
the short-run *ATC* curve is above the *LAC* curve, a profit-maximizing firm will

___(expand/contract)___ its scale of operation.

8.30

It is useful to think of this expansion as shifting the short-run cost curves to the
right. In terms of Figure 8.2 there is a new set of short-run *MC* and *ATC* curves

that lies to the ___(right/left)___ of *MC* and *ATC*, for which it is true that q_2
can be produced at a lower average total cost. For this reason, in the long run,
our farmer will expand his operations by, let us say, acquiring more land.

8.31

How far will the farmer expand? He will expand until the new short-run *ATC*
curve, at the short-run equilibrium level of output, just touches the *LAC* curve.
This is shown in Figure 8.2 by point *a*, where ATC_2 and *LAC* are tangent to

each other at output ___q_3___ . At this scale of operation the short-
run equilibrium position is at output q_3, because it is only at this level of output
that price equals ___marginal   cost___ . The long-run equilibrium
position is also at output q_3, because it is only at this level of output that price

equals long-run ___marginal   cost___ .

8.32

Also at q_3 the long-run average cost is ___(the same as/different from)___ the short-run
average cost.

8.33

The reason why the long-run equilibrium is q_3 in Figure 8.2 can be better understood if the relationship between the short- and long-run cost curves is made

clear. As was indicated earlier, in the long run the firm has ___(one/many)___

Answers
29. will · expand
30. right
31. q_3 · marginal cost (MC_2) · marginal cost (MC)
32. the same as
33. many

set(s) of short-run cost curves from which to choose. Each set of short-run cost curves corresponds to a different scale of operation. In our tomato farmer example, there would be one set of cost curves for 100 acres of land, another for 200 acres, a third for 300 acres, and so on. We can think of long-run adjustment as choosing the best set of ____*(short/long)*____ -run cost curves, that is choosing the best scale of operations.

8.34
The long-run average cost curve is made up of small segments of these many short-run average total cost curves. The *LAC* curve shows for each level of output the segment of that short-run *ATC* which has the ____*(highest/lowest)*____ cost for that level of output. This can be seen in Figure 8.3.

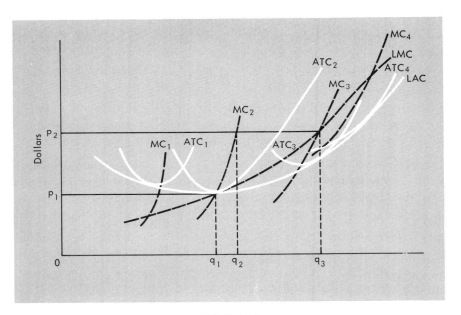

FIGURE 8.3.

For each level of output there will be a different scale of operation which can produce that output most efficiently, or at the lowest cost. As a result, for each level of output there will be a different ____ATC____ curve that is best.

Answers
    33. short
    34. lowest · *ATC*

8.35

Consider output q_3 in Figure 8.3, produced in plant size (2) with ATC_2, in plant size (3) with ATC_3 and in plant size (4) with ATC_4. Which plant can

produce q_3 at the lowest average cost? ___*3*___. How do you know?

8.36

Does another plant size exist which could produce q_3 cheaper than 3?

___*No*___. How do you know? _____

8.37

Note that the minimum point of ATC_4 occurs at an output q_3, but that this minimum point exceeds the tangency point of ATC_3 and LAC. How do we

know minimum ATC_4 occurs at q_3? _____

8.38

Thus, given a price of p_2 in the long run the entrepreneur would build that plant size which would produce that level of output which would give the

___*highest*___ level of profit. To be in long-run equilibrium price would

have to equal ___*long - run*___ marginal cost.

8.39

However, once the optimum plant size was decided upon and once the plant was

built, then price would also have to equal ___*short - run*___ marginal cost.

Answers

    35. 3 · because at q_3, ATC_3 is less than ATC_4, which in turn is less than ATC_2
    36. no · because ATC_3 at q_3 equals LAC
    37. because MC_4 intersects ATC_4 at q_3
    38. highest · long run
    39. short-run

8.40

Thus in long-run equilibrium, not only will long-run average cost equal the

_____Short____-____ron_____ ____Average_-_Cost_____ ,

but *LMC* and the ____Short____-_____run____ __marginal__

____Cost____ will also be equal. All this can be seen at output q_3 in Figure 8.3.

8.41

At a price of p_1, what level of output will the optimum-sized plant produce?

____Q_1_____ What is the long-run equilibrium size of plant? ____2____

How do you know? __$p_1 = LMC$_____

Given that plant size 2 is built, will the firm be in short-run equilibrium?

____yes____ How do you know? __$p_1 = MC_2$_____

8.42

What is unique about the long-run equilibrium size of plant at a price of p_1?

This is an important point to which we shall return.

8.43

After some level of output (q_1 in figure 8.3), it is likely that it will be more difficult to manage the firm as efficiently. This is not necessarily true, but we will assume in this chapter that it is true and defer until Chapter 13 discussion of those cases for which efficiency does not decrease with size. Given this assumption the *LAC* after some given output will slope ____upward____ from left to right.

8.44

Let us repeat our discussion with our farm example. Now we see why in Figure 8.2 the farmer will move to output q_3 in the long run. For price p_2 he will choose that scale of operation for which the short-run profit-maximizing

Answers
   40. short-run average cost · short-run marginal cost
   41. q_1 · 2 · $p_1 = LMC$ · yes · $p_1 = MC_2$
   42. output q_1 will be produced at minimum *ATC* and also minimum *LAC*
   43. upward

level of output is also that scale of operation for which that output can be

produced at the lowest ___cost___ . If there were another scale of operation that could produce output q_3 at a lower cost, then it

(would/would not) pay the farmer to change his position. If there is no better

place to move, then we say that he has attained long-run ___equilibrium___

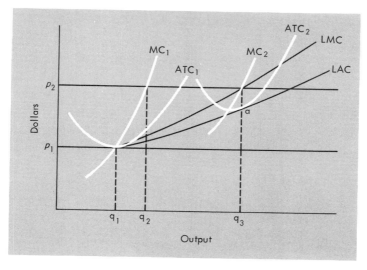

FIGURE 8.2.

8.45

As can be seen in Figure 8.2, output q_3 is also the point where the long-run

marginal cost curve is equal to the ___price___ . We know that in the short run the competitive firm will maximize profit if it expands to the point where price equals marginal cost and that the marginal cost curve is the

___supply___ curve.

8.46

The same is true in the long run. The long-run profit-maximizing output is

where price equals long-run ___marginal cost___ , and the

Answers
44. cost · would · equilibrium
45. price · supply
46. marginal cost

LMC curve is the long-run ___Supply___ curve. Refer to Figure 8.1. There the relationship between the short- and long-run cost curves and the supply curves is made clear.

8.47
Having mastered demand theory and now basic supply theory, let us put them together and consider price, output, and resource allocation in a free enterprise economic system. Let us explore both the advantages and disadvantages of such a type of economic organization. This frame almost did not have a

___blank___ in it!

REVIEW QUESTIONS

8.1
In the long-run which costs to the firm are fixed? ___D___.

a. Variable costs.
b. Average costs.
c. Marginal costs.
d. No costs.

8.2
In the long-run, to remain in business a firm must receive sufficient revenue to

cover ___D___.

a. its opportunity cost.
b. its fixed cost.
c. its total cost.
d. all of the above costs.

Answers
   46. supply
   47. blank
    1. d
    2. d

8.3

In long-run equilibrium, a firm will be producing that output where price equals

 _____ .

a. minimum long-run average cost.
b. long-run marginal cost.
c. a short-run minimum average cost and a short-run marginal cost.
d. all of the above.

8.4

The difference between short-run and long-run is that _____ .

a. the short-run is any period less than 2 years.
b. some factors of production are in fixed supply to the firm only in the short-run.
c. marginal cost rises only in the short run.
d. profits are always greater in the short run.

8.5

i. A firm's short-run supply curve is its MC curve above the minimum point on its AVC curve.

ii. A firm's long-run supply curve is made up of the minimum points of all possible short-run ATC curves.

Which of the preceding statements are correct? _____ A _____

a. Only i.
b. Only ii.
c. Both i and ii.
d. Neither i nor ii.

Answers
3. b
4. b
5. a

9

Price Determination

9.1

In previous chapters we learned that a _____ curve of a consumer tells the quantities of a good that would be demanded in a market at various prices, other things remaining equal. The normal demand curve slopes

_____ from left to right indicating that more of a good would be

demanded at _____ prices.

9.2

The position of a demand curve is determined by a set of _____ such as income and the prices of other goods, which for any consumer are assumed to be constant.

9.3

Movements along a demand curve tell us how the quantity demanded will vary

as _____ varies, *ceteris paribus*. A shift of a demand curve will

occur when one of the _____ determining the position of the curve changes.

Answers
1. demand · downwards · lower
2. parameters
3. price · parameters

9.4

A _____ curve of a firm tells the quantities of a good that would be supplied at various prices, *ceteris paribus*. The normal supply curve slopes

_____ from left to right, indicating that businessmen normally will

supply more of a good only at a _____ price.

9.5

The position of a firm's supply curve is determined by a set of _____, such as the level of technology and the prices of productive factors which for any particular firm are assumed to be constant.

9.6

A firm's response to changes in the price of the commodity it is producing is

observed by <u>*(movements along/shifts of)*</u> the supply curve. A firm's response

to changes in a parameter is shown as a <u>*(movement along/shift of)*</u> the supply curve.

9.7

From the demand curves of individual _____ and the supply curves

of individual _____, it is possible to derive the industry or market demand and supply curves.

9.8

The industry _____ curve shows the amounts of a commodity that all consumers taken together would demand at different prices. The

_____ demand curve is derived by adding together, for each possible price, the quantities that individual consumers would demand.

9.9

In a similar way, the industry _____ curve shows the amounts of a commodity that all firms taken together would produce at different prices.

Answers
4. supply · upwards · higher
5. parameters
6. movements along · shift of
7. consumers · firms
8. demand · industry
9. supply

Given the prices of factors of production, the _____ supply curve can be derived by adding together, for each possible price, the quantities that individual firms would supply.

9.10
As we shall see, for any commodity, the interaction of the industry demand and supply curves, in competitive markets, will determine the equilibrium price and quantity. Thus, while all consumers and firms will act as though they had no

effect on the _____ of a commodity, the actions of all consumers

and firms will determine the _____ demand and supply curves and, therefore, will determine the equilibrium price of the commodity.

9.11
Let us see how the equilibrium price and quantity of a commodity are de-

termined in the market by the interaction of the industry _____

and _____ curves. We can begin with the short-run equilibrium position of the industry.

9.12
Consider now Table 9.1. The first two columns, if plotted, would give a

normally shaped _____ curve for the good in question (let us call it

good *X*). This _____ curve would slope _____
from left to right. The position of this curve would be determined by a set of

_____, the independent variable being _____ and the

dependent variable being _____ .

9.13
If one of the _____, determining the position of the demand curve, were to change, the quantities in column 2 corresponding to the various prices

(would/would not) be as they are in Table 9.1.

Answers
   9. industry
  10. price · industry
  11. demand · supply
  12. demand · demand · downwards · parameters · price · quantity
  13. parameters · would not

Table 9.1
Demand and Supply Schedules

(1)	*(2)*	*(3)*
	Quantity That Would	*Quantity That Would*
Price Per Unit	*Be Demanded*	*Be Supplied*
0	200	0
1	180	0
2	160	40
3	140	80
4	120	120
5	100	160
6	80	200
7	60	240
8	40	280
9	20	320
10	0	360

9.14
If each unit of good X were priced at \$7, the quantity that would be demanded at this price would be _____ .

9.15
If the price of good X were to change to \$6 per unit, the demand curve represented by columns 1 and 2 would shift. _____ *(true/false)*

9.16
The figures in columns 1 and 2 are for a time period of a given length, say one week. If we were to draw the demand curve for a time period of five weeks, it would be to the _____*(left/right)*_____ of the demand curve for a time period of one week.

9.17
In a similar fashion, if we were to draw a curve for columns 1 and 3 in Table 9.1, we would have a _____ curve which would slope upwards from

Answers
    14. 60
    15. false
    16. right
    17. supply

_____ to _____ . This curve would be similar to our demand curve in the sense that its position would be determined by a set of

_____ . The dependent variable would again be _____

and the independent variable _____ .

9.18

Imagine that all potential buyers of good X get together with all the potential suppliers of good X, and they hire an auctioneer. Imagine that the auctioneer starts with a price of $3, saying to the potential buyers, "How many units of good X would you buy at a price of $3?" The potential consumers will

answer _____ . Then, the auctioneer asks the suppliers, "How many units of good X would you be willing to supply at $3?" The potential suppliers

will answer _____ . The auctioneer will see that at a price of $3

the quantity that would be demanded is _____ than the quantity that would be supplied.

9.19

Since it is the purpose of the auctioneer to achieve an equilibrium solution, he will not be willing to keep the price at $3. As long as the quantity that would be supplied is less than the quantity that would be demanded, some consumers

would not be in _____ , because they would be willing to buy the good at the market price but would be unable to find any of the good left for sale. In order to reach an equilibrium, the auctioneer must change the

_____ .

9.20

The auctioneer has taken a course in economics and knows about normally shaped demand and supply curves. He knows that if he chooses a higher price,

the quantity that would be demanded will be _____ , and the

quantity that would be supplied will be _____ than the corresponding quantities at a price of $3.

Answers

    17. left · right · parameters · quantity · price
    18. 140 · 80 · greater
    19. equilibrium · price
    20. less · greater

9.21

Suppose the next price he chooses is $6 per unit. Again he asks the potential buyers how many units of good *X* they would buy at a price of $6, and they

reply _____ . And the potential suppliers tell him they would

supply _____ units of good *X* at a price of $6.

9.22

However, he sees at a price of $6 that the quantity that would be demanded is

_____ than the quantity that would be supplied. At a price of $3 we would have excess demand (the quantity that would be demanded is in excess of the quantity that would be supplied), and, as you might expect, at a price of

$6, we would have a situation of excess _____ .

9.23

It is only when the auctioneer reaches a price of $ _____ per unit that the quantity that would be demanded is equal to the quantity that would be supplied in that time period. Thus, we would say that in the market under con-

sideration, a price of $ _____ per unit of good *X* is the *equilibrium*

price, and a quantity of _____ is the *equilibrium quantity.*

9.24

This price is known as the equilibrium price because once this price has been established in this market, there will, *ceteris paribus*, be no tendency for the price to move from $4 because at this price the quantity that would be de-

manded just _____ the quantity that would be supplied.

9.25

We saw that at a price of $3 in this market we had excess _____

and at the price of $6 we had excess _____ . But, at a price of

$4, both excess _____ and excess _____ are zero.

Answers
21. 80 · 200
22. less · supply
23. 4 · 4 · 120
24. equals
25. demand · supply · demand · supply

Thus, at a price of $4, the market is just cleared. The quantity that would be demanded equals the quantity that would be supplied. Excess demand and excess supply are both zero, and consequently, $4 is the _____ price.

9.26
In Figure 9.1, we have drawn the demand curve and supply curve from the data in Table 9.1. As you can observe, those curves intersect at a price of

$ _____ and at a quantity of _____.

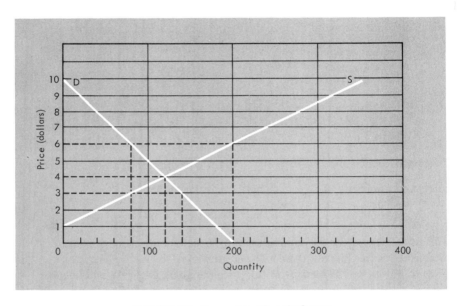

FIGURE 9.1. Demand and Supply Curves

9.27
We can observe in Figure 9.1 what we saw in Table 9.1. At a price of $3, the quantity that would be demanded is _____ and the quantity that would be supplied is _____. The difference of 60 is a measure of excess _____ at a price of $3 per unit.

Answers
   25. equilibrium
   26. 4 · 120
   27. 140 · 80 · demand

9.28

Similarly, at a price of $6 per unit the quantity that would be demanded is

_____ , and the quantity that would be supplied is _____ .

The difference of 120 is a measure of excess _____ at this price. At
a price of $4 per unit and only at this price is the quantity that would be de-

manded _____ to the quantity that would be supplied, and, con-

sequently, excess supply and excess demand both equal _____ .
Given the shape of the demand and supply curves in Figure 9.1, is it possible

for any price other than $4 per unit to be an equilibrium price? _____
Given that the demand and supply curves remain in the same position as they
are in Figure 9.1 for several time periods, would the equilibrium price change?

_____

9.29

Thus, $4 would remain the _____ price, and 120 units would re-

main the _____ quantity, because there would be no economic
forces at work tending to change either that price or quantity.

9.30

Let us analyze the example we have chosen in Figure 9.1 and see how in the

actual market, economic forces will drive the price to the _____
level of $4 per unit. Again imagine our auctioneer starting off the price of
$2 per unit and asking each supplier individually how many units of good X
he would supply in time period t at this price. He also asks each buyer how
many units he would purchase at this price. He then tells the assembled sellers

and buyers in the market that the quantity that would be supplied at a price of

$2 is _____ and the quantity that would be demanded is

_____ .

Answers

28. 80 · 200 · supply · equal · zero · no · no
29. equilibrium · equilibrium
30. equilibrium · 40 · 160

9.31

Now, if this auctioneer were to close the market at this price, it

(would/would not) be possible to satisfy all the buyers, because there is

an excess _____ of _____ units at a price of $2
per unit.

9.32

Some of the buyers whose demand is not satisfied at a price of $2 per unit
(those who cannot have the quantities of X they desire) may think that if
they just increased their offer price slightly, they would be able to get the
quantity they wished. This is the competitive higgling of a free market, when
buyers are bidding against each other to acquire the good they desire and when
suppliers are also bidding against each other in trying to sell the good. Let us
see what happens if we now choose a price of $3 per unit. Compared with the
previous price, the total quantity that would be demanded at this price is

(smaller/larger) , implying that some buyers have reduced the quantity that
they are willing to buy at the higher price and/or some buyers have fallen out
of the market. Comparing those two prices, we are really observing a movement

_____ the demand curve in Figure 9.1.

9.33

However, if we now observe the supply aspects of the market, a _____
quantity would be supplied at a price of $3 per unit than at $2. This is repre-

sented in Figure 9.1 by a *(movement along/shift of)* the supply curve.

9.34

Are we nearer an equilibrium solution at a price of $3 than we were at a price

of $2? The answer is _____ because excess demand at $3 per unit

is _____ , which is _____ than excess demand at $2

per unit, which is _____ .

Answers
    31. would not · demand · 120
    32. smaller · along
    33. larger · movement along
    34. yes · 60 · less · 120

9.35

Thus, economic forces are driving this market towards an equilibrium solution. Those buyers who cannot purchase the quantities they desire at a certain price

are forced to offer a _____ price in the hope that a greater supply

will be forthcoming at this _____ price and that demands will be

satisfied, or they hope that by offering a _____ price, they will outbid a competitive buyer.

9.36

When we consider the supply aspects, we see another economic force at work.

At higher prices, the quantity that sellers are willing to supply _____ as more suppliers enter the market or as the amount that each seller is willing to

_____ increases.

9.37

When we arrive at a price of $4 per unit in Figure 9.1, we see that the quantity

that would be demanded at this price just _____ the quantity that

would be supplied. And consequently, $4 per unit is the _____ price of good X.

9.38

The reason why buyers will not be prepared to offer a price higher than $4 per unit is because each buyer can purchase the quantities he desires at $4 per unit.

The total quantity demanded in this market at $4 per unit is _____

units which just _____ the total quantity that would be supplied at this price.

9.39

If we choose the price of $5 per unit, a similar process occurs. At this price, we

have excess _____ of _____ units. In this situation,

Answers
35. higher · higher · higher
36. increases · supply
37. equals · equilibrium
38. 120 · equals
39. supply · 60

some suppliers will obviously not be able to sell the quantities of good X they have, and each, acting individually, will think that if he lowers his price slightly

he will be able to sell all he has, because then he will be charging a _____ price than the other suppliers. But, at the lower price, some suppliers will either drop out of the market or reduce the quantities that they are prepared to sell. Conversely, looking at the demand side, at the lower price, the quantity

that buyers are willing to take at the lower price will be _____.

Again, the market will be moving towards _____ .

9.40
This higgling in the market will continue until the equilibrium price and quantity are reached. In the real world, however, there are factors existing in markets which may prevent ideal market situations from occurring. While an equilibrium price may never be established or, if established, may never remain at equilibrium long, the market mechanism we have just analyzed describes what happens in many markets in the United States. That is, in the free market situation, price

tends toward the _____ level.

9.41
We must now investigate what happens when we relax our *ceteris paribus* assumptions, or in other words, what happens when other things do not remain equal in our market. Let us return to our example in Table and Figure 9.1. Let us imagine that the number of potential buyers in this market increases, and this causes the quantity that would be demanded in time period t to double at every price.

Thus in Table 9.2, at a price of $1 per unit of good X, the new quantity that would be demanded will be 360 and at the price of $3 per unit, the new quantity

that would be demanded will be _____.

9.42
What has happened in this example is that one of the _____ determining the position of the demand curve has changed, and this has caused us to have a new demand curve for good X. Let us represent the old and the new market situations in Figure 9.2.

Answers
39. smaller · greater · equilibrium
40. equilibrium
41. 280
42. parameters

Table 9.2
Shift in Demand

(1) Price Per Unit	(2) Original Quantity That Would Be Demanded	(3) New Quantity That Would Be Demanded	(4) Quantity That Would Be Supplied
0	200	400	0
1	180	360	0
2	160	320	40
3	140	280	80
4	120	240	120
5	100	200	160
6	80	160	200
7	60	120	240
8	40	80	280
9	20	40	320
10	0	0	360

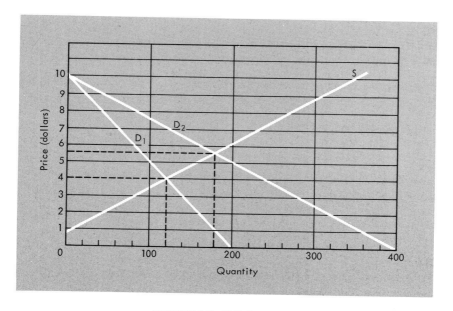

FIGURE 9.2. Shift in Demand

9.43

We can see from Figure 9.2 that the intersection of D_1 and S occurs at a price of

$ _____ per unit and at a quantity of _____ units of X.

Answers
43. 4 · 120

Thus, if we were discussing our original demand curve, D_1, and the supply curve, S, we would know that the intersection of those curves would give us the

_____ price and quantity.

9.44
Let us now consider the shift of the demand curve. We have a shift of the de-

mand curve because one of the _____ determining the position
of the demand curve has changed. (In this case, it is the number of consumers.)
If we observe where D_2 intersects S, we shall discover what the new

_____ price and quantity are. In this example, the new _____

price lies between $ _____ and $_____ per unit, and

the new _____ quantity is _____ units of good X.

9.45
What we are observing in Figure 9.2 is a movement of the demand curve upwards
and to the right. When this occurs, we say we have an increase in demand. Thus,

an increase in demand occurs when a) one of the _____ determining
the position of a demand curve changes and b) this change causes the demand curve

to move upward and to the _____ .

9.46
As you might expect, a decrease in demand occurs when one of the _____
determining the position of the demand curve changes in such a way that the

demand curve moves _____ and to the _____ .

9.47
Thus, when we speak of an increase or a decrease in demand, we are talking of a

_____ of the demand curve. This has to be carefully distinguished
from a movement along a demand curve.

Answers
    43. equilibrium
    44. parameters · equilibrium · equilibrium · 5 · 6 · equilibrium · 180
    45. parameters · right
    46. parameters · downward · left
    47. shift

9.48

When we have a movement along a demand curve, none of the parameters determining the position of the demand curve change, but we are considering the

hypothetical situation of the different _____ of a good that

_____ be demanded at various prices.

9.49

Now, of course, a demand curve could shift its position so that it intersected
a previous demand curve. If, for instance, we would consider D_1 in Figure 9.2
and imagine a new demand curve D_3 intersecting D_1 at a price of $4 per unit

and at a quantity of _____ , such that at prices above $4 the part
of our new demand curve lay upwards and to the right of D_1, and at prices
below $4 the part of our demand curve D_3 lay below and to the left of D_1,
we could say we had an increase in demand for prices above $4 and a

_____ in demand for prices less than $4.

9.50

It is important that you distinguish between movements along and movements
of a demand or a supply curve. Failure to do so can cause analytical errors in
economics. If the market depicted in Figure 9.2 by D_2 and S were in equilibrium,
which of the following would cause:
a. a movement along the demand curve,
b. an increase in the demand curve,
c. a decrease in the demand curve?
1. An increase in the incomes of consumers who normally purchase good X.

_____

2. A decrease in price of a competitive product. _____
3. An increase in the price of a complementary product caused by a leftward

shift of the supply curve for that product. _____
4. An increase in the price of a complementary product caused by an increase

in the demand for that product. _____

5. A shift of S down and to the right. _____

Answers
    48. quantities · would
    49. 120 · decrease
    50. b · c · c · b · a

6. A decision by the suppliers of good X to offer smaller quantities of good X at

each price. _____
7. The discovery that consumption of good X is detrimental to health.

_____

8. Given that we have very competitive sellers supplying good X, a technological
breakthrough that makes the production of good X much cheaper than it was

previously. _____

9.51
Let us now consider some rather special cases in demand and supply analysis
where you can bring your knowledge of elasticity to bear on the problems involved. Consider a street in a residential area where there are no vacant plots.

Thus, the supply of houses on this street _____*(is/is not)*_____ fixed, and consequently, the supply curve of houses for this street would be represented on a

figure by a _____ line, which would have the property of being

completely _*(elastic/inelastic)*_ .

9.52
If each house on this street is identical, then the _____ price of
houses on this street will be determined by where the demand curve for houses
in this street intersects the supply curve. Let us imagine the equilibrium price
to be $50,000 per house.

9.53
If there is now an increase in demand for houses on this street, the demand

curve will shift _____ and to the _____, the equilib-

rium price will _____, but the equilibrium quantity will

_____ _____, since the supply curve is completely

_____.

Answers
  50. a · c · a
  51. is · vertical · inelastic
  52. equilibrium
  53. upwards · right · increase · remain unchanged · inelastic

9.54

Thus, we can see that if we start off from a position of equilibrium and if we have an increase in demand, the higher will be the new _____ price, the more _____ is our supply curve.

9.55

When considering most of the goods and services we consume in our daily lives, we would expect that suppliers would be willing to supply _____ of a good at higher prices. But many examples exist in the real world where an increase in supply will not be forthcoming no matter the price offered. We have examples of the number of original Mona Lisa paintings, the number of Rose Bowl tickets, and many more you can think of where the supply is completely _____. In those cases, an increase in demand in a competitive market will lead to a _____ equilibrium _____.

9.56

At the other end of the spectrum, we can consider a completely elastic supply, which would be represented in a figure by a _____ line. Given that we start off from an equilibrium position once more, an increase in demand _(will/will not)_ lead to a higher equilibrium price. What we would have in this situation would be a larger _____ _____.

9.57

The supply curves, representing most of the goods we consume in our daily lives, lie somewhere between the extremes of complete elasticity and complete inelasticity. Consequently, an increase in demand normally results in a _____ equilibrium price and a larger _____ quantity.

9.58

You should now be able to see rather easily why it is that some goods that are very valuable cost so little. If you take a good such as air, that is very valuable

Answers
54. equilibrium · inelastic
55. more · inelastic · higher · price
56. horizontal · will not · equilibrium quantity
57. higher · equilibrium

because without it life could not exist, it should become obvious why we do not

pay for air. The demand curve for air is obviously *(elastic/inelastic)* but the

supply of air is unlimited at _____ cost.

9.59

Thus, while we might be prepared to pay a very high price for air if we had to,
if we look at the demand for, and the supply of air in a figure similar to the demand and supply figures we have already analyzed, we would have an

_____ demand curve which would intersect a horizontal supply

curve at a price of $ _____. That is, for all practical intents and

purposes, the supply curve for air in the world would be the *(vertical/horizontal)*
axis.

9.60

Goods with this type of supply curve are known as free goods. They are free

goods, because the _____ is essentially limitless, and there is zero
cost of production. Thus, while air is extremely valuable—without it, we could
not survive—it is also extremely cheap; not so cheap, however, in Los Angeles!

9.61

Let us now use our knowledge of demand and supply analysis to discover what
happens when a central body, such as a government, interferes with this free
price system. In Figure 9.3, we have the demand and supply schedules of steak
in a local community. Under competitive conditions, the equilibrium price

per pound of steak would be $ _____ and the equilibrium quantity

would be _____ pounds, per time period under consideration.

9.62

Let us imagine, however, that for some reason the local government decides to
fix a price ceiling on the price of steak. Suppose that this price ceiling is $2 per
pound. In other words, the legal maximum price that may be charged for steak

is $2 per pound. At a price of $2 per pound, however, we can see from Figure 9.3 that we have a situation of excess _____, since the quantity that would be demanded at this price is _____ pounds and the quantity that would be supplied is _____ pounds. Thus, the amount of excess _____ at $2 per pound is _____ pounds.

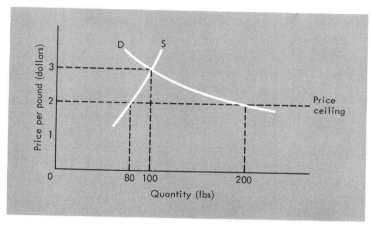

FIGURE 9.3. Demand for and Supply of Steak

9.63
Without a price ceiling existing in this market, and if indeed suppliers of steak had started off by selling steak at $2 per pound, they would have discovered

that this price was _____ the equilibrium price and consequently,

price would have _____ to $ _____ per pound.

9.64
At the equilibrium price, the question of who obtains steak is relatively simple. Those people who are prepared to pay $3 per pound for steak will be able to

buy as much steak as they want at that price, because $3 is the _____
price.

Answers
62. demand · 200 · 80 · demand · 120
63. below · risen · 3
64. equilibrium

9.65

However, with a price ceiling of $2 per pound, not all demands will be satisfied,

because the quantity that would be demanded at that price is _____
than the quantity that would be supplied. Thus, we have a situation of excess

supply. ___*(true/false)*___

9.66

With a price ceiling of $2 per pound as we have in Figure 9.3, the price mech-
anism is obviously inadequate in allocating steak amongst potential buyers,
and some other allocating mechanism will have to be sought, since there are

only _____ pounds of steak available from suppliers at a price of $2

per pound to be distributed to buyers who actually want _____
pounds of steak at this price.

9.67

One method would be to have a rationing system in which each household would
be limited to a certain quantity of steak. Another way to allocate the 80 pounds
of steak would be on a first-come-first-served basis. Or, the suppliers of steak
may sell steak to regular customers to the exclusion of nonregular customers.

But, whichever method is adopted, the _____ _____
will not be the allocating mechanism as it is in a freely competitive market
situation.

9.68

Consumers and suppliers might also resort to a black market system, which would
be an illegal mechanism for circumventing the price ceiling and which would be

essentially resorting to an illegal, but competitive, _____ system.

9.69

The reason why a case such as that depicted in Figure 9.3 is important is because
many countries resort to price ceilings during wars when there are shortages of
many basic commodities. Since many of these basic commodities are essential
to the survival of families, it is felt unfair that those individuals who cannot pay
the high equilibrium prices should be deprived of such commodities. Thus, a

Answers
   65. greater · false
   66. 80 · 200
   67. price mechanism
   68. price (market)

price ceiling system is often adopted for many goods, and this, together with a rationing scheme, ensures a distribution of available supplies that seems more equitable to many people. Thus, in situations similar to the one we have in Figure 9.3, price ceiling and rationing schemes can be used in situations of excess

_____, and from the point of view of economic analysis, we see

that the goods in question will not be allocated completely by a _____

_____ .

9.70

The opposite of a price ceiling is a price floor, and if we look at Figure 9.4, we have a situation of a price floor. If, in the time period under consideration, we were to allow competitive forces to operate in the market depicted in Figure

9.4, the equilibrium price per bushel of wheat would be $_____,

and the equilibrium quantity would be _____ million bushels.

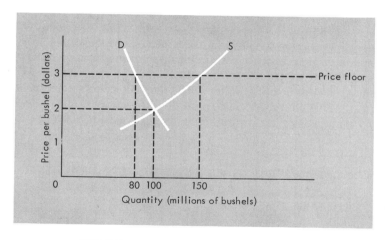

FIGURE 9.4. Demand for and Supply of Wheat

9.71

However, let us imagine that the government decides, in order to help raise the incomes of farmers, to enforce a price floor of $3 per bushel of wheat. This means that no one may legally sell wheat for less than $3 per bushel, and that no one may legally buy wheat for less than $3 per bushel. With the price floor enforced, the quantity of wheat that will be demanded at this price per time

period will be _____ million bushels, and the quantity that will be

supplied will be _____ million bushels.

9.72
Thus, with a price floor of $3 per bushel, we will have a situation in this market

of _____ _____ to the extent of _____ million bushels of wheat.

9.73
The question now arises, what will happen to the excess supply of wheat? One solution would be for the government to buy the excess supply of wheat, which

in this case amounts to _____ million bushels per time period, and distribute or sell this to other nations.

9.74
Another possible solution would be for the farmers to dispose of, let us imagine by burning, this excess supply of wheat. Would this action ever be profitable for the farmers? Before we can answer that question, we must, of course, discover the revenues and costs involved. What will be the farmers' total revenue in this market per time period if there are no price floors (remember total revenue is derived by multiplying price per bushel by number of bushels sold)?

_____

What will be the farmers' total revenue under a price floor situation as depicted

in Figure 9.4? _____

9.75
Thus, we can see total revenue is actually _____ under a situation of a price floor than it is under competitive conditions.

Answers
71. 80 · 150
72. excess supply · 70
73. 70
74. $200 million · $240 million
75. greater

9.76

In a situation such as that depicted in Figure 9.4, the government may also restrict the supply of wheat. We can see from the supply schedule in Figure 9.4

that at a price of $3, farmers would be willing to supply _____ million bushels of wheat per time period. What the government might do is require farmers to reduce the amount of wheat they would supply at this price so that the amount of wheat that would be produced would just equal the amount of wheat that would be demanded at that price. If this were to occur in Figure 9.4,

the government would require farmers to produce only _____

million bushels of wheat per time period instead of _____ million bushels of wheat, which they would normally produce were the price floor

_____ per bushel.

9.77

Now, at a price of $3 we would have farmers producing exactly the amount of

wheat that people would demand at $3 per bushel, i.e. _____ million bushels of wheat per time period. Under this type of situation the

farmers are definitely *(better off/worse off)* than they would be in a freely competitive system, because in a freely competitive system total revenue from

the sale of _____ million bushels of wheat would amount to

$ _____ million, whereas under the new system, total revenue from

sales of wheat will amount to $ _____ million per time period at a

production level of _____ million bushels of wheat. Farmers are

also definitely *(better off/worse off)* in this situation, because if we assume that the supply schedule of wheat is normally shaped and reflects cost of production, then the total costs of producing 80 million bushels of wheat will be

(less than/greater than) the total cost of producing _____ million bushels of wheat per time period which the farmers would do in the freely competitive situation.

9.78

Using our knowledge of elasticity, we can see why indeed farmers get a larger total revenue at a price of $3 compared with a price of $2 per bushel. It is

Answers
76. 150 · 80 · 150 · $3
77. 80 · better off · 100 · 200 · 240 · 80 · better off · less than · 100

because the demand curve for wheat in this price range is ___*(elastic/inelastic)*___,

since a 50 percent increase in price leads to __*(less than/greater than)*__ a 50 percent
decrease in quantity that would be demanded.

9.79
Let us now turn to Figure 9.5. *D* and *S* are the demand and supply schedules of
a hypothetical good *Y*. We see that the demand for this good in the price range

in the figure is completely _____. The equilibrium price per unit is

$ _____ and the equilibrium quantity is _____.

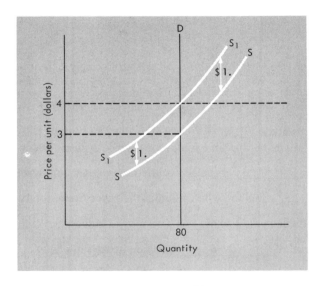

FIGURE 9.5. Tax Effect

9.80
Now let us imagine that the government imposes a $1 tax on each unit of the
good which the suppliers sell. Before the imposition of this tax, as is shown by

SS, suppliers would be willing to supply _____ units of this good
at $3 per unit, but since they now have to pay the government $1 on each unit

Answers
   78. inelastic · less than
   79. inelastic · 3 · 80
   80. 80

they sell after the imposition of a tax, they will be willing to supply_____ units of this good only at a price of $4 per unit as is shown by S_1S_1. We see that the imposition of a tax has caused an upwards and leftwards shift of the

_____ schedule.

9.81
Thus, the new effective supply schedule will be S_1S_1. The new equilibrium

price will be $ _____, and the new equilibrium quantity will be

_____ .

9.82
In the situation before the tax, total revenue, if the market were in equilibrium,

would amount to $ _____. After the tax has been imposed, total

revenue will amount to $ _____, of which the supplier will receive

$ _____ and the government will receive $ _____.

9.83
Now obviously, the suppliers of this good are no worse off than they were before,

since _____ _____ received by the suppliers has not changed. Thus, the whole burden of the tax has been borne by the consumers,

since each individual who now buys a unit of the good is paying $ _____

instead of $ _____ as he would have in the nontax situation.

9.84
In the case depicted in Figure 9.5, therefore, we would say that the incidence of the tax is completely on the consumers, and as you might guess, this is be-

cause the demand curve for this good is completely _____ .

Answers
80. 80 · supply
81. 4 · 80
82. 240 · 320 · 240 · 80
83. total revenue · 4 · 3
84. inelastic

9.85

Now consider the case in Figure 9.6. In this situation we have a completely

_____ demand curve, and in the pretax situation, the equilibrium

price is $ _____ per unit and the equilibrium quantity _____.

After the tax has been imposed, the equilibrium price is $ _____

per unit, and the equilibrium quantity is _____.

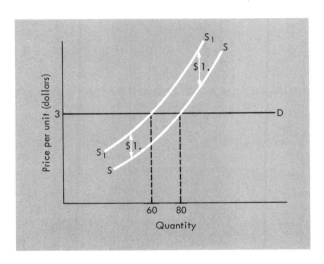

FIGURE 9.6. Tax Effect

9.86

Again we can see that the imposition of a $1 per unit tax has caused the

_____ schedule to shift upwards and to the left. Now, had consumers purchased only 60 units of the good in the pretax situation, the total

revenue collected by the suppliers would have been $ _____. After
the tax has been imposed, however, the equilibrium quantity that will be purchased will actually be 60 units. And in this case, the total revenue will again

be $ _____, but out of this sum suppliers will have to give

$ _____ to the government. Thus, we see that the total incidence

of the tax in this situation is on the *(consumers/suppliers.)*

Answers
    85. elastic · 3 · 80 · 3 · 60
    86. supply · 180 · 180 · 60 · suppliers

9.87

We have chosen extreme examples to show how to determine the incidence of the tax. You should now work through some examples for yourself with normally shaped demand and supply curves, bearing in mind that the more elastic the demand curve is relative to the supply curve, the greater will be the burden of tax

borne by the _____, whereas the more inelastic the demand curve is relative to the supply curve, the greater will be the burden of the tax borne by

the _____.

REVIEW QUESTIONS

Questions 1 and 2 are based on the following information:

Typically, the Rose Bowl football game is sold out. In fact at the printed prices, twice the number of seats could be sold.

9.1

Which of the following are correct? _____

a. The printed price is less than the competitive market price.
b. The printed price is greater than the competitive market price.
c. The printed price is equal to the competitive market price.
d. Insufficient information exists to determine which of the above is correct.

9.2

Which of the following are correct? _____

a. The supply curve of Rose Bowl seats is inelastic with respect to price.
b. Total revenue is not being maximized.
c. Profit is not being maximized.
d. All of the above are correct.

Answers
   87. suppliers · consumers
   1. a
   2. d

9.3
"If, at the going price there is excess demand, competitive firms will shift
their supply curves to the right causing prices to rise and quantity to increase
until an equilibrium is reached."

With regard to competitive markets, the above statement _____

a. is essentially correct in describing how equilibrium is reached.
b. is correct regarding how suppliers behave, but ignores buyers' reactions.
c. is incorrect, because the supply curves will not shift.
d. is incorrect, because it confuses shifting supply curves with shifting demand
curves.

9.4
If you were given the industry demand curve and equilibrium price of a product,

you would know _____ .

a. the price at which the industry demand and supply curves intersected. .
b. the quantity at which the industry demand and supply curves intersected.
c. one point on the industry supply curve.
d. all of the above.

9.5
If, after a competitive market has achieved equilibrium, there is a shift to the
right of its demand curve and, at the same time, a shift to the right of its supply

curve _____ .

a. the new equilibrium price will be higher; the new equilibrium quantity greater.
b. the new equilibrium price will be lower; the new equilibrium quantity greater.
c. the new equilibrium price could be higher or lower; the new equilibrium quantity greater.
d. the new equilibrium price could be higher or lower; the new equilibrium could
be greater or less.

Answers
   3. c
   4. d
   5. c

10

Market Equilibrium

10.1

Let us now analyze price determination in the short run and then in the long run in a freely competitive market. Consider Figure 10.1, which is a repeat of Figure 7.7.

At prices below P_1 the firm would not produce any output since it could not cover its _____ cost. Consequently for prices below P_1, the loss incurred in closing down is _____ cost, which is less than the loss incurred for any positive level of output.

10.2

For prices above P_1, the profit-maximizing firm will produce up to the point at which _____ _____ equals marginal cost. At P_2, the firm will produce _____ and at P_3 the firm will produce _____. Thus for prices greater than P_1 the _____ _____ curve of the firm will be its short-run supply curve.

10.3

Throughout, we have assumed perfect competition. One of the conditions of perfect competition is that each competitive firm supplies such a small portion

Answers
1. variable · fixed
2. marginal revenue · q_2 · q_3 · marginal cost

of the market as to be unable to affect the price in the market. That is, each firm is a price taker—it accepts the going market price and can produce and sell as much as it wants without affecting this _____, which is determined by the intersection of the aggregate _____ and the aggregate supply curves in the market.

Because of this in Figure 10.1, the price line is equal to _____

_____, and marginal revenue. All will be independent of the level

of _____ of any one firm. Also this average revenue line will be the demand curve faced by any individual firm.

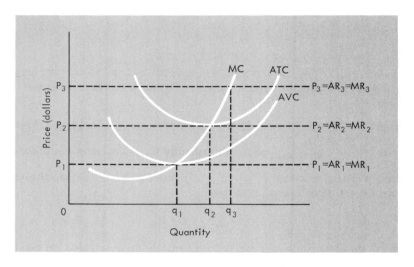

FIGURE 10.1. Short-Run Equilibrium of the Firm

10.4

In Figure 10.2 D_1 and S represent the monthly demand and supply curves for sets of bedroom furniture. Thus, in this time period the equilibrium price is

_____ and the equilibrium quantity _____. From the supply side this quantity is the summation of the outputs of all the competitive firms in the market (Q_{2_s}) at a price of _____. From the demand side the quantity is the summation of all the individual demands, (Q_{2_D}).

Answers
    3. price · demand · average revenue · output
    4. P_2 · Q_2 · P_2

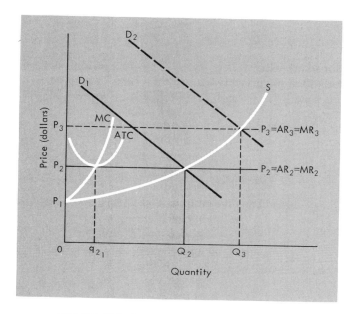

FIGURE 10.2. Price Determination in the Short Run

10.5

We have superimposed Figure 10.1 onto Figure 10.2, and we see that the firm
(1) in Figure 10.1 will supply per month an output of q_{2_1}. Given the assumption

of perfect competition, this firm ___(will/will not)___ be able to affect the market
price, i.e. this firm, like all other firms making up the supply of Q_2, will be a

price _____.

10.6

Given that firm 1 is a profit-maximizing firm, the entrepreneur in charge of this

firm will produce up to the point at which _____ _____
equals marginal revenue, which is, as we see from Figure 10.2, an output equal
to q_{2_1}. Q_2, the output of all the competitive firms in the market, will be
composed of the output of all firms under a similar output policy. Thus, the
demand curve facing each of those firms will be the $AR_2 = MR_2 = P_2$ line.

Answers
   5. will not · taker
   6. marginal cost

10.7

We also see that for prices less than P_1, the industry output (i.e. output of all

firms in that market) will be _____ ; i.e. profit maximization (or
loss minimization) shows that it is less costly for firms to shut down for prices
lower than P_1, since losses for each firm will then be composed only of

_____ _____ .

10.8

If there is a shift in the aggregate demand curve to D_2 (i.e. if at least one of the

_____ determining the position of the demand curve changes), the

new equilibrium price will be _____ and the new equilibrium quan-

tity _____ , which again will be the summation of the individual
firms' quantities that would be supplied at that price.

10.9

Just as the short-run supply curve of the individual firm is its _____

_____ curve above the minimum point of its average variable cost
curve, so the aggregate supply curve S will be the summation of all the firms'

short-run supply curves, i.e. a summation of their _____

_____ curves.

10.10

In Figure 10.2 therefore, after the shift in the demand curve from D_1 to D_2,

the equilibrium price will be _____ and the equilibrium quantity

will be _____ . Each firm will be making _____ ,
over and above a normal return on investment by producing that level of output

where marginal revenue equals _____ _____ equals
average revenue equals P_3.

Answers
7. zero · fixed costs
8. parameters · P_3 · Q_3
9. marginal cost · marginal cost
10. P_3 · Q_3 · profit · marginal cost

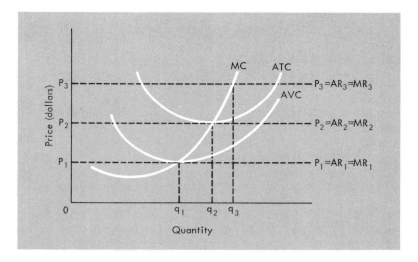

FIGURE 10.1.

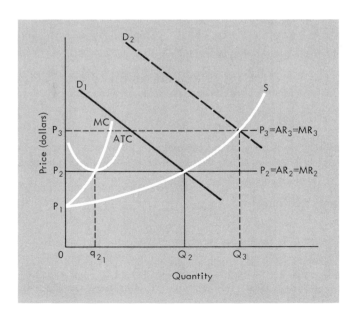

FIGURE 10.2.

10.11

At a level of aggregate demand of D_2 what will be the output of each profit-

maximizing firm in the short run? _____

10.12

This quantity $\times$ number of firms = _____ = quantity that would be
demanded at a price P_3.

10.13

At a level of output of q_3, what profit will the firm make on the q_{3rd} unit, i.e.

the last unit produced (*careful*)? _____ How do you know?

_____

10.14

At a level of output of q_3 what will be the average level of profit on each unit

of output? _____ The total profit (i.e. profit above the normal

return)? _____

_____

10.15

Now consider what will happen in the long run. Businessmen will observe

_____ being made by firms in the industry depicted in Figure 10.2
and, being profit-motivated, will divert resources into the industry.

10.16

First, consider the case in which the movement of new firms into the industry
does not increase the prices of the factors of production employed in this in-

dustry. Thus, the _____ of producing a unit of output will not
increase as new firms move in.

Answers
  11. q_3
  12. Q_3
  13. zero · because $MR = MC$, i.e. the revenue received from selling the q_{3rd} unit just
      equals its cost
  14. $AR_3 - ATC$ at q_3 · $(AR - ATCQ_3) \times q_3$, i.e., average revenue minus average
      costs at q_3 times output q_3.
  15. profit
  16. cost

10.17

In the long run, new firms will continue to move into the industry as long as

_____, over and above a normal return, exists. Profit will exist

as long as _____ is greater than the average total cost of production;

that is, as long as the _____ line is above the minimum point of
the average total cost curve.

10.18

As the quantity supplied increases as new firms move in, however, the

_____ necessary to clear the market will decrease and will continue to decrease as long as firms move in. When will firms stop moving into
the industry? Only when it is no longer profitable for them to move in; that
is, only when profits in excess of normal returns are eliminated in the industry.
This will occur when each firm, old and new, is operating at the minimum

point of its average _____ _____ curve.

10.19

Since we assume no increase in factor prices as new firms move into the industry, the new long-run equilibrium price will be the same as the previous
equilibrium price before the increase in demand. That is, the minimum point

of each firm's average total _____ curve will not change as firms
move into the industry.

10.20

Thus the long-run industry _____ curve will be a horizontal line.

10.21

This can be shown in Figure 10.3. Initially the market is in long-run equilibrium.

The price P_1 is determined by the intersection of the aggregate _____

schedule, D_1, and the aggregate _____ schedule, S_1. The equilibrium

quantity is _____, and each firm (there are n firms) is operating at the

Answers
    17. profit · price · price
    18. price · total cost
    19. cost
    20. supply
    21. demand · supply · Q_1

_____ point on its average total cost curve. Each is earning only a normal return on investment. Profit is zero.

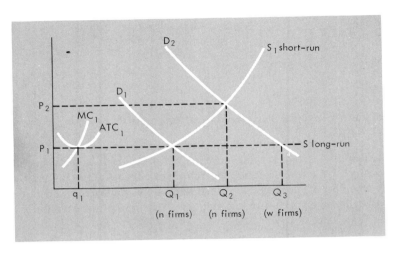

FIGURE 10.3. Long-Run Supply (Constant Cost)

10.22

Now suppose the aggregate demand schedule shifts to D_2. In the short run,

the new equilibrium price and quantity are _____ and _____

respectively. Each firm will be making _____ and maximizing

profit by operating up to the point at which _____ _____

equals _____ _____.

10.23

The additional output that each firm will supply will be determined by each

firm's _____ _____ curve which is its short-run supply curve. Thus, the aggregate supply curve S_1 with which we are interested in

Answers
   21. minimum
   22. P_2 · Q_2 · profit · marginal revenue · marginal cost
   23. marginal cost

the short run will be found by adding horizontally the short-run supply curves of each firm. Thus, a supply of Q_2 will be a summation of the quantities supplied by each firm at its profit-maximizing level of output.

10.24
Firms now move into the industry seeking _____, and continue to do so until only a normal return on investment remains in this industry. From Figure 10.3 we see that this will occur when there are w firms in the industry, each

operating at the _____ point on its average total cost curve.

10.25
Thus when the industry reaches long-run equilibrium after the shift in the demand curve, the long-run equilibrium price will be _____ and long-run equilibrium quantity will be _____.

10.26
In this example, the long-run supply curve will be represented by a

(horizontal/vertical) line and supply will, therefore, be completely

(elastic/inelastic) with respect to price in the long run.

10.27
Remember the assumption we have made, however, to arrive at such a long-run supply schedule. We have assumed that an increase in demand for factor inputs

will not cause any increase in their _____, and consequently, there

has been no increase in the average _____ _____ of producing additional output in the long run. How realistic this assumption is may depend on the size of the industry. Most industries compete in the same markets for factor inputs. The automobile industry, the ship-building industry, the consumers' durables industries and many more all compete, for instance, for steel just as they all compete for labor and many more factor inputs. Now,

Answers
  24. profit · minimum
  25. P_1 · Q_3
  26. horizontal · elastic
  27. prices · total costs

if an industry is very small relative to all others competing for those factor inputs, then a small increase in its demand for, let us say, steel may have a negligible influence on the market price of steel; and thus, as far as steel is

concerned, this industry could expand without _____ the price of steel to itself, or to the other industries using steel as a factor input.

10.28
Thus, if one industry is small and is only one of many using certain factor

input, the ___*(more/less)*___ likely it will be to have an influence on the

_____ of any factor input, and, thus, the more _____ will be this industry's long-run supply curve. In the limiting case where the industry can expand without increasing the price of any factor input, the

long-run supply schedule will be completely _____. That is, given any increase in demand for the output of this industry, the price of the product will return to its former equilibrium level when, *ceteris paribus*,

the industry again reaches long-run _____.

10.29
For most industries, however, if we assume that additional factor inputs are

forthcoming only at higher prices, the long-run industry _____

curve will not be a _____ line (i.e. completely elastic), but will be upward sloping.

10.30
Consider Figure 10.4. In this instance, in contrast to the situation depicted in

Figure 10.3 as firms move into the industry in their search for _____ the increased demand for factor inputs causes their price to rise.

10.31
As factor prices increase, the cost of producing a unit of output _____ and, consequently, the average total cost curve of each firm rises.

Answers
    27. increasing
    28. less · price · elastic · elastic · equilibrium
    29. supply · horizontal
    30. profits
    31. increases

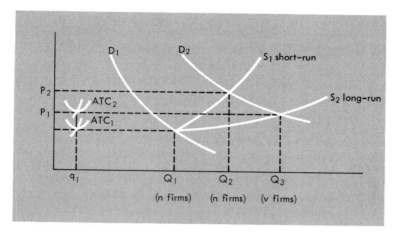

FIGURE 10.4. Long-Run Supply (Increasing Cost)

10.32

If we consider the firm's cost curves as shown in Figure 10.4 we see that before the increase in demand the firm was in long-run equilibrium operating at the

minimum point of ATC_1 producing an output of _____.

10.33

The new demand curve, D_2, causes the short-run equilibrium price to be P_2

and short-run equilibrium output to be _____. As firms move into the industry, however, factor prices rise, ATC_1 rises to ATC_2, and when the industry is again in long-run equilibrium when there are v firms, each firm will

still be operating at the minimum point of its average _____

_____ curve but the minimum will be higher than it was previously.

10.34

Thus in the increasing cost case, the long-run supply curve will not be a horizontal line but will be positively inclined. While not perfectly elastic, however, we can

see from Figure 10.4 that the long-run supply curve is ___*(more/less)*___ elastic than the short-run supply curve.

Answers
32. q_3
33. Q_2 · total cost
34. more

10.35
It could be possible, of course, to have a situation in which an increase in demand for factors of production would lead to a decrease in their prices. If this did happen, then, as the demand for a commodity increased, the prices of productive factors would decrease and the minimum point of a firm's average

total cost curve would _____*(rise/fall)*_____. In this situation the long-run supply

curve of the industry would be *(positively/negatively)* inclined.

Having analyzed short-run and long-run equilibrium for firms and industries, let us briefly summarize what we have learned so far before we turn to Chapter 12 and consider equilibrium of markets in the economy as a whole.

REVIEW QUESTIONS

10.1
If a perfectly competitive firm in equilibrium were to lower its price,

_____.

a. it would receive a larger share of the market.
b. other firms would lower their prices also.
c. it would operate at a loss.
d. it would drive all other firms out of business.

10.2
The short-run supply curve of a perfectly competitive industry is _____.

a. made up of the minimum points of each firm's average total cost curve.
b. the horizontal summation of firms' marginal cost curves.
c. the horizontal summation of firms' marginal cost curves above the intersection point of the marginal cost and average variable cost curves.
d. horizontal if factor prices are constant.

Answers
    35. fall · negatively
      1. c
      2. c

10.3

The long-run supply curve of a competitive industry is _____ .

a. the horizontal summation of the long-run marginal cost curves of all firms in the industry.
b. the horizontal summation of the long-run marginal cost curves above the average cost curves of all firms in the industry.
c. the horizontal summation of the long-run average cost curves of all firms in the industry.
d. none of the above.

10.4

If a firm sells its product at the market price, whatever that price may be, and wants to earn as much profit as that price makes possible, it should

_____ .

a. try to produce and sell that quantity of output at which marginal cost has risen to equality with price.
b. try to sell all the output it can produce.
c. try to produce and sell that quantity of output at which marginal cost has reached its minimum possible load.
d. never let marginal cost reach equality with price, since this is the point at which profits become zero.

10.5

In the long run, if marginal cost is equal to marginal revenue, and selling price is just below total average cost, the firm will _____ .

a. leave the industry.
b. maximize profits.
c. incur losses, but continue to operate.
d. increase output.

Answers
   3. d
   4. a
   5. a

11

A Brief Summary

11.1

In introducing the subject matter in the beginning of this book, we explained the basic problem an economic system has to solve. While we have concentrated our attention on how a free enterprise system solves this problem, we saw that the basic problem faced by any economic system was the allocation of scarce

_____ among alternative uses to satisfy consumer _____ as fully as possible. We saw how, in a competitive free enterprise system, the allocation of resources was determined by the independent decisions of

_____ and firms.

11.2

We then analyzed the behavior of consumers and firms respectively and their interaction in competitive markets. More precisely, we analyzed the theory of

_____, the theory of _____ and the interaction of

demand and supply in competitive _____.

11.3

It was assumed throughout that all consumers and firms are competitors. This means that when making consumption and production decisions, consumers and firms act as price takers. That is, they do not consider that their decisions

Answers
1. resources · wants · consumers
2. demand · supply · markets

224

to buy or produce a good will have any noticeable effect on the _____ of that good, in the competitive markets.

11.4

In the discussion of demand, we assumed that consumers would spend their

_____ according to their preferences.

11.5

Formally, we say that consumers allocate their limited income in such a way as

to maximize total _____. The marginal equivalency condition for

such a maximum to be attained is that the _____ utility from the last dollar spent be the same for all goods and services.

11.6

When the price of a particular good falls, the amount of that good that a dollar

can buy *(increases/decreases.)*

11.7

Consequently, when the price of a good falls, the marginal utility derived from

the last dollar spent on a good will *(increase/decrease.)* This will encourage

consumers to buy more of that good to meet the marginal _____ condition necessary for a maximum.

11.8

Thus we have seen why, when the price of a good falls, the quantity demanded

by consumers will *(increase/decrease.)*

Answers
3. price
4. income
5. utility · marginal
6. increases
7. increase · equivalency
8. increase

11.9
Another way to say the same thing is that the demand curve, which shows the

quantity that will be demanded at different prices, slopes *(upward/downward)*
from left to right.

11.10
In the discussion of supply, it was assumed that firms try to maximize

_____. You learned that the marginal equivalency condition for
profit maximization can be stated two ways: either in terms of marginal product
or marginal cost.

11.11
One way of stating the marginal equivalency condition is that in order to maximize profit it is necessary to hire that amount of each resource where the value

of the marginal _____ and the cost per unit, or price, of the resource
are equal.

11.12
The value of the marginal product of a resource tells how much extra

*(revenue/cost)* will result from hiring an extra unit of the resource. The

price of the resource tells by how much _*(revenue/cost)*_ will increase from
hiring an extra unit of the resource.

11.13
If, for any resource, the value of the marginal product is greater than the price

of the resource, then the firm will add more to _____ than it will

to _____ by hiring an extra unit. That is, profit will

*(increase/decrease)* if an extra unit is hired in this case.

Answers
    9. downward
  10. profit
  11. product
  12. revenue · cost
  13. revenue · cost · increase

11.14

The reverse argument can be made if the value of the marginal product is less than the price of the resources. In this case, it is possible to increase profit by

(increasing/decreasing) the amount of the resource hired.

11.15

Only if the value of the marginal product and the price of the resource are equal will there be *no* gain from changing the amount of the resource hired.

In other words, only when the value of the _____ _____

and the _____ of a resource are equal will profit be at a

_____.

11.16

This condition for profit maximization can be stated another way. In order for a competitive firm to maximize profit, it is necessary to produce that level of

output for which the _____ of the product is equal to _____ cost.

11.17

The price of a product tells how much will be added to the ___*(revenue/cost)*___ of a competitive firm if an extra unit is produced. The marginal cost tells how

much will be added to _____ if an extra unit of output is produced.

11.18

If price is greater than marginal cost, the production of an extra unit of output

will add ___*(more/less)*___ to revenue than to cost; that is, profit will

(increase/decrease) if an extra unit is produced. If price were less than marginal

cost, it would be possible to add to profit by *(increasing/decreasing)* output.

Answers
14. decreasing
15. marginal product · price · maximum
16. price · marginal
17. revenue · cost
18. more · increase · decreasing

11.19

Only at the level of output where price equals marginal cost will _____
be at a maximum.

11.20

This way of expressing the marginal equivalency condition for profit maximization enables us to derive the supply curve for a firm. The supply curve of a firm,

of course, shows the _____ that a firm will be willing to produce at

different _____ .

11.21

A profit-maximizing competitive firm will always expand output to the point

where _____ equals _____ _____ . As a
result, for any particular price, the quantity that will be produced will be given

by the marginal _____ curve. In other words, the marginal cost
curve shows the quantity that a competitive firm will supply at different prices.

That is to say, the marginal cost curve is the competitive firm's _____
curve.

11.22

Since most firms operate in the range where the law of diminishing returns

applies, marginal cost will _____*(rise/fall)*_____ as output increases. This is true
because, if an extra unit of a resource adds less to output as more of that resource is employed, more resource units will be required to produce an extra
unit of output as more of that resource is employed. Thus, according to the
law of diminishing returns, as a firm expands output the marginal product of a

factor of production _____ and the marginal cost of output

_____ .

Answers
19. profit
20. quantities · prices
21. price · marginal cost · cost · supply
22. rise · decreases · increases

11.23

Since the marginal cost curve is a firm's supply curve, the law of diminishing

returns implies that the typical supply curve will slope *(upwards/downwards)*
from left to right.

11.24

The foregoing discussions were put to use to show how, in the market for any

commodity, the equilibrium _____ and _____ of that
commodity would be determined by the forces of supply and demand.

11.25

In any market, unless the quantity that consumers demand equals the quantity
that firms supply, competition among consumers and among firms will lead to

changes in _____ until supply and demand are equal.

11.26

The importance of this result can be easily seen. Suppose, for example, that
consumers' preferences change so that they consider books to be more satisfying commodities than was previously the case. This would have the effect

of shifting the demand curve for books _____ and to the

_____.

11.27

At the old price for books, the quantity demanded will now exceed the quantity

supplied, and the price of books will _____. As the price increases

publishers will be induced to *(move along/shift)* their supply curve and produce
more books. This process will continue until supply and demand are

_____.

11.28

To take another example, suppose that publishers discover a new, more efficient
way to produce books. This will have the effect of shifting down firms' cost

Answers
    23. upwards
    24. price · quantity
    25. price
    26. upwards · right
    27. increase · move along · equal

curves with the result that they will be prepared to produce more books at each

price. This change in technology, then, shifts the supply curve _____

and to the _____ .

11.29
At the old price, the quantity _____ will be greater than the quan-

tity _____ and competition among firms will lead to a fall in

_____ .

11.30
As the price of books falls, consumers will respond by *(moving along/shifting)*

their demand curves. This process will continue until _____ and

_____ are equal.

11.31
In both of these examples we have seen how the utility and profit-maximizing
behavior of consumers and competitive firms led to a change in the amount of
resources used in the production of a commodity as conditions changed. In
the first example, the change in consumers' preferences was reflected in a shift

in the _____ curve. This led to a change in _____
which signaled firms to increase production.

11.32
In the second example the change in costs was reflected in a shift in the

_____ curve. This led to a change in _____ which
induced consumers to increase expenditures on the commodity in question.

11.33
In each case the change in price acted as a signal. In the first case the rise in

price signaled to _____ that consumers would prefer to consume

Answers
    28. downward · right
    29. supplied · demanded · price
    30. moving along · demand · supply
    31. demand · price
    32. supply · price
    33. firms

more books and also made it profitable for firms to produce more books. In the second case the fall in price signaled to _____ that books could be produced with fewer resources and enabled them to purchase books at a lower price.

REVIEW QUESTIONS

11.1

After a change in commodity prices, or a change in income an individual finds the marginal utilities of the goods he consumes have declined. This means that

he is _____ .

a. worse off in his new situation.
b. better off in his new situation.
c. worse off only if his income has changed.
d. better off only if commodity prices have changed.

11.2

A profit maximizing firm will always hire an additional worker as long as the

value of his marginal product _____.

a. is positive.
b. is zero.
c. exceeds the worker's wage.
d. is less than the worker's wage.

11.3

A perfectly competitive firm will always expand output as long as _____.

a. rising marginal cost is less than price.
b. rising marginal cost is less than marginal revenue.
c. rising marginal cost is less than average revenue.
d. any of the above is true since price equals both marginal and average revenue.

Answers
  33. consumers
    1. b
    2. c
    3. d

11.4

The Law of Diminishing Returns implies that _____.

a. long-run industry supply curves are positively inclined.
b. a firm's supply curve is positively inclined.
c. demand curves are negatively inclined.
d. none of the above.

11.5

Other things remaining equal, a change in technology which increases efficiency

in a perfectly competitive industry will _____.

a. lower price.
b. increase price.
c. leave price unchanged.
d. insufficient information exists to determine what will happen to price.

Answers
  4. b
  5. a

12

General Equilibrium and Economic Efficiency

12.1

We have just analyzed the way in which supply and demand interact and determine the equilibrium _____ and _____ in the market for any single commodity. In so doing we have analyzed the basic mechanics of a market economy. But the solution, or equilibrium, determined in any single market, constitutes only a partial equilibrium, because it does not take into account the interdependence among markets.

12.2

What happens in the market for trucks is certainly going to have an effect on the market for steel, since steel is needed to produce trucks. What happens in the market for steel is certainly going to have an effect on the market for iron ore, since iron ore is needed to produce steel. What happens in the market for iron ore will have an effect on the market for trucks, since trucks are needed to carry iron ore. This is just a simple example of what it means to say that

_____ are interdependent.

12.3

But while it would be difficult, in fact impossible, to describe the millions of such interdependencies that exist in an economy like the United States',

Answers
    1. price · quantity
    2. markets

competitive markets automatically take these interdependencies into account.

It is possible for _____ to perform this complex task for two reasons.

12.4
First, no single individual or organization has to make all the decisions. Con-

sumers and firms all pursue their own interests and the general _____
solution is the result of all those individual decisions taken together.

12.5
Second, markets can give out signals which convey to the many individual decision makers the information necessary to plan their expenditure or production.

These signals are, of course, _____.

12.6
As individual consumers and firms make their decisions they affect the

_____ of commodities. In turn the prices which are signals to
consumers and firms will influence their decisions. Changes in prices and in
quantities supplied and demanded will occur until equilibrium in *all* markets is

achieved. This solution we call _____ equilibrium.

12.7
Thus, through individuals pursuing their own ends—utility in the case of the consumer and profit in the case of the entrepreneur—in a competitive economy,

_____ will be allocated according to those ends.

12.8
The decisions of individual consumers and firms, acting freely and independently,

are recognized in the many competitive _____ that exist in a competitive free enterprise system. Equilibrium is reached in all markets when the
combination of commodities demanded is equal to the combination of commodi-

ties supplied, just as _____ is reached in any individual market when

Answers
3. markets
4. equilibrium
5. prices
6. prices · general
7. resources
8. markets · equilibrium

the amount of a commodity consumers are willing to buy just equals the amount firms are willing to produce.

12.9

We have not yet seen, however, if, when equilibrium is reached in a competitive market economy, we have an efficient solution to the problem of resource allocation. In the remaining part of this chapter, we will show that a competitive

_____ economy will, though with some exceptions, tend toward an efficient equilibrium.

12.10

What is meant by the term "efficiency?" One kind of efficiency can be called technological efficiency. If a firm, in producing a given output, uses up the smallest possible quantity of resources, then it would be technologically

_____. That is, it would incur the least possible cost in producing a given output.

12.11

For an economy as a whole, if a given combination of commodities is produced with the smallest possible cost (quantity of resources) then it will be

_____ efficient.

12.12

Will an economy with competitive markets tend to be technologically efficient? Suppose, for example, that some firms in the construction industry were not

efficient in this sense. This would mean that they were using more _____ to build houses than necessary. As a result these firms would be incurring

greater costs and earning smaller _____ than would be the case if they were efficient.

12.13

If these firms are trying to maximize profit, then clearly it would be in their own

interest to reduce costs by becoming technologically _____.

Answers
9. market
10. efficient
11. technologically
12. resources · profit
13. efficient

12.14
But if, for some reason, these firms did not adopt efficient methods of production, it would be profitable for competing, more efficient, firms to produce and sell

houses at a lower _____ and bid away the customers of less efficient firms. The more efficient firms would be able to sell houses at a lower price and

still earn a profit because their _____ are lower.

12.15
The effect of this competitive behavior would be to force inefficient firms to reduce costs or, eventually, to force them out of business. Thus, if self-interest

does not bring about technological efficiency, then the force of _____ will.

12.16
Thus, a competitive market economy will tend to be technologically efficient,

because, for any combination of commodities produced, _____ will force firms to adopt the least-cost methods of production.

12.17
But, before an economy can be called economically efficient, it must be more than just technologically efficient. In other words, economic efficiency requires something more than that the combination of commodities produced use up

the fewest possible _____ , i.e. something more than the combination being produced at least cost.

12.18
It would be possible, for example, for an economy to produce nothing but paper-weights and still be technologically efficient. Such an economy would not be

_____ efficient, however, because it clearly would not be producing the best (from the viewpoint of consumers) combination of commodities.

Answers
14. price · costs
15. competition
16. competition
17. resources
18. economically

12.19

Economic efficiency requires that resources be allocated among the production of different commodities in such a way that the utility of consumers be maximized. The paperweight economy would not be efficient, because it would be possible

to increase the _____ of consumers by shifting at least some

_____ from the production of paperweights to the production of goods such as food and clothing.

12.20

We have seen that a competitive market economy will tend to be _____

efficient. Will it also tend toward _____ efficiency? Let us see.

12.21

Earlier, it was shown that a consumer who spent his income in such a way as to

maximize utility would make the _____ utility from the last dollar spent equal for all goods.

12.22

For simplicity, consider only two goods, *A* and *B*. For the _____ maximizing consumer it must be true that

$$\frac{\text{marginal utility of } A}{\text{price of } A} = \frac{\text{marginal utility of } B}{\text{price of } B}$$

12.23

This says, of course, that if *A* costs twice as much as *B*, its marginal utility would

have to be ___*(twice/half)*___ that of *B* to make it worthwhile to buy the last unit of *A*.

12.24

It has also been shown that a profit-maximizing competitive firm will produce that

level of output for which price equals marginal _____ . For goods

Answers
19. utility · resources
20. technologically · economic
21. marginal
22. utility
23. twice
24. cost

A and B, it will be true, in a _____ market economy, that price of A = marginal cost of A and that price of B = marginal cost of B. If we consider

together the behavior of _____ -maximizing consumers and

_____ -maximizing firms in a competitive economy we can see that there will be a tendency for resources to be allocated efficiently.

12.25
Using symbols, we know in equilibrium that

(1) $$\frac{MU_A}{P_A} = \frac{MU_B}{P_B}$$ for all consumers.

In words: in equilibrium, the ratio of marginal utility to price for any commodity must be equal to the ratio of marginal utility to price for any other commodity. If, for any consumer, for any two commodities, the ratios were not equal, the consumer would not be in equilibrium.

Again, using symbols, we also know in equilibrium that

(2) $P_A = MC_A$ and $P_B = MC_B$ for all producers of A and B.

In words: in equilibrium the price of a commodity must equal its marginal cost. Consider (1) and (2) together.

(1) $$\frac{MU_A}{P_A} = \frac{MU_B}{P_B}$$

(2) $P_A = MC_A; \quad P_B = MC_B$

Let us substitute the prices (P's) in (1) with the relevant marginal costs (MC's) from (2). Thus in (1) we will replace P_A with _____ and P_B with _____ .

This gives the result

(3)
$$\frac{MU_A}{MC_A} = \frac{MU_B}{MC_B}$$

What does this mean?

12.26

Since MU_A is the utility gained from consumption of the last unit of A and MC_A is the dollar amount of resources used to produce the last unit of A, $\frac{MU_A}{MC_A}$ is the _____ gained from the last dollar's worth of

_____ in the production of A. Pause here and make sure you understand frame 26.

12.27

Likewise $\frac{MU_B}{MC_B}$ is the _____ gained from the last dollar's worth of

_____ used in the production of B.

12.28

Equation (3), then, says that for each consumer in a competitive economy the utility gained from the last dollar of resources used in the production of A,

that is $\left(\frac{MU_A}{MC_A}\right)$ _____ the utility gained from the last dollar of

resources used in the production of B, that is $\left(\frac{MU_B}{MC_B}\right)$.

12.29

Suppose that this equality does not hold. Suppose, for example, that $\frac{MU_A}{MC_A} = \frac{4}{2}$ and $\frac{MU_B}{MC_B} = \frac{3}{2}$. Suppose that $2 worth of resources were shifted

Answers
26. utility · resources
27. utility · resources
28. equals

away from the production of B to the production of A. Since the MC_B is

_____ this will mean one less unit of B. What will be the loss in

utility just from this reduction in the amount of B? _____

12.30

Since the MC_A is also $2, the resources obtained from industry B, when put to

use in industry A, will produce _____ unit(s) of A. What will

be the gain in utility just from this increase in the amount of A? _____

12.31

Will it be worthwhile in this case for the economy to shift resources from B to

A? ____*(yes/no)*____ . Why? Because there will be a net gain in _____
by doing so.

12.32

It will pay to shift resources from one industry to another until $\dfrac{MU_A}{MC_A} =$

$\dfrac{MU_B}{MC_B}$. In other words, this is the marginal equivalency condition for utility

maximization for the economy as a whole. And, as we saw before, a competitive

economy will move toward an equilibrium where this condition ____*(is/is not)*____
met.

12.33

For this reason we say that a competitive economy is economically _____ .
When a competitive economy attains equilibrium, there can be no gains made

by reallocating _____ .

Answers
   29. 2 · 3
   30. 1 · 4
   31. yes · utility
   32. is
   33. efficient · resources

12.34

In other words, a _____ market economy will allocate scarce

_____ among alternative uses in such a way as to satisfy consumers'

_____ as fully as possible.

12.35

In the preceding frames we have seen that a competitive market economy will tend to be efficient. By this is meant two things: first, such an economy will tend to produce the combination of commodities that is most in accordance

with the preferences of _____; second, it will tend to produce that combination of goods and services with the smallest possible quantity of

_____.

12.36

Underlying this discussion was an important assumption, which was never stated explicitly. It was assumed that whenever a firm produced a commodity it would have to pay all the costs of production, and in turn would be paid by all consumers who benefited from its product. Knowing the going market price of any good, a profit-maximizing firm when making its decision about what to produce

will consider the _____ it has to pay and will disregard whatever

_____ it does not have to pay. It will also base its decision, not on how many consumers could be benefited by its product, but on how much con-

sumers will _(enjoy/pay for)_ its product.

12.37

As we shall see, when the costs that firms must pay differ from total costs, or when all consumers do not have to pay to enjoy the benefits of firms' products,

a competitive economy will not tend to allocate _____ efficiently.

12.38

In order to understand why this is true let us consider two examples, one in

which firms do not have to pay for all the _____ of production of a

Answers
34. competitive · resources · wants
35. consumers · resources
36. costs · costs · pay for
37. resources
38. costs

commodity, and one in which consumers can enjoy the benefit of a commodity

without having to _____ for it.

12.39
Imagine a large power plant that supplies electricity to a city. Suppose that this
power plant burns coal to obtain energy to drive its turbines, and that it is located
in the middle of the city. What are the costs of producing electricity? There are

the costs of the scarce _____ needed to produce electricity. The firm
must pay for the land, labor, and capital it uses because these resources are

_____ .

12.40
There is another cost, however, that this firm does not have to pay. In the
burning of coal the power plant gives off large quantities of smoke that pollutes
the air. As a result, for persons living in this city, health suffers, residences are
more difficult to keep clean, and the general tenor of life is less pleasant. Air

pollution, then, is a real _____ of producing electricity which the

firm *(does/does not)* have to pay.

12.41
In a competitive market economy nothing exists to force the firm to take
the costs of air pollution into account. As a result, in a competitive market

economy resources will be allocated as if such costs *(do not exist/are too great)* .
Let us see why, when some costs are not taken into account, the allocation of
resources in a competitive market economy will not be efficient.

12.42
You will remember that a competitive firm will maximize _____
if it produces the level of output where price equals marginal cost.

Answers
  38. pay
  39. resources · scarce
  40. cost · does not
  41. do not exist
  42. profit

12.43

If the firm pays only some of the costs of production, it will maximize profit

producing the level of output where _____ equals the

_____ _____ paid by the firm.

12.44

If consumers spend their income to maximize utility, then, in general equilibrium
for a competitive economy, it will be true that the extra utility obtained from the

last dollar paid of production cost of a commodity will be *(the same/different)*
for all commodities.

12.45

Returning to our example, if we consider for simplicity just two commodities,
electricity (E) and gas (G), then it would be true in equilibrium for a competitive
economy that

$$\frac{MU_E}{\text{paid } MC_E} = \frac{MU_G}{\text{paid } MC_G}$$

But we know that, in this example, the costs of producing electricity are

_____ than the costs paid by firms producing electricity. As a
result, in terms of all costs (whether paid by firms or not) it will be true in
equilibrium that

$$\frac{MU_E}{MC_E} \text{ is } \underline{\quad\textit{(less/greater)}\quad} \text{ than } \frac{MU_G}{MC_G}.$$

12.46

Since it is a necessary condition for efficiency that the utility gained from the
last dollar of cost be the same for all commodities, we can see from the preceding

frame that a competitive economy __*(will/will not)*__ be efficient when some
costs are not paid by producers.

Answers
43. price · marginal cost
44. the same
45. greater · less
46. will not

12.47

Historically, communities have recognized this problem and have tried to solve it
by modifying the competitive economy in different ways. In terms of our smoke
example, zoning has sometimes been used to require that plants, which make
surrounding areas unpleasant to live in, be located in areas distant from residential
areas. This approach forces firms to take into account the costs of air pollution

by locating in an area where these costs are ____*(high/low)*____ .

12.48

An alternative approach that has been used is to require power plants to use
filters and other devices to prevent smoke from pouring out into the air. In
this case firms are forced to take into account the possible costs of air pollution

by the requirement that they do whatever is necessary to *(eliminate/create)*
harmful quantities of smoke.

12.49

Such policies constitute a kind of interference in the workings of a competitive
market economy, but it is interference directed at situations which a competitive

economy ___*(can/cannot)*___ handle efficiently.

12.50

To summarize briefly, when there are costs of producing a certain commodity
that firms do not have to pay, then a competitive market economy will tend to

allocate resources _____ . By having society impose restrictions
that force such firms to take into account all costs of production, it may be possible to restore the tendency of a market economy toward economic

_____ .

12.51

Let us consider now an example of a *public good.* Here consumers are able to
enjoy the benefits of a commodity without having to pay for it. Suppose there
is a mosquito swamp that makes life miserable for everyone in the neighboring
town. It would appear that such a situation would make it profitable, in a
competitive market economy, for a firm to produce and sell swamp-clearing

Answers
   47. low
   48. eliminate
   49. cannot
   50. inefficiently · efficiency

services. Since a large number of persons would like to enjoy the benefits of

such services, presumably, they *(would/would not)* be willing to pay for them.

12.52
Now suppose some swamp-clearing firm could perform such services. Would it
be able to sell this service? Now, there is no economic reason why any consumer in this town would be willing to pay for this service after the swamp had

been cleared since now it *(would/would not)* be necessary to pay in order to
enjoy a mosquito-free evening. That is, a resident could enjoy (consume) a
mosquito-free evening at zero cost.

12.53
Thus, after the service is rendered (after the swamp is cleared), consumers are

able to enjoy the benefits of this service without having to _____
for it.

12.54
Suppose the firm recognizes this problem and decides to have consumers agree
to pay before the swamp is cleared. Since, in a competitive economy, consumers make their expenditures individually, not as a group, our firm would

have to deal with consumers *(as a group/individually)* .

12.55
It is unlikely, even though he might be bothered by mosquitos a great deal,
that any one consumer would be willing on his own to hire a firm to clear the
swamp. He might say to himself: "It really isn't worth it to me to have the
swamp cleared if I have to pay the entire cost. Besides, if any one else decides
to have the swamp cleared, I will benefit just as much as if I paid for it myself.
What's more, if I were to have the swamp cleared, everyone else would benefit

without paying any of the cost." As a result, *(no one/some one)* is likely to
buy the services of the swamp-clearing firm.

Answers
    51. would
    52. would not
    53. pay
    54. individually
    55. no one

12.56
An enterprising firm might then hit upon the idea of selling shares so that no single individual would have to pay the entire cost. Unfortunately, however, if consumers really were to behave independently and in their own interest they would reason to themselves: "Why should I buy a share? The small amount of my contribution is not going to make any significant difference. If everyone else buys a share, the swamp will be cleared, and I will benefit, whether I buy a share or not. If no one else buys a share, the swamp will not be cleared, even if I were to buy a share." As a result, once again, our firm

___(will/will not)___ find swamp clearing a profitable activity.

12.57
Because there is no way of preventing people who do not pay for the service from consuming it, it is very difficult in a competitive market economy to get anyone to pay for a service like swamp clearing. This is unlike most commodi-

ties. If you want to wear a coat, you must _____ for your own

coat. If you want to drive a car, you must _____ for your own car. But if you want to be free of mosquitos, you can be so just as well if someone else clears the swamp as if you clear the swamp.

12.58
Thus, even though everyone would benefit by having the swamp cleared, it

___(will/will not)___ be cleared in a competitive market economy if no one is willing to pay for it.

12.59
There is a way, however, in which the swamp can be cleared to most people's satisfaction. This solution requires that consumers do not behave independently or competitively. If all consumers got together as a group and agreed that each citizen would be taxed to pay part of the cost of clearing the swamp, then it would be possible to pay for the project. But collective or group consumption of this kind is different from the behavior assumed when we talk about a

_____ _____ economy.

Answers
   56. will not
   57. pay · pay
   58. will not
   59. competitive market

12.60

Society has long recognized the need for collective consumption. In fact, one of the principal activities of governments is to make expenditures, on behalf of consumers as a group, for goods that most people want but that will not be produced in a competitive market economy. These goods are frequently called

"public goods." Examples of _____ goods are national defense, police and fire protection, scientific research, education, public highways, parks, and recreational areas. For each of these it is at least partially true that consumers will be free to enjoy them whether or not they pay for them.

12.61

When governments make expenditures, they "interfere" with the workings of a

competitive market economy. But when these expenditures are for _____ goods, they make it possible for goods to be produced that consumers want produced, but that would not be produced in adequate quantities in a _____

_____ economy.

12.62

In this chapter we have seen why a competitive market will tend to be

_____ as long as firms pay for all costs of production and consumers pay for all those goods that they consume. This is a very important result, which is the ultimate justification for reliance on market forces in an economy, and which also makes clear the legitimate role for government in influencing the allocation of resources as a means to achieving efficiency.

12.63

In Chapter 13, we shall again consider a situation in which a free enterprise

system does not lead to the most efficient allocation of scarce _____.

This will be a situation of imperfect competition. Despite the exceptions, however, a large bulk of economic activity takes place in our economy as though it were a competitive free enterprise economy. Thus, it is important that you understand how such an economy functions and also be aware of exceptions to general rules.

Answers
60. public
61. public · competitive market
62. efficient
63. resources

12.64

Without overemphasizing them, you should also be aware of exceptions to our assumptions on the demand side: Consumers, for instance, are undoubtedly influenced to some extent by advertising. If advertising "forces" consumers to buy goods they really do not want, then they ___*(will/will not)*___ be maximizing utility.

12.65

When we analyze the economic efficiency of a competitive free enterprise system, we take as given the initial distribution of resources. That is, the initial distribution ___*(is/is not)*___ questioned; no value judgment is made as to whether such a distribution is fair or just.

12.66

It is possible to have an _____ allocation of resources in a competitive market system with a very uneven distribution of resources and output. The existence of a population made up of 10 percent millionaires and 90 percent paupers *(must/does not necessarily)* imply that resources are being inefficiently allocated.

12.67

Conversely, we could imagine an economy in which everyone had the same amount of resources and income might be thought of by some as having an ideal distribution. Would this imply that resources were being efficiently allocated?

_____

12.68

In our economy, opinions are often sharply divided. Many people believe that the _____ of income is too uneven; and as evidence they point to the poverty of the 20 percent of the population having the lowest incomes, and to the relative affluence of the 20 percent with the top incomes. The transfer of income from the top 20 percent to the lowest 20 percent would ensure a

Answers
    64. will not
    65. is not
    66. efficient · does not necessarily
    67. no
    68. distribution

more equal _____ of _____ but would not guarantee a

more efficient _____ of _____ .

12.69
Many argue that as an economy we should be prepared to sacrifice economic

efficiency for a most equitable _____ distribution. Others are con-

cerned primarily with an _____ allocation of resources.

12.70
Perhaps the greatest concern is, or should be, that attempts to make the distribution of income more equitable have led to inefficiency in the allocation of

resources. Such a situation is ___*(less/more)*___ preferable than one in which
equity and efficiency are both achieved.

12.71
For instance, the minimum-wage law, according to which employers must pay
employees at least $1.75 per hour, is defended as a weapon of the government
to promote a more equitable distribution of income. This argument implies that

a man receiving $1 per hour will have a _____ income when the
minimum-wage law is enforced. Further, since such low wages are those received
by the lowest-income workers, the minimum-wage law will ensure a more

_____ distribution by raising the amount of income received.

12.72
However, while the government can insist that an employer pay the

_____ _____, it cannot insist that the employer provide
jobs. If indeed the demand for such labor decreases as the wage rate increases,
the enforcement of a minimum wage, higher than that being paid, will lead to

less labor being demanded and, consequently, ___*(higher/lower)*___ employment.

Answers
68. distribution · income · allocation · resources
69. income · efficient
70. less
71. higher · equitable
72. minimum wage · lower

12.73

Figure 12.1 shows both situations.

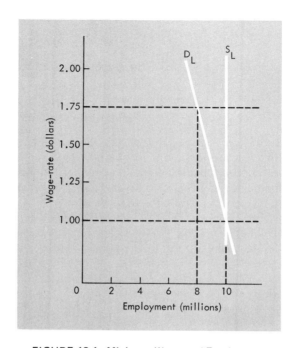

FIGURE 12.1. Minimum Wages and Employment

At $1 per hour the labor market in Figure 12.1 is cleared, the quantity de-

manded and the quantity supplied are _____ and no unemployment
exists.

12.74

At $1.75 per hour, however, the labor market ____*(is/is not)*____ cleared. The

quantity demanded is _____ though the quantity supplied is the

same and unemployment of _____ million workers exists.

12.75

The ten million workers, taken as a group, now have a __*(larger/smaller)*__ income

per hour, i.e. $14 million (8 million X $1.75) vs $ _____ . But two

million of those workers do not share in this income, since they are _____.

12.76

In addition the output of goods and services which the two million (now unemployed) were producing previously is no longer being produced, i.e. the total

output of goods and services is _____ than it otherwise could be and to this extent society is worse off.

12.77

Thus, while the introduction of a minimum-wage law, in this example, has

produced a more equitable distribution of _____ (the ten million as a group now have a higher income), total output and income in the economy

are _____ than before. Therefore resources __*(are/are not)*__ being allocated efficiently.

12.78

The ideal solution, given the redistribution-of-income goal, would be to achieve

the goal __*(by/without)*__ sacrificing efficiency in the allocation of resources, though conflicts are possible between efficiency and equity. An analysis of resource allocation in a competitive market system, however, deals with economic

_____ , not _____ .

12.79

Let us briefly summarize how the competitive free enterprise system functions. Consumers allocate their incomes on the goods and services they want most. In

so doing each consumer attempts to maximize his total _____ .

Answers
> 75. larger · 10 million · unemployed
> 76. less
> 77. income · lower · are not
> 78. without · efficiency · equity
> 79. utility

12.80
Businessmen attempting to maximize _____ produce the goods and services demanded by consumers. Businessmen will produce additional output as long as the revenue from the production of one extra unit is greater than the

_____ of producing that unit. More technically, as long as marginal

_____ exceeds _____ _____, more will

be added to revenue than to _____ and profit will increase.

12.81
Businessmen compete with each other in resource (land, _____, and capital) markets and attempt to combine resources (factors of production) in the most efficient manner. Thus, the average cost of each unit of output

will be least when factors are purchased at the minimum _____ and combined as efficiently as possible.

12.82
The prices that businessmen pay for those resources will be the incomes received by the resources' owners. Thus, what are costs to the businessmen are

_____ to the resources' owners, who in turn attempt to maximize

_____ by allocating their income on the goods and services they want most.

12.83
In the markets for goods and services, competition will force down the

_____ of each commodity to the minimum average cost of production. Profit will disappear and only a normal return on investment will remain.

12.84
If in any industry prices move higher than average minimum production cost,

_____ will exist, and resources will move into that industry in

search of _____. This process will continue until profit (over and

Answers
80. profit · cost · revenue · marginal cost · cost
81. labor · price
82. incomes · utility
83. price
84. profit · profit

above a normal return) disappears. On the other hand if price is below average

minimum production _____, resources will move out of that in-

dustry in search of _____ elsewhere.

12.85
Thus in equilibrium, businessmen will be producing just as much of each product
as consumers are willing to buy at the price which just covers production cost.

The _____ which just covers production cost is the price that is just
necessary to command the factors of production needed to produce the amount
demanded.

12.86
In equilibrium, therefore, the price that consumers must pay for any good will
equal the marginal cost of production. Since in equilibrium this will be true for

all commodities, there would be no way to allocate resources more _____.

12.87
Also in equilibrium, the price a businessman must pay for a factor of production
will equal the value of its marginal product. If the value of the marginal product

is _____ than the price paid for the resource, it will add more to
revenue than to cost, if the businessman continues to hire additional units of the
factor. This will be true for any factor input until the value of its marginal

product equals its _____.

12.88
Thus in equilibrium, each factor will be paid a price equal to the value of its

_____ _____. The income, therefore, that any re-

source owner will earn, will be determined by the value of the _____

_____ of the resource owned, which in turn will be determined by

the _____ for and _____ of the commodities that require that resource in the production process.

Answers
84. cost · profit
85. price
86. efficiently
87. greater · price
88. marginal product · marginal product · demand · supply

12.89

In equilibrium therefore, when the _____ of each resource equals

the value of its _____ _____, no resource could earn a
higher return by moving to any other field of production.

12.90

We can now see how, in a competitive free enterprise system, scarce

_____ are allocated efficiently through innumerable interdependent
markets. In this remarkable system there is no central control or planning. The
actions of utility-seeking consumers and profit-motivated entrepreneurs lead,

ceteris paribus, to a general _____ solution, in which resources
will be allocated in the most efficient fashion. Earlier in the chapter, we noted
exceptions to the above. In turning to Chapter 13, we shall note still other
exceptions, which are also important. Let us first consider monopoly.

REVIEW QUESTIONS

12.1

Which of the following statements are true?   _____

a. Technological efficiency implies economic efficiency.
b. Economic efficiency implies technological efficiency.
c. Both (a) and (b) are true.
d. Economic efficiency together with technological efficiency implies an optimum
income distribution.

Answers
    89. price · marginal product
    90. resources · equilibrium
     1. b

12.2

If $\dfrac{MU_A}{MC_A} > \dfrac{MU_B}{MC_B}$ ($>$ = is greater than) in a perfectly competitive economy

with no externalities, _____.

a. it would be possible to increase utility by reallocating resources from Industry B to Industry A.

b. it would be possible to increase utility by reallocating resources from Industry A to Industry B.

c. $\dfrac{MU_A}{P_A}$ must be greater than $\dfrac{MU_B}{P_A}$

d. $\dfrac{MU_B}{P_B}$ must be greater than $\dfrac{MU_A}{P_A}$

12.3

A firm producing commodity X, dumps wastage in the local river causing pollution and killing all salmon and trout. Does the pattern of river utilization

constitute an economical use of resources? _____

a. No, because rivers should be preserved for fishing.

b. No, because the firm does not take into account all the costs of using the river for dumping of waste.

c. Yes, if more consumers buy X than buy fish.

d. Yes, if X can be produced more cheaply by using the river to dispose of the firm's waste.

12.4

Suppose all consumers voting independently and honestly, indicated that they would be willing to pay the same amount for public good Y. If each consumer contributed this amount, all of which was devoted to producing this good,

then, in terms of economic efficiency,_____.

a. too much of Y would be produced.

b. too little of Y would be produced.

c. just the right amount of Y would be produced.

d. without more information you cannot tell which of the above is correct.

Answers

 2. a

 3. b

 4. a

12.5

In a perfectly competitive economic system _____.

a. incomes will be equal if all men are born with equal ability.
b. incomes will be sufficiently high so that no individual will starve.
c. incomes will differ only insofar as people differ in how long or hard they work.
d. None of the above are necessarily true.

13

Imperfect Competition

13.1

So far we have been analyzing markets in which competition prevails, i.e. markets in which many consumers compete with each other on the demand side, and in which many suppliers compete with each other on the supply side.

The price of a commodity is determined by the forces of _____

and _____. In those competitive markets, no single buyer or

seller has a significant influence on the _____ of the commodity being sold in the market, though each can buy or sell as much of the commodity

as he wishes at that _____.

13.2

Obviously, in the U.S. economy not all markets are characterized by perfect competition. The automobile industry, for instance, has its giants, each of whom can have a substantial effect on the price of automobiles. Thus, the

automobile industry in the United States is not a _____ _____ industry. Many other real-life examples spring to mind and the study of the deviations from perfect competition could fill a book. To begin with, however, discussion will be limited to the complete opposite of perfect competition: monopoly.

Answers
1. demand · supply · price · price
2. **perfectly** competitive

13.3

For the non-Greek scholars, we should explain that "monopoly" means "one

seller." Between the extremes of _____ and perfect competition, we have duopoly (two sellers), oligopoly (a few sellers) and monopolistic competition (a substantial number of sellers but fewer than the number required for perfect competition). To the question of whether monopoly is a "good thing" or a "bad thing," we shall return, but, for now, we shall analyze how price and output are determined in pure monopolistic situations.

13.4

Suppose the demand schedule for good X is represented by the following data and further suppose that the supplier in the market is a monopolist. If a consumer wishes to purchase some of good X, he must purchase it from that

monopolist. Should the _____ decide not to produce any of good X, then there will be none available in this market, since he is the only producer. (We assume that X is a good, such as insulin, for which there is no close substitute.)

Table 13.1
Demand Schedule

Price Per Unit	Quantity That Would Be Demanded
$10	0
9	20
8	40
7	60
6	80
5	100
4	120
3	140
2	160
1	180
0	200

13.5

From Table 13.1 we can draw a normally shaped _____ curve. Suppose the profit-maximizing monopolist has access to these data. He will wish to know how many units of good X he should produce per time period or how much he should charge for each unit of good X. Now it is important to note that, given the market demand schedule, he cannot decide both how

Answers
   3. monopoly
   4. monopolist
   5. demand

much to produce (sell), and also what price to charge. For instance, if he decides to produce and sell 140 units per time period the only price that will clear the

market of excess demand or excess supply will be $_____ per unit. Thus, once he makes either an output or a selling-price decision, the market, if it is to be cleared, will automatically determine the other for him.

13.6

Since the monopolist is a profit-maximizing entrepreneur, we must discover

which output and price will yield maximum _____. For any given level of output, this will be found by subtracting the total costs of producing

from the total _____ received from selling that level of output.

Table 13.2
Demand and Revenue Schedule

(1) Price Per Unit	(2) Quantity That Would Be Demanded	(3) Total Revenue	(4) Average Revenue	(5) Marginal Revenue
10	0	0	—	
				9
9	20	180	9	
				7
8	40	320	8	
				5
7	60	420	7	
				3
6	80	480	6	
				1
5	100	500	5	
				−1
4	120	480	4	
				−3
3	140	420	3	
				−5
2	160	320	2	
				−7
1	180	180	1	
				−9
0	200	0	0	

13.7
In Table 13.2 we have calculated total, average, and marginal revenue from the

data in Table 13.1. Total revenue is found by multiplying each_____
by the quantity that would be demanded at that price. Thus $TR = P \times Q$.

13.8
Average revenue is _____ _____ divided by quantity.
In symbols $AR = \dfrac{TR}{Q}$.

_____ revenue is the extra revenue from the sale of one additional

unit of output. Thus _____ revenue is the increase in revenue
divided by the increase in output. That is $MR = \dfrac{\Delta TR}{\Delta Q}$.

13.9
The data from Table 13.2 have been plotted in Figure 13.1. The average revenue
curve is, of course, the same as the demand curve. We saw in perfect competition

that the _____ curve facing the firm was also the firm's average

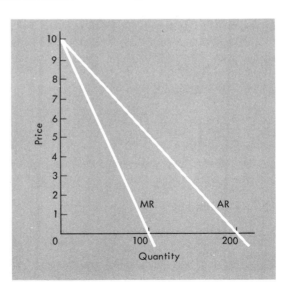

FIGURE 13.1. Average and Marginal Revenue

Answers
   7. price
   8. total revenue · marginal · marginal
   9. demand

revenue curve. In the monopoly case, however, the *industry* demand curve will be the demand curve faced by the monopolist, since the monopolist has the only firm in the industry. Thus the demand curve facing a monopolistic firm

___(will/will not)___ be a horizontal line as was the case in the demand curve facing a competitive firm.

13.10
We can also see from Figure 13.1 that marginal revenue no longer equals

_____ revenue. Thus for any positive level of output, for the monop-

olist price ___(will/will not)___ equal marginal revenue.

13.11
Imagine that the demand (equals _____ _____) curve in Figure 13.1 is for some magic elixir, which comes from only one spring owned by a monopolist. Let us further imagine that the elixir rises from the ground and thus costs nothing to produce. If the monopolist's aim is to maximize profit, how many gallons of elixir should he put up for sale each month? Alternatively, what price per unit should he charge if his aim is profit maximization?

13.12
Profit, of course, equals total _____ minus total _____ .
Since in this example production cost is zero, the monopolist's profit will be

the same as _____ _____. Thus profit will be a maxi-

mum when _____ _____ is a maximum.

13.13
From Table 13.2, we see that total revenue will be a maximum when the

monopolist charges a price of $_____ per unit and sells

_____ units. Total profit will equal total _____ will

equal $_____ .

Answers
   9. will not
  10. average · will not
  11. average revenue
  12. revenue · cost · total revenue · total revenue
  13. 5 · 100 · revenue · 500

13.14

In studying competitive firms, we saw that the profit-maximizing level of output

was that output where marginal revenue equaled _____ _____.
As long as a firm could add more to its revenue than to its cost by producing an
extra unit of output, it would be profitable for the firm to do so. Thus firms

would produce up to the point at which marginal _____ equaled

_____ cost.

13.15

The same holds true for a monopolist. In our example, however, the marginal

cost of producing an extra unit of elixir is _____. If the monop-

olist wishes to maximize _____, he will produce elixir up to the
point at which the extra revenue from the sale of one additional unit of elixir
equals the cost of producing that unit. In the case of zero marginal cost, there-

fore, the monopolist will produce elixir up to the point at which _____
revenue equals zero. From Figure 13.1, we see that marginal revenue is zero at

_____ units of output.

13.16

If the monopolist were to produce beyond this point, marginal revenue would

be _____ than marginal cost, since marginal revenue would be

negative and marginal cost would be _____.

13.17

Thus by producing beyond this point, while the monopolist adds nothing to

_____, he actually detracts from total revenue and _____
would, therefore, fall were he to produce more than 100 units.

13.18

Most monopolists do not have the fortune of owning a magic-elixir spring but
have to pay positive prices for factors of production. Imagine, therefore, that

Answers
14. marginal cost · revenue · marginal
15. zero · profit · marginal · 100
16. less · zero
17. cost · profit

our monopolist is the sole supplier of an exotic liquor, but that his cost curves are similar in shape to those of the competitive firms we studied earlier. Assume, however, that the demand curve for this liquor is the demand curve in Figure 13.1.

This then will be the _____ _____ facing our monopolist.

13.19

In Figure 13.2 we show the revenue and cost curves.

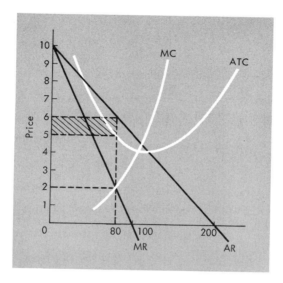

FIGURE 13.2. Monopolistic Equilibrium

If the monopolist wishes to maximize _____, he will produce up to that point at which marginal revenue equals marginal _____. As long as producing an extra unit of output adds more to _____ than it does to _____ it will be profitable to produce that unit.

13.20

If the production of an additional unit adds more to _____ than it does to _____ however, it will not be profitable to produce

Answers
18. demand curve
19. profit · cost · revenue · cost
20. cost · revenue

that unit. Thus in Figure 13.2 the profit-maximizing level of output will be

_____ units.

13.21
Once the monopolist has decided what is his _____- m *imizing
level of output, the maximum price he can charge will be determined by the

demand or _____ _____ curve. In Figure 13.2 we

see that this price is $ _____.

13.22
From the *ATC,* we see that the average cost of producing one unit of output

at this output level is $ _____ and thus, average _____
per unit is $1. Total profit will, therefore, be average profit × the number of

units of output, or $1 × _____. Total profit is represented by the
shaded area in Figure 13.2.

13.23
Thus, our monopolist will be in equilibrium producing an output where marginal

revenue _____ marginal cost and he will be making a _____
over and above a normal return.

13.24
If our monopolist will not allow others to see his secret recipe for his liquor or
if the government has granted him the sole rights of production, other firms will

not be able to enter this industry seeking the _____ that exists.
Does the presence of the monopolist therefore lead to an inefficient allocation
of resources in the economy?

13.25
To answer this question, let us see whether the marginal equivalency condition
for efficient allocation of resources will be satisifed when there is monopoly.

Answers
  20. 80
  21. profit · average revenue · 6
  22. 5 · profit · 80
  23. equals · profit
  24. profit

If you recall, we showed that resources would be efficiently allocated only if

$$\frac{MU_A}{MC_A} = \frac{MU_B}{MC_B} = \cdots = \frac{MU_N}{MC_N}$$

If this did not hold true, it _(would/would not)_ be possible to make consumers better off by reallocating resources.

13.26
From Figure 13.2 we can see that at the profit-maximizing level of output marginal cost is $ _____ and the price is $ _____.

13.27
Thus, price exceeds marginal cost and the marginal equivalency condition for efficient resources allocation _(does not hold/holds.)_

13.28
As far as consumers are concerned, therefore, the price they must pay if they wish to purchase this liquor exceeds the _____ _____ of production.

13.29
We saw in earlier chapters that in equilibrium, a consumer maximized utility in spending his income when the last dollar spent on each commodity yielded him the same _____ utility. Symbolically, we expressed this in the following way:

(1) $$\frac{MU_A}{P_A} = \frac{MU_B}{P_B} = \cdots = \frac{MU_N}{P_N} \cdots$$

Answers
25. would
26. 2 · 6
27. does not hold
28. marginal cost
29. marginal

13.30

If each industry were competitive, then in long-run equilibrium, for each

commodity, _____ and marginal cost would be equal. Symbolically:

$$P_A = MC_A$$
$$P_B = MC_B$$

(2) $\vdots$

$$P_N = MC_N$$

13.31

Since for each industry under perfect competition, _____ equals
marginal cost (equation (2), frame 30), we can substitute MC whenever there
is a P.

13.32

The result is as follows:

(3) $$\frac{MU_A}{MC_A} = \frac{MU_B}{MC_B} = \cdots = \frac{MU_N}{MC_N}$$

Thus under perfect competition the marginal _____ condition for
efficiency is satisfied.

13.33

What happens if we now introduce our liquor-producing monopolist (producing
commodity B—Bramduie) into this picture? Clearly, for commodity B we cannot
substitute MC_B for P_B in equation (1) because, for the monopolist, marginal cost

is _____ than price.

Answers
    30. price
    31. price
    32. equivalency
    33. less

13.34

Suppose that for a competitive industry A, $\dfrac{MU_A}{MC_A} = \dfrac{3}{2}$. Therefore for commod-

ity A we know that, in equilibrium, $\dfrac{MU_A}{P_A}$ = _____ because in

equilibrium P_A = _____ .

13.35

Consumers, being price takers, observe the prices of all commodities including A and B (Bramduie) and allocate their income to _____ utility. For commodities A and B the equivalency condition is that $\dfrac{MU_A}{P_A} = \dfrac{MU_B}{P_B}$. We know however that $\dfrac{MU_A}{P_A} = \dfrac{3}{2}$; therefore $\dfrac{MU_B}{P_B}$ = _____ .

13.36

Now reconsider Figure 13.2.

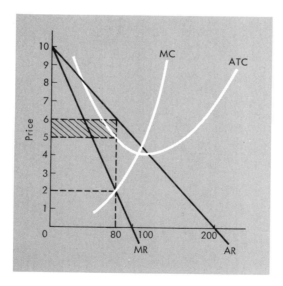

FIGURE 13.2.

Answers

34. $\dfrac{3}{2} \cdot MC_A$

35. maximize $\cdot \dfrac{3}{2}$

What is the price at the profit-maximizing level of output? $ _____

What is the marginal cost at that output? $ _____ . Therefore we can write

$$P_B = 3\,MC_B.$$

13.37
Let us bring together this information on Bramduie:

$$\text{first } \frac{MU_B}{P_B} = \frac{3}{2}$$

$$\text{second } P_B = 3\,MC_B$$

Substituting yields:

$$\frac{MU_B}{3\,MC_B} = \frac{3}{2}$$

and multiplying each side by 3 yields:

$$\frac{MU_B}{MC_B} = \frac{9}{2}.$$

Remember we know that $\dfrac{MU_A}{MC_A} = \dfrac{3}{2}$ for a competitive industry, and we now

see that for a _____ industry $\dfrac{MU_B}{MC_B} = \dfrac{9}{2}$, i.e. those ratios

_____ identical.
(are/are not)

Answers
36. 6 · 2
37. monopolistic · are not

13.38

Suppose we were to give up one unit of commodity A which is produced competitively. Since $\frac{MU_A}{MC_A} = \frac{3}{2}$, we know that utility would be reduced by

___*(two/three)*___ and given that MC_A = $2, one unit of resources would be freed.

13.39

Suppose that one unit of resources is put to use producing Bramduie. Since the marginal cost of producing Bramduie is also _____ unit of resources (i.e., MC_B = $2 as is shown in Fig. 13.2), it will be possible to produce one unit of Bramduie with the one unit of freed resources.

13.40

Is the gain of one unit of Bramduie sufficient to offset the loss of one unit of A? ___*(yes/no)*___ . By reallocating resources, in this example, utility is *(increased/decreased.)* By the switch of one unit of resources described above, utility is increased by *(three/six/nine.)*

13.41

We can see this result in a different way. We can rewrite the _____ equivalency condition which is

$$\frac{MU_A}{MC_A} = \frac{MU_B}{MC_B} \text{ to read}$$

$$\frac{MU_A}{MU_B} = \frac{MC_A}{MC_B} .$$

Suppose for some other example that $\frac{MU_A}{MU_B} = \frac{3}{1}$, but $\frac{MC_A}{MC_B} = \frac{5}{1}$. In this example again assume A is produced competitively and B is produced under

Answers
  38. three
  39. one
  40. yes · increased · six
  41. marginal

monopoly. As in the Bramduie example, the marginal equivalency condition

(does/does not) hold.

13.42
Consider the equation

$$\frac{MU_A}{MU_B} = \frac{3}{1}.$$

The marginal utility of one extra unit of A is _____ times the marginal utility of one extra unit of B.

13.43
Consider now the equation

$$\frac{MC_A}{MC_B} = \frac{5}{1}.$$

That is, the marginal cost of an extra unit of A is _____ times the marginal cost of an extra unit of B. Thus as far as production costs are concerned, businessmen could produce five additional units of B by giving up one unit of A.

13.44
Now reallocate resources. Since $\frac{MC_A}{MC_B} = \frac{5}{1}$, by producing one less unit of A

we can produce _____ more units of B. Since $\frac{MU_A}{MU_B} = \frac{3}{1}$, the

consumer values three additional units of B as equivalent to one additional unit of A. Given our resource allocation, however, we can now give the consumer five additional units of B for one less unit of A. Thus the consumer's

utility will _____ if we reallocate resources.

13.45

In short, the presence of a monopolist in our free enterprise system causes re-

sources to be allocated in a(n) _(optimal/nonoptimal)_ fashion because, as we have seen, we could make at least one consumer better off (increase his

_____) without making any other consumer worse off.

13.46

Why, then, does any economy tolerate firms which are not perfectly competitive? Would welfare and efficiency not be increased if a government forced all
firms to become perfect competitors? Economics would be a very simple subject if the answers in the previous sentence were always yes. Let us see why the
answers are not necessarily yes. If, as a firm expands, the average cost of producing a unit of output decreases, then the average total cost curve of that firm

will _____(rise/fall)_____ as output increases. This must mean that the marginal

cost of production is _____.

13.47

There are many reasons why such a situation is possible. Each employee can
become highly specialized and very efficient in doing only one job. Assembly
line production and the installation of very expensive equipment, such as com-
puters, may be profitable if the output level is sufficiently high. Bulk buying of
raw materials may result in a lower per-unit cost. For those and for many other

reasons therefore, it is quite conceivable that average _____ of
production can be lower, the higher the level of output.

13.48

Imagine that Figure 13.3 represents the average total cost curves for a firm for
different possible scales of operation.

It is quite clear that the minimum average total _____ of produc-

tion occurs with ATC_4, at an output level of _____.

Answers
    45. nonoptimal · utility
    46. fall · decreasing
    47. cost
    48. cost · q_4

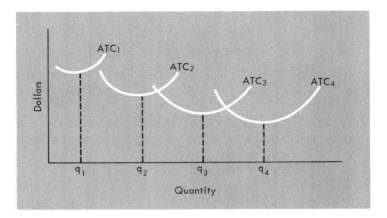

FIGURE 13.3. Economies of Scale

13.49

Let us now superimpose on Figure 13.4 the aggregate demand curve for the commodity whose cost curves appear in the figure.

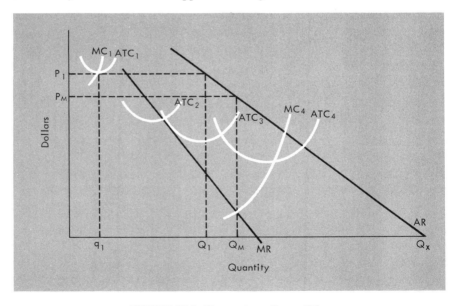

FIGURE 13.4. Monopoly vs. Competition

If we insist on this being a competitive industry, we require a large number of firms. In order to have a large number of competitive firms, we cannot allow any firm to produce more than q_1. Thus all firms would produce q_1 at minimum cost for that output level, which means that all firms would operate the scale of output given by ATC_1. In "equilibrium," aggregate demand would equal aggregate supply. The equilibrium price would be _____ and the equilibrium quantity for the industry would be _____.

13.50

Each firm would be producing at the minimum point of ATC_1 and, important for our efficiency considerations, marginal cost would equal _____.

13.51

Consider now the monopoly solution if we have only one firm with ATC_4.

The monopolist will maximize _____ by producing up to that output at which marginal revenue equals marginal cost. The equilibrium price will be _____ and the equilibrium output will be _____.

13.52

Now the monopolist is certainly not producing that level of output where $MC = P$ but is producing where $MC =$ _____. Consequently, P is ___*(greater/less)*___ than MC. We have just seen, however, that under the marginal equivalency condition of a competitive price system, resources are _____ allocated when price does not equal _____ _____.

13.53

Consider, now, the situation in Figure 13.4, when we insisted on many competitive firms rather than a monopoly. It was certainly true that we had _____ equal to marginal cost but, in this situation, the "equilibrium" price was _____ and the equilibrium quantity Q_1. In the monopoly situation the equilibrium price is _____ and the equilibrium quantity is _____. That is, in this example, under monopoly price is lower and quantity greater than in the competitive case.

Answers
49. $P_1 \cdot Q_1$
50. price
51. profit $\cdot$ $P_M \cdot Q_M$
52. MR $\cdot$ greater $\cdot$ inefficiently $\cdot$ marginal cost
53. price $\cdot$ P_1 $\cdot$ $P_M \cdot Q_M$

13.54

Consider this case from the viewpoint of consumers. Under monopoly, compared with competition, consumers can enjoy a _____ quantity at

a _____ price. Thus obviously, in the case where we have decreasing-cost industries, competition will not lead to optimum resource allocation, nor will perfect competition prevail.

13.55

If we begin with many competitive firms, each one will realize that average total

_____ can be reduced by expanding the scale of operation. In Figure 13.4 however, we can see that if each firm expanded to a size represented

by ATC_4 and if each produced only Q_M (___*(less/more)*___ than output at the minimum point of ATC_4), the aggregate quantity supplied would be in excess

of the aggregate quantity demanded, which is _____ at a price of zero.

13.56

In this example, only one firm would find it profitable to remain in this industry

in the long run, i.e. that firm which would be allowed to be a _____ .

13.57

If you consider the real world, there are many examples of firms that, while not pure monopolists, are certainly far removed from being perfect competitors. The local gas and electricity companies and the telephone company are a few examples. You do not need to be an economist to imagine the inconvenience, inefficiency, and waste of resources that would result if there were thousands of telephone poles and cables side by side on the highways belonging to thousands

of competitive telephone companies. The saving of scarce _____ is obviously large by having only one telephone company.

13.58

It is in society's interest to have large firms in decreasing-cost industries. Since

such firms, however, will not equate _____ with

Answers
54. larger · lower
55. cost · less · Q_x
56. monopolist
57. resources
58. price

_____ _____, there may be a legitimate role for government to regulate prices in those industries. And the government often does so in industries such as public utilities. The telephone company for instance must apply to the Federal Communications Commission (FCC)—an agency of the federal government—for permission to change telephones rates. Also, if the FCC considers the telephone company's profits too high, it can force the telephone

company, in the public interest, to charge ___*(lower/higher)*___ prices.

13.59
So far we have considered the extremes in types of firms—the perfectly

_____ firm and the _____ firm. In between those extremes lie the majority of the firms we observe daily. They are known as imperfect competitors and to those firms we now turn.

13.60
One of the assumptions of perfect competition is that suppliers in a given industry

produce an identical product. Consequently consumers ___*(are/are not)*___ indifferent as to whose output they consume. Most consumers, for instance, are

_____ as to which particular farmer's wheat was used to make today's loaf of bread.

13.61
Another assumption is that the number of suppliers is sufficiently _____

that no single supplier has an appreciable effect on _____ through changing his rate of output.

13.62
If you stop for a moment and consider the commodities you consume daily, you will realize that relatively few meet these "perfect competition" tests. Do you randomly shop for beer or hamburgers or books, or are you like most people and frequent your favorite or most convenient store? If the answer is

yes, then obviously you ___*(are/are not)*___ indifferent about suppliers, and

perfect _____ is not ruling in those markets.

Answers
58. marginal cost · lower
59. competitive · monopolistic
60. are · indifferent
61. large · price
62. are not · competition

13.63
If you were an automobile producer you might be indifferent as to which company's steel you purchased, i.e. the steel could be identical. But when you realize that relatively few companies produce the bulk of steel in the United

States, you know that the steel industry is not perfectly _____

and that each large company can have a significant effect on the _____
of steel.

13.64
In what way does the presence of imperfectly competitive firms affect efficient resource allocation in our economy? The answer, you might guess, is that, simi-

lar to monopoly, equilibrium price does not equal _____ _____

in imperfectly competitive industries and thus our marginal _____
condition for efficient resource allocation is violated.

13.65

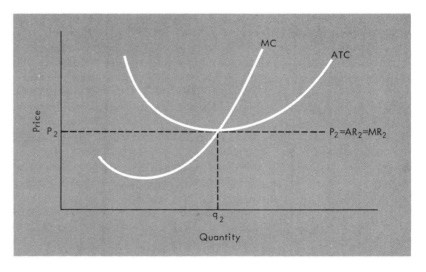

FIGURE 13.5. Perfectly Competitive Firm in Equilibrium

Figure 13.5 shows a perfectly competitive firm in equilibrium producing output

_____ at a price of p_2. We know the firm has no incentive to change output because q_2 is the equilibrium output—marginal revenue equals

_____ _____; any other output would cause a

_____.

13.66

The demand curve D facing this firm is a _____ line (at a height equal

to _____ = _____ = _____), and consequently

is completely _(elastic/inelastic)_. This means that if the supplier attempted to charge a price greater than P_2, he would not sell any of his commodity. All his buyers would switch to a competitor's indistinguishable product at a price of

_____.

13.67

In imperfect competition the demand for the product of a firm is *not* completely

elastic. The more elastic is the demand curve facing a firm, the _(greater/smaller)_ will be the response of buyers to a price change. While the demand curve facing

many imperfect competitors is highly elastic, i.e. a small _____ increase will cause a relatively large decrease in quantity demanded, it is not completely elastic as is the case under perfect competition, where a small

_____ increase causes the firm's sales to fall to zero.

13.68

In imperfect competition therefore, a firm can raise its _____ and although some consumers may switch to a competitor's output, not all will. Thus

the demand curve facing this firm _(will/will not)_ be a horizontal line but

will slope _____ from left to right.

13.69

The decision of consumers to switch to a competitor's product will depend upon how close a substitute they consider the competitor's product and how much

Answers
65. q_2 · marginal cost · loss
66. horizontal · P_2 · AR_2 · MR_2 · elastic · P_2
67. greater · price · price
68. price · will not · downward

cheaper it is. Most cigarette smokers have some loyalty to one brand, but given an increase in the price of only their brand many smokers would switch to a close _____. To the extent that some smokers, however, remained loyal to their brand and paid the higher price, the demand curve for that brand, although highly _____, would not be completely so and, consequently, would slope _____ from left to right.

13.70
If the information in Frame 69 is correct, we know that the demand for cigarettes irrespective of brand is elastic. ___*(true/false)*___ How do you know? _____

13.71
Figure 13.6 represents a typical imperfectly competitive firm.

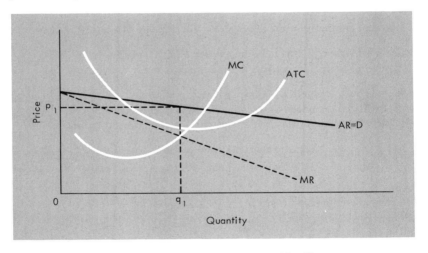

FIGURE 13.6. Imperfectly Competitive Firm

This profit-maximizing firm will produce output Oq_1 at a price p_1 and will make a profit (over and above a normal return) equal to _____.

Answers
   69. substitute · elastic · downward
   70. false · we were given information on the elasticity of demand for one brand, not for all cigarettes
   71. $(AR\text{-}ATC)\,q_1$, i.e. average revenue minus average cost at q_1 × number of units of output

13.72

We know this is an imperfectly competitive firm because _____

_____ .

13.73

If a situation such as that depicted in Figure 13.6 existed in the short run, what would happen in the long run? Other resources' owners would see above normal

_____ being made in this industry and would divert _____
into it.

13.74

To the extent that some buyers switch to the newcomers' products the demand

curve facing the firm in Figure 13.6 will shift to the ____*(right/left)*____ ; i.e. one of

the _____ determining the position of *D* will have changed.

13.75

Firms will continue to enter this industry until all excess _____
disappears. Figure 13.7 depicts the **long-run equilibrium position.**

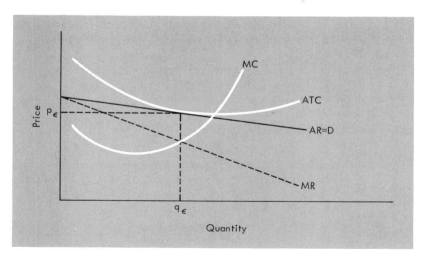

FIGURE 13.7. Imperfectly Competitive Firm in Long-Run Equilibrium

Answers
72. the demand curve it faces is not horizontal (perfectly elastic)
73. profit · resources
74. left · parameters
75. profit

13.76
How do you know that only normal returns are being earned by resources in

Figure 13.7? _____

13.77
How do you know q_E is the equilibrium output of the firm in Figure 13.7?

_____

Why does the firm not charge a higher price than P_E? _____

_____

13.78
Now consider Figure 13.8 in which we have placed a perfectly competitive firm
B in long-run equilibrium alongside our imperfectly competitive firm A of
Figure 13.7.

When firm A is in equilibrium _____ exceeds MC. In addition, the

firm _____*(is/is not)*_____ producing at minimum average cost; unused capacity
exists in the firm.

13.79
Thus in comparing A with B we see that in imperfect competition price is

_____ and output is _____.

13.80
Because price exceeds MC for firm A, then $\dfrac{MU_A}{MC_A}$ ___*(will/will not)*___ equal

$\dfrac{MU_B}{MC_B}$ and utility could therefore be increased by diverting resources towards

industry A.

Answers
    76. at output q_E $ATC = AR$, i.e. neither profit nor loss is being made
    77. at output q_E $MR = MC$ · any price other than P_E would involve a loss to the firm
    78. price · is not
    79. higher · lower
    80. will not

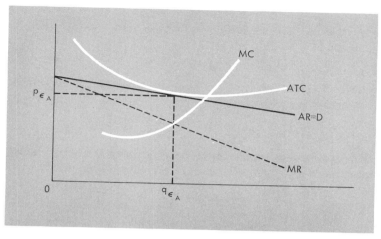

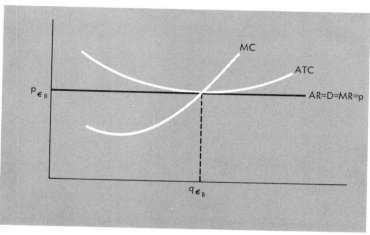

FIGURE 13.8. Long-Run Equilibria Compared

13.81

If of course consumers believed that one brand of cigarettes, soup, gasoline, or aspirin were a perfect substitute for another and acted accordingly, and if entry to each industry were free, we could imagine the D curve for firm A tilting until it was a horizontal line, i.e. until we had a _____

_____ firm. Then MR would equal MC and our _____

_____ condition would be established.

Answers

81. perfectly competitive · marginal equivalency

13.82

To the extent that no real product differentiation exists, i.e. to the extent that brand X aspirin at 89¢ per fifty tablets is not at all different from ordinary aspirin at 15¢ per 50, not only are consumers being duped and do they buy

imaginary differentiation, but _____ are being misallocated and welfare is lower than it could be.

13.83

To the extent that product differentiation is real, i.e. soup *K* is better than soup *L,* the manufacturers of soup *K* have some discretionary power, that is they

can _____ the price and sales will not fall to zero.

13.84

Real or imagined product differentiation gives a downward sloping _____

curve, an intersection of *MR* with _____ at an output less than

minimum *ATC,* an equilibrium price greater than _____ and a

ratio of *MU* to *MC* ___*(greater/less)*___ than the corresponding ratio for a perfectly competitive industry.

13.85

As we have shown in the case of monopoly, as long as $P \neq MC$ it is always possible

to reallocate _____ so that society is better off, i.e. so that at least one person is better off and no one is worse off. This means that as long as such

a reallocation can take place society ___*(is/is not)*___ using its resources as efficiently as possible.

13.86

As we move from the perfectly competitive firm to the imperfectly competitive firm and towards the monopolist, we encounter the *oligopolistic* firm that is relatively large in its industry and that has an appreciable effect on

_____ —not as much as the monopolist, but more than the imperfect competitor.

Answers

82. resources
83. raise
84. demand · *MC* · *MC* · greater
85. resources · is not
86. price

13.87

We could categorize much of our heavy industry in the United States as being oligopolistic (e.g. automobile manufacturers—three major firms), since a

___*(small/large)*___ number of ___*(small/large)*___ firms produces the bulk of the industry's output.

13.88

Again the demand curve facing an oligopolist is _____ sloping.

Again a firm will maximize _____ by producing that output where marginal revenue equals marginal cost. And once again, since price will

exceed _____ _____, the marginal equivalency condition will not hold.

13.89

In the oligopolistic industry, compared with the imperfectly competitive industry, entry by other firms is often extremely expensive and the existence of

above normal _____ often will not attract resources into this industry.

13.90

In an attempt to lessen the power of oligopolists and monopolists, laws known as antitrust laws have been introduced. Those laws are not only aimed at limiting the power of oligopolists but also constitute an attempt to achieve efficient resource allocation.

Considerable attention has been given to the exceptions to efficient resource allocation in a competitive free-enterprise system. This is because they are important; they require your further study. Of prime importance right now, however, is your understanding of the basic competitive system. The United States has a mixed free-enterprise system—some government, some monopoly, some oligopoly, some monopolistic competition, mixed in with much activity that approaches a competitive free-enterprise system. Crucial to an understanding of many important economic issues facing us today, from smog control and river pollution to an inefficient educational industry, is a thorough understanding of the free-enterprise system. If you have conscientiously completed this programmed text, you now have that understanding and are ready for further analysis.

Answers
87. small · large
88. downward · profit · marginal cost
89. profit

REVIEW QUESTIONS

13.1

Suppose a fully employed economy had only two industries, one monopolistic, the other competitive. Assuming that there are no economies of large scale production, government action to break up the monopoly into many com-

petitive firms would lead to _____ .

a. an increase in output for the monopolised industry and a decrease in output for the competitive industry.
b. a decrease in output for the monopolised industry and an increase in output for the competitive industry.
c. an increase in output for both industries.
d. a decrease in output for both industries.

13.2

If, for a manufactured commodity, a monopolist were allowed to charge that price which maximized profit, which of the following would be true? _____ .

a. The price would not equal the cost of the last unit produced.
b. The revenue received from the last unit produced would equal the cost of producing that unit.
c. Total revenue (price $\times$ quantity) for the monopolist would not be maximum.
d. All of the above.

13.3

The government has decided to allow the major automobile companies to merge and become one firm. It rejected the advice of a panel of economists who argued that the government should prohibit the merger and apply anti-trust laws to restore rigorous competition.

Which of the following arguments would suggest that the government's decision would lead to greater economic efficiency than would the economists'

proposal? _____ .

a. Larger firms can produce automobiles at lower cost.
b. Competitive firms would attempt to maximize profits.
c. Prices in competitive markets are determined by the forces of supply and demand.
d. If there were many firms, too many different models of automobiles would be produced.

Answer
  1. a
  2. d
  3. a

13.4

An imperfectly competitive firm discovers that at its present level of output average total cost, which is minimal, is $8.25 and average revenue is $9.00.

Marginal revenue is $6.00. To maximize profit the firm should _____.

a. leave price and output unchanged.
b. increase price and leave output unchanged.
c. increase price and decrease output.
d. decrease price and decrease output.

13.5

To maximize your understanding of economics you should _____.

a. buy another copy of this book.
b. buy another two copies of this book.
c. try and apply what you have learned to real world problems.
d. study sociology.

Answers

4. c
5. how about c?